The Waiter

THE WAITER

MANOJ KUMAR YADAV
Assistant Lecturer
Institute of Hotel Management and Catering Technology,
Gwalior (M.P.)

AMAN PUBLICATIONS
NEW DELHI

Published by
Rajiv Jain for Aman Publications
LG-4A, Ganpati Bhawan,
4675-B/21, Ansari Road,
Darya Ganj, Delhi - 110002
PH: 23255012, 23282127
E-mail: sshjbs@yahoo.com

First Published – 2011

ISBN : 81–8204–064-7
978-81-8204-064-9

SOLE DISTRIBUTOR
JINDAL BOOK SERVICES
LG-4A, Ganpati Bhawan,
4675-B/21, Ansari Road,
Darya Ganj, Delhi - 110002

Printed by:
Sachin Printers, New Delhi, India.

Preface

A waiter is a person who works in either the catering or restaurant industry, and is invaluable to the food service process. Traditionally most waiters were male, but this has changed significantly, leading to the term waitress. Eventually many felt that differentiating waiter from waitress was sexist, and many have suggested less gender-centric terms for people in this profession, including server, or waitperson.

In the F& B Department, the product does not only include the Food & Drinks. It also includes any member of the staff coming into contact with the customer. Hence the total product would be a sum of food, drinks as well as the service rendered by the staff. Service is very difficult to standardize, yet some form of ideal standards can be laid down for the smooth and efficient performance.

A waiter is a male member of the service staff at a bar or restaurant. The waiter performs the essential function of taking the food and beverage orders of a customers, delivering their order to their table, and assuring that they have everything they need during their dining experience. In addition to these basic responsibilities, the waiter may also be responsible for settling the bill at the end of the meal, clearing away used dishes, and cleaning the tables after the customers have left. Almost all waiters will have some type of additional side work, typically tasks like rolling silverware, sweeping floors, or any other work that needs completed in the establishment.

—Editor

Contents

1

Introduction

WHAT IS A WAITER?

A waiter is a person who works in either the catering or restaurant industry, and is invaluable to the food service process. Traditionally most waiters were male, but this has changed significantly, leading to the term waitress. Eventually many felt that differentiating waiter from waitress was sexist, and many have suggested less gender-centric terms for people in this profession, including server, or waitperson.

A waiter's job in a restaurant includes greeting people once they are seated at a table. If it is a particularly busy night, the waiter should still attempt to acknowledge people seated in the section of the restaurant he or she is responsible for and let them know that he'll be back in a moment or two. The waiter then takes orders of guests, informs guests about specials, and answers questions regarding ingredients or preparation methods. If you are in this profession, it is very helpful to be aware of how the kitchen staff prepares meals. After taking an order, the waiter gives this order to the kitchen staff, and if multiple courses are involved, servers may let staff in the kitchen know when first courses are finished in order to maintain good progress of meals from the kitchen to a guest's table. The typical order with multiple courses is usually "fire table X." Most waiters are assigned a specific amount of tables for each shift, which are numbered. Waiters serve dishes to guests, and may additionally clear dishes, especially if buspersons are also busy. They may consult on wines to be served, though in some restaurants this is the responsibility of the sommelier. When a meal is finished, they may present guests with dessert and dessert wine menus, or some restaurants have a dessert cart, which the waiter brings by, so delicious seeming desserts can visually tempt guests.

Throughout the course of a meal, waiters check back with guests making sure the meal is to their satisfaction, and that nothing else is required (sauces, knives, additional water, or more drinks). Dishes need to be cleared promptly, so guests don't have to sit at tables with dirty dishes, but not so promptly that some of the guests haven't finished eating. A waiter also has to adapt him or herself to the pace of each diner. Some people are interested in quickly eating a meal and leaving, and others are interested in more leisurely dining experiences.

Depending on the state they're working in, the base wage of a waiter can range from a little over $2.00 US Dollars (USD) to minimum wage per hour. Waiters are able to make more money by getting tips, which must be claimed as income on tax reports. According to the U.S. Department of Labour, in 2006 the median hourly earnings of a waiter, including wages and tips, was a little over $7 USD. The standard tip in the US is 15%, when service has been adequate. When service is less than adequate, customers should take into account the business of the restaurant, and what other factors may have contributed to a poor meal. If the food is poorly prepared, this really isn't the waiter's fault and doesn't warrant a deduction in tip.

Waiters can work in the catering industry too, and here their jobs may be only the carrying of food and drinks to table, or for elaborately catered affairs, they may also be taking orders as well as delivering food. Hallmarks of a good waiter include the ability to be attentive and polite to guests, careful delivery of food to the table, and an attitude that makes a dining experience pleasurable to guests. He is the main functionary of the service area and does much of the labour oriented work in his area of service. He should be courteous, graceful and maintain stamina enough for long hours of work. He should keep all his senses active throughout his entire service period. Usage of common sense and quick thinking is a must for the waiters to handle any unexpected situations. His general duties would include:

1. Setting up the restaurant and doing the mise-en-place for operation
2. Assist the Captain in welcoming and seating the guests
3. Pour water and make the guests feel comfortable with a few genuine words of concern and eagerness.
4. Collect the KOT/BOT from the Captain and ensure that the order is place correctly in the right area of the kitchen.
5. Add/remove cutlery, glassware and flatware as required.
6. Serve the beverages in the correct order of service to the guests.
7. Service of food should follow the set rules of the organization; therefore the waiters must comply with it.
8. Clear the tables and ask the guest comments and report the same to the Captain.
9. Assist all other waiters during their pressure work times in speeding up the service.
10. Present the bills and do the correct payment procedures and return the change to the guest.
11. Do not hover over the guest or hold prejudices in serving certain clientele in anticipation of tips.

12. Ensure that the restaurant is properly closed down at the end of service.
13. A room service waiter has to follow certain procedures while doing service of food and beverages in the room. Refer to the Room Service operations to know the procedures and tasks to be completed.

Trancheur/Carver

The carver is responsible for the carving trolley and the carving of meat joints at the guest's table as required. This is still predominantly a Western/European style of service which has yet to see the lights of mass revolution in India. The carver has to carve a whole cooked carcass of turkey, duck, capon, rooster, and leg of lamb/mutton or a saddle of beef at the guest's choice at his table. The carving of such joints requires great skill and the carver has to master the fine art of Garde Manger.

Sommelier/Wine Waiter

He is responsible for the service of all alcoholic drinks at the table during the service of meals. He should have tremendous knowledge on wines with respect to quality of wine, age, taste, be able to read labels, right service temperatures, vintages and the correct form of service. Traditionally a wine waiter'sduty included the service of cigars, cigarettes, chewing tobacco and tobacco rolls. He should also be able to know which wines are complemented best with which food.

Interdepartmental Coordination

The various departments of a hotel are so closely interlinked that none can do without the other. Therefore it becomes imperative for us to understand what communication exists between these departments so that we may practice the same in our work experiences. Coordination as the word says implies that "it is a process whereby work which has been subdivided is brought together and pre-unified into specific tasks or objectives". The need for coordination and synchronization of the work of individuals is one of the most important managerial activities. This is not a periodic activity and has to be an ongoing process.

If this coordination is not achieved then it will lead to clients not being satisfied, loss of trade and reputation and bad balance sheet for the organization. Let us look into this area keeping in view the F&B Department as the central focal point. The F& B Department has to coordinate with the other departments as depicted in the illustration for the following purposes:

Kitchen: The various outlets of the F& B department are solidly backed up with the kitchen department for the production of food and accompaniments. Staffs on both sides have to coordinate in functions like receiving and placing of food orders.

House Keeping: This department plays a major role in keeping the various F& B outlets neat, hygienic and clean at all times. The maintenance of furnishings and upholsteries, linen, electrical and electronic fixtures are normally the responsibility of the house keeping department. Staffs on both sides have to coordinate to maintain high standards of professional upkeep.

Front Office: The F & B outlets receive information to arrivals & departure dates of the guests which is important. By this the F&B staff knows whether the guests are room guests or walk-ins into the various outlets. All F & B bills of room guests are to be sent to the cashier at the Front office for computing the Grand Master bill for the guest. Any outside reservations for dining in the F&B outlets are routed by the front office personnel to the respective outlets.

Sales & Marketing: The personnel in this department strike deals with various people and organizations for corporate meetings, conventions, celebrative parties, etc. normally these parties are routed to the Banquets department in the F & B service area.

HRD: This is an important department as F & B relies here in procuring skilled manpower for running their operations smoothly. The salaries and other benefits, training etc. of the F & B staff are given by the HRD department.

Security: This department takes care of the valet parking services of the guest's vehicles that arrive to dine in the various F&B outlets. They are also concerned in keeping anti social elements at bay as well as handling any guests that turn anti social.

Purchase and Stores: F&B procures their stationery, alcoholic & non alcoholic beverages, crockery, cutlery, hollowware, glassware and other proprietary requirements that are not given by any other departments, from the Purchase and Stores.

ATTRIBUTES OF A WAITER

In the F& B Department, the product does not only include the Food & Drinks. It also includes any member of the staff coming into contact with the customer. Hence the total product would be a sum of food, drinks as well as the service rendered by the staff. Service is very difficult to standardize, yet some form of ideal standards can be laid down for the smooth and efficient performance. Standards can be laid down on two levels, namely:

Professional and Hygienic Appearance

The first impression is the lasting impression. How professionally and hygienically you present your self will determine the standards of your establishment and the quality of service that will follow. It therefore becomes important for all staff to be aware of the factors listed below and becomes their individual responsibility to ensure that they put it into practice:

1) Take a bath everyday.
2) Aftershaves, perfumes or deodorants used should not be too strong.
3) Male staff should keep well-trimmed short hair and female staff should tie up their hair and bundle them up in a hairnet.
4) Excessive makeup and jewellery should be avoided. Avoid use of rings (finger &ear) or bracelets.
5) Nails should be clean and well trimmed and free of nicotine stains and any sort of odour.
6) Your mouth should be brushed or cleaned with Listerine before coming on duty.
7) Your uniform should be well kept, neatly ironed and starched as appropriate.
8) Shoes must be well polished and shining. Avoid use of fashion/designer shoes or high heels. Safety and foot comfort is of more importance.
9) Cuts and burns should be covered with the correct dressings.
10) Any colds or other possible infections should be reported immediately.
11) Your hands should be washed immediately after using the toilet, smoking or dealing with waste. Use hot water and disinfectant.
12) Try to avoid bad mannerisms like running your fingers through your hair, chewing/biting nails or scratching your face, etc.

Personality Traits

Personality can be defined as the sum total of a person's behaviour, attitude, manners, composure and training.

Behaviour: An individual must be able to tolerate people and be nice to others without any particular reason.

Attitude: Staff can be trained to change their attitudes into positive ones, if found lacking to the benefit of the person as well as the hotel. Some attitudes required would be:

- To have good, healthy humour at all times.
- To remain cheerful under all circumstances.
- To speak and feel good about all people at all times.
- To enjoy serving others.
- Getting rid of negative ideas and wrong inter-pretations.

Manners: Manners are taught at home and schools, but with respect to the Hospitality industry few mannerisms have to be developed. The list is endless, but a few major ones are listed below to understand the nature of the manners required:

- How to greet people and receive them?
- How to make the guest feel comfortable?
- How much to say and what not to say?
- How to respond?
- How not to argue?

Composure: This is an individual's response to work under stressful conditions. Personal feelings like irritation, anger tragedy or misfortune should not reflect in our behaviour towards guests.

Training: With respect to the hotel whatever training one receives need to be put into practice and eventually train others too. This over a period of time adds to the personality value. Apart from the above a few other attributes are required. They are as follows:

1) *Punctuality*: It is very necessary to be on time for duty. Coming in late for work shows lack of interest and

respect towards work, oneself, management as well as the guests.

2) *Memory*: A very important quality that can help in various ways towards achieving quality service. E.g. Knowing the likes & dislikes of the guests, where they like to sit, their favourite drinks, etc.

3) *Honesty & Loyalty*: If one needs to receive trust and respect then the triangle of staff, guest and management has to be based on honesty & loyalty. Staffs have to realize that their loyalty belongs to the management that has employed them. All their dealings with the guest and the management have to be honest.

4) *Efficiency*: Staff have to develop the following attributes to increase their efficiency:

Knowledge About: Various foods & beverages on the menu as well as the latest market trends. Local information to be able to advise guests on the various forms of entertainment offered best means of transport, sightseeing locales, etc. Various types of cutlery, crockery, glassware, china & earthenware, furniture, fixtures, table appointments, operating procedures, etc.

Sales Ability: The F&B staffs are the front force in the service areas. It therefore becomes necessary to develop skills to sell the food and beverage to the maximum possible.

Complaint Handling: All forms of complaints should be tried to resolve without causing any discomfort or ill feeling to the guest. If any situation becomes beyond ones control then it should be immediately referred to a senior member. Remember that loss of time in dealing with complaints only makes the situation worse.

WAITING TABLES

A waiter is a male who "waits" on tables, often at a restaurant or a bar. A female who "waits" on tables is often called a waitress. The gender-neutral server and collective waitstaff can also be used.

Waiting tables is one of the most common occupations in the U.S. (along with nursing, and teaching). The Bureau of Labour Statistics estimates that, as of May 2005, there are over 2.2 million persons employed as waiters and waitresses in the U.S.

Waiters' duties include preparing tables for a meal, taking customers' orders and serving drinks and food in a restaurant. Depending on the restaurant, other less common duties may be required, such as singing birthday songs to customers who are celebrating a birthday. A theme restaurant may even require waiters to dance (e.g. Joe's Crab Shack).

There are now event caterers that outsource waiter/s/esess to events and specific functions. "Silver Service" waiters are specially trained to serve at banquets or high-end restaurants. They follow specific rules of service and it is a skilled job. They generally wear black and white with a long, white apron (extending from the waist to ankle). The head waiter or waitress is in charge of the staff of waiters and/or waitresses, and is also responsible for assigning seating. Some restaurants employ busboys or busgirls to assist the waiters and/or waitresses.

TIPPING

In the United States and some other Western countries, it is customary to tip a waiter or waitress after a meal. In the U.S., waiters and waitresses, like other "tipped" employees, can be paid a lower minimum wage than other occupations. For example, waiters and waitresses in Georgia are generally paid around $2.13 an hour. It is appropriate that you tip between 10% and 20% of the total bill depending the service you received.

In contrast, waiters and waitresses in many East Asian countries refuse tips, which are sometimes even considered an insult. Many cultures in the region believe that leaving a tip implies that the waiter or waitress is not being paid enough by his or her employer.

Tipping is not customary in Australia or New Zealand and is not factored into wages of waitstaff. However, tips are appreciated especially if the customer or party has been unusually difficult or has left a mess. Many parents of small children leave a small tip. Tips in Australia, because they are not a significant part of the income of the service staff are usually token amounts rather than a percentage of the bill.

How to Create a Waiter Costume

Every restaurant is in need of a great waiter. Whether you tried and simply couldn't carry 4 plates at once or simply never had the chance to try out this in-demand job, you can live out your dream of waiting tables by dressing as a waiter for Halloween. No, you won't have to listen to a customer screaming at you because his soup is not quite hot enough, but you will be able to enjoy the pleasure of wearing a man's tie, even if you're a woman. Be sure to tie it a bit too tight to appease your fictitious crazy restaurant manager. Yes, in order to wear this costume, you best prepare yourself for seeing the insanity of humanity!

Step 1: Get a white, button down professional shirt. If you're a woman, get a man's dress shirt. Borrowing it from a dad, boyfriend or brother is recommended. An Oxford shirt is the best choice, but as long as it's white, crisp and button down, it will do for this costume.

Step 2: Grab a tie! Orange and black are the preferred colours here. If you are borrowing a lot of this costume, ask to borrow any tie that you can get your hands on. Knot the tie securely around your neck. Make sure you button down the collar if you've chosen an Oxford.

Step 3: Pull on a pair of black dress slacks. They should be neatly pressed. Tuck your white dress shirt into the pants. It should look nice, clean and neat.

Step 4: Put on a black apron. It should be long and match the dark shade of your pants. You should put several pens, a wine opener, a crumber and a notepad into your apron. A pen and a pad is a must. Besides, if you're going to be at a party, a wine opener just may come in handy, anyway.

Step 5: Put on a pair of black shoes. These should be nonslip if possible or at least look like they are. Nonslip black footwear is a must for most restaurant workers. You can find these cheaply at store like K-Mart and Payless Shoe Source.

Step 6: Pull your hair up. It must be out of your way so that no strands fall into that delicious food you serve up! You can opt for a bun, a pony tail or a braid.

Step 7: Grab a tray and a bottle of wine as accessories for your costume. While you don't want to carry this around all night, fun props that are believable for a restaurant add to the fun and credibility of your costume.

HOW TO BECOME A WAITER OR WAITRESS

Most chain restaurants provide server training for members of their staff, either on-or off-site. This may involve learning in a classroom setting and/or shadowing an experienced server for a period of time. A high school diploma is usually the maximum educational requirement for such positions and oftentimes, even this isn't necessary.

Fine dining facilities, such as those owned by celebrity chefs, at hotels like the Ritz-Carlton, high-end clubs and banquet halls and resort/cruise ship operators, might also provide server training. However, to secure a position with such employers, one often has to show evidence that they have a sustained history of serving in mid-to-upper level dining establishments. Such businesses may also want documented evidence that an applicant has training in sommelier arts or other cuisine skills; this might, for example, include experience gained at culinary arts schools, like Le Cordon Bleu, The Art Institutes or any number of on-line education providers.

At whatever level one aspires to work, most servers acquire the bulk of their training on-the-job, that is, while working as a waiter or waitress. The one exception would be private, domestic serving, where one might be expected to attend a domestic service training program such as those that educate chauffeurs and butlers in their duties. The requirements for serving at the residences of political figures, for example, presidents, governors and ambassadors or at assisted living facilities may be even stricter, requiring background checks, government oversight and even some form of licensing.

What does a Waiter do?

Waiters and waitresses attend customers or employers in domestic and assisted-living settings, by serving food and beverages. As this suggests, waiting staff work for a diverse range of employers, including hotels, restaurants, private and public clubs, banquet facilities, cruise ships, vacation resorts and households. Most servers wear uniforms, either as extensions of a given restaurant's brand or as required by the formal atmosphere maintained by their employer.

Such a diverse set of opportunities means serving is one of the most popular jobs in the world. Frequently, it is also one of the most flexible in terms of scheduling. That, combined with its relative lack of off-the-clock demands, means it's frequently the preferred day-job of aspiring creative professionals, writers, musicians, actors etc. However, many servers, especially those in high-end restaurants, resorts, cruise ships, and in domestic settings, consider themselves career professionals and aspire to work in top restaurants, households and other facilities around the world.

What Skills or Qualities do I need to become a Waiter/ Waitress?

Any effective server must be able to constructively interact with people. This is the occupation's primary skill and the quality that defines successful waiters and waitresses. Clearly, this means working well with often irritable, hurried customers, but also with management staff, domestic employer, kitchen team and/or fellow servers.

Servers must also be at least somewhat physically capable, as the corporeal realities of serving can be demanding. Carrying large, heavy trays; nimbly moving about crowded rooms; arranging and serving complex orders, these are a few of the physical demands a server faces in the course of their daily work. Since servers are also almost constantly on their feet during a shift, a basic level of physical fitness can help mediate the effects of long hours spent exerting oneself.

Servers must also possess good memories and have the ability to organize large amounts of data, which is often given in a hurry, by customers, managers and employers. In a restaurant setting, a basic knowledge of maths will help a server recognize and deal with inevitable billing errors. Moreover, a good level of computer literacy, including major point of sale software systems, will prevent many of these errors from occurring.

How much does a Waiter Make?

Since the American restaurant industry demands its customers subsidize its labour costs with tips, most servers work for less-than minimum wage, just over $2/hour. Therefore, the type of restaurant in which a server works is crucial in determining take-home pay. Since tips are most commonly paid by calculating 10-20% of a bill, waiters and waitresses at establishments whose average bill runs into the hundreds of dollars and those whose run much less, experience a great discrepancy in pay.

Full-time servers working at casual-dining restaurants can usually expect to make between $20-25,000/year in most markets. Servers at higher-end restaurants and banquet halls can make many times that; up to six figures in markets like New York and Los Angeles. In the same cities, domestic servers and those working in assisted living facilities can make between $60-80,000 per year. As they often operate under different international laws and employ diverse sets of nationals, the salaries of servers at vacation resorts and on cruise ships can vary greatly.

THE 5 COMMON COMPLAINTS IN A RESTAURANT AND HOW THE WAITER CAN AVOID THEM

Every Food and Beverage waiter relies on what a customer tips, not on their hourly wage, in order to make a decent living. So with the consumer's eroding disposable income and more restaurants to choose from in history, it is imperative the waiter provides great service to get that person to leave a good tip. A waiter always has to be thinking ahead, highly organized, and able to prioritize quickly on the fly if they are to succeed. Most important of all is to avoid the service complaint. Having been on the front lines since 1980 serving guests in all different kind of venues here are my top five things a waiter can do to ensure the successful outcome to a dining experience. You may be surprised at what my top five are.

The first complaint that usually surfaces is when a waiter has not acknowledged the table yet and they have been sitting there wondering if anyone will come over. This is always a bad start so the waiter always must go to the table and even if they are too busy at that moment to stay, they must tell the guest they will be right with them as soon as they can. Even if it takes a few minutes to get back to them they are expecting you now, but be ready to take the whole order when you get back. Drinks and all. Don't let them wait further. If they are not in a hurry they may only want to have drinks but in some restaurants where people just want to eat and run then take the whole order. You probably would want that anyway if you have a big, busy section.

The second complaint can occur if there is a delay in the

food order coming out of the kitchen. A lot of waiters at this point, noticing that their guests are becoming mean looking, avoid the customer at all cost until the food is ready. Don't ! Check with the kitchen and get the time as to when it will be ready. Go over to the table and tell them when it will be coming out and apologize for the delay.

The third complaint that takes place is usually when the food is immediately delivered and something does not come out the way the guest ordered it. To avoid this complaint make sure you take your time and listen to what the guest is ordering and write it down properly. If you do not understand something ask them to repeat it and then repeat it back to them especially if it has special instructions. I always write everything down. I never rely on my memory as what could happen is you have an order memorized and while heading to the terminal someone interrupts you and presto you are trying to remember what was just in your head. The fourth complaint will happen if you do not do a table check that takes place approximately 3-5 minutes after they have started eating. Let's say they received the steak they ordered which is fine but was it cooked at the required doneness? Make the eye contact and if the guest is answering in not so a positive fashion offer to get the meal correctly cooked. At this moment you have done your job correctly. You wrote the order out correctly, punched it up right, it came out fine but the kitchen did not do their part. So we have to fix the problem and get the meal redone. Get the manager to deliver the cook up as we call it in the business. The point here is do your table checks! The fifth complaint happens when during the table checks you are not offering to replenish their drinks, remove empty glasses, and filling up their water glass. Nothing worse than a guest with an empty glass of anything in front of them.

Notice I did not mention menu knowledge, wine knowledge or any kind of education whatsoever. If a waiter does not do the above 5 the guest will not care how much a waiter knows. Remember people do not care how much you know only how much you care. That is service on a high level. Always affirm with the guest while clearing their plates on how they appeared to enjoy their meal and get their reaction. Let the guests dictate the conversation on a topic of their choice. Be friendly and never appear to be stressed out. Always make eye contact with the guest. During the meal service I shut up while the guests are eating. Remember they are there to enjoy their own company not myself. I believe if a waiter follows these five service rules and does their job with a smooth delivery they will make money.

WAITER SALARY

A waiter is a male member of the service staff at a bar or restaurant. The waiter performs the essential function of taking the food and beverage orders of a customers, delivering their order to their table, and assuring that they have everything they need during their dining experience. In addition to these basic responsibilities, the waiter may also be responsible for settling the bill at the end of the meal, clearing away used dishes, and cleaning the tables after the customers have left. Almost all waiters will have some type of additional side work, typically tasks like rolling silverware, sweeping floors, or any other work that needs completed in the establishment.

To be a good waiter, you must have a positive and social personality. The majority of the work a waiter will be performing is customer service in a food service environment. This job will involve dealing with children and adults alike. Most restaurants and bars only require that you have a high school diploma and some experience in the field. Having effective communication skills and strong math skills will always help, since you may be responsible for settling bills and dealing with cash provided from the customer.

You must also meet certain legal requirements for working in the establishment, mainly pertaining to liquor sale and distribution. Most states and countries have legal age limits to be allowed to serve or even handle alcohol in a restaurant or dining establishment. The average guaranteed waiter salary (their hourly base rate of pay) is between $2.50 and $8.00 an hour. It is very rare to find a waiter job that pays more than $5, making the median waiter salary around $4.25. This makes the average waiter salary range between $5,200 and $16,640 a year for a 40 hour a week waiter job. The median annual salary would then be around $8,840.

While this may seem very low, this is not including tips. In most areas, the standard for tipping is to leave between 15 and 20 percent of the customers bill for the service staff. This greatly increases the amount of money a waiter brings home on any given day. Some waiters can make $40 in a shift while other can easily pull in over $500 a shift. This fluctuation depends entirely on the clientele of the establishment and the type of restaurant the waiter is working in. Being a waiter may not be a glamorous job, but many people work as a restaurant server in order to make ends meet. While the job may have its hardships, working at the right place can lead to a very comfortable life. Typically, waiters at more upscale restaurants make more simply based on the average price of the bill. The phrase waiter can be applied to all restaurant servers, but they tend to be the ones who work in the high class restaurants.

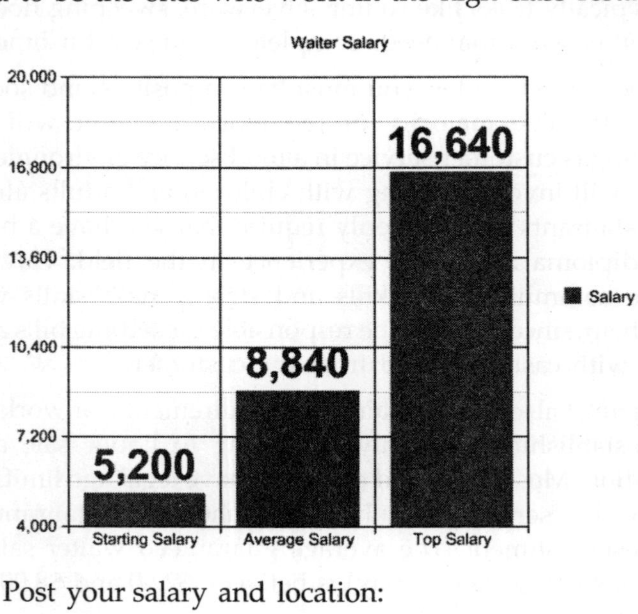

Post your salary and location:

WAITER/WAITRESS PREPARE FOR TABLES

Waiters/waitresses prepare tables in a restaurant before guests arrive, take orders, serve food and drink, and clear tables. They might have to add up the bill for the meal and take payment for it.

Work Activities

Waiters/waitresses are also known as waiting staff. Wherever people have food brought to their table-restaurants, cafes and so on-you will find waiting staff. Before a restaurant is open or before the guests arrive at a function (such as a wedding) the waiting staff may have several jobs to do. They might have to lay out the tables-putting out tablecloths, napkins, cutlery, crockery and table decorations. They might have to move tables around and polish the cutlery.

If people have to sit in certain places, for example, at a function, the waiting staff put out the name cards at each place. They will also have to check that there are enough menus available, and that any other equipment they use (trays, serving trolleys, warmers) is clean and to hand.

Once the restaurant is open or guests start to arrive, the waiting staff help to make sure people feel comfortable. They might show people to their tables and hang up their coats, though sometimes this is the job of a head waiter/waitress. When people sit down, the waiting staff show them a menu and ask if they would like a drink. The waiting staff take orders for meals and explain any unusual items on the menu. The orders are written on a pad and handed in to the kitchen. A waiter/waitress usually looks after a set area or group of tables. When the food is ready, the waiting staff bring it from the kitchen and serve it to the guests. Sometimes the food is put on the plate in the kitchen (this is known as 'plate service'). Otherwise the waiting staff bring out the food on trays and serve it onto the plates at the table. This takes some skill and is known as 'silver service'.

While people are eating, the waiting staff need to stay alert in case the diners ask for anything else, and they should be ready to refill drinks glasses. Once the meal is over, the staff clear the table, serve teas and coffees, and give the customers their bill. When the guests leave, the staff may need to reset the table. In some places the waiting staff may have to take payments for meals by cash, credit or debit cards.

When the function ends or the restaurant closes, the waiting staff clear the tables and put the linen aside for washing. They polish and put away the cutlery and generally help to tidy up. Some staff specialise in serving wine and drinks and are known as wine waiters/waitresses. Waiters/waitresses may have to wear a uniform.

Personal Qualities and Skills

This can be a very busy job, full of pressure. You must be able to stay calm and be tactful and patient with customers. As waiting staff you are the public face of a restaurant or cafe. It can often be down to you whether people will come back or will recommend the place to their friends.

You need to have energy and stamina for this job as you are on your feet all the time. You must be able to work quickly and efficiently. You should be polite and friendly, and able to communicate clearly. You should also be interested in food-customers might ask for your recommendation, so it helps to know something about what is on the menu. You need good personal hygiene and a smart appearance. Number skills are important for handling money.

Pay and Opportunities

Wages vary depending on the type of employer. The pay rates given below are approximate. Waiters/waitresses earn in the range of £220-£280 a week, rising to around £320 a week.

Waiters/waitresses usually work 37-40 hours a week, which may include shift work, split shifts, early starts, late finishes, weekend work and public holidays. Overtime may be available. Part-time, temporary and seasonal employment is also possible.

Waiters/waitresses work throughout the UK, in pubs, hotels and restaurants. Holiday parks and other leisure centres, both indoors and outdoors, also employ waiters/waitresses. There are many opportunities for promotion and rapid career development to supervisory or management level is possible. Vacancies are often advertised in the local newspapers and at Jobcentre Plus.

Adult Opportunities

It is illegal for any organisation to set age limits for entry to employment, education or training, unless they can show there is a real need to have these limits. Some entrants have relevant skills and abilities gained in working with the public and handling cash.

Colleges will usually consider applications from candidates who don't meet their usual entry requirements. You should check the admissions policy of individual colleges.

- 72% of waiters/waitresses work part-time.
- 4% have flexible hours.

CHEFS AND WAITERS

You have decided to cook for a living. Maybe you were brought up in a restaurant or you discovered cooking was a hidden talent that you could nurture and perhaps even make money doing something that you enjoy. But in order to share your art with the world at large, it has to pass through my hands. Little of what you produce will ever touch a person's tongue if I'm not there to serve. I'm a waiter. I have been working at a "fine dining" level of service for 10 years and before that I worked at the deli and diner level for more years than I care to remember. I became a waiter because I was born into a restaurant family. Service is as natural to me as breathing. That doesn't mean I like it all the time. Let's face it, even the air stinks occasionally. But I've tried other professions and I have always come back to service.

The relationship between the front of the house and the back of the house breaks down to this, its most basic element: we need each other. In order to be a waiter, I need food to serve. I would prefer to serve food that I am proud of and can recommend without reservation. In order to be a chef, you need to have your menu represented and served the way you like. And if the communication between the chef and the waiter is as it should be, then the customer will be satisfied and will come back again and again. The waiter makes decent tips and the chef gets a glowing reputation and the business grows. What could be sweeter?

If only it were that simple. It isn't always easy to get information from a chef. There's lots going on in a kitchen as the line crew starts gearing up for service. So there should be a moment before the doors open when the chef is accessible and can go over menu items that any waiter might be unsure of. This includes tastings. Nothing is as valuable to a waiter as seeing the presentation and understanding all the important elements of a dish before the customer arrives. And nothing is more frustrating than a chef who doesn't do this on a regular basis.

But this means that the waiter has a responsibility to listen and remember the information when it's offered. I have known waiters who will get up from a pre-shift meeting and go blank. They have no idea what the specials are and can't remember the difference between sautéing and braising. How should you deal with them?

I'm sorry to say that the only way a chef can be sure whether the waitstaff gets the menu or not is by administering tests. This can be done in the few extra minutes before service with the entire staff or you can sit down with each server individually and quiz them verbally. It shows the waiters that you are serious about your food and want the same commitment from them. With the confidence that having the correct information gives, a waiter can then be an effective salesperson and offer complete service to any guest.

HEAD WAITER

Responsibilities of Head Waiter

A head waiter manages the waiting staff and is involved in customer service and sales. He supervises and controls the waiters' work and matters of customer service and the serving of alcoholic drinks. He also sells restaurant products and services, and makes bids for functions and celebrations. He may work, for example, in a hotel restaurant, a restaurant proper, a dance restaurant or the restaurant/bar on board a ship, or in a nightclub.

It is shift work and you often also have to work at weekends. At the busiest times the working days can be very long. Noise and poor lighting may cause stress at work.

Skills of Head Waiter

Head waiters need to be well organised and have an ability to work with others. They need to be creative, have sales skills and be friendly.

WAITING STAFF

Waiting staff, wait staff, or waitstaff are those who work at a restaurant or a bar attending customers — supplying them with food and drink as requested. Traditionally, a male waiting tables is called a "waiter" and a female a "waitress." Some people prefer to use gender-neutral language, using *waiter* indiscriminately for males and females, server, waitperson, or waitron, an Americanism coined in the 1980s. Waiting staff may also be employed in (mainly, large) private households, but there such specialization is rarer, with the general domestic staff performing the function of waiting staff. Waiting on tables is (along with nursing and teaching) part of the service sector, and among the most common occupations in the United States. The Bureau of Labour Statistics estimates that, as of May As of 2005, there were over 2.2 million persons employed as servers in the U.S. Many servers are required by their employers to wear a uniform.

Duties of Waiting Staff

The duties of waiting staff include preparing tables for a meal, taking customers' orders, serving drinks and food, and cleaning up before, after and during servings in a restaurant. Most servers carry certain items such as a pad and pen for orders, a lighter for candles, or some form of corkscrew or sommelier knife. Depending on the restaurant, other less common duties may be required, such as singing birthday songs to customers who are celebrating a birthday. Singing waiters were a commonplace specialty in the early to middle 20th century, and some modern theme restaurants require servers to dance (e.g. Texas Roadhouse, Johnny Rockets or Joe's Crab Shack). Event caterers outsource waiting staff to events and specific functions.

Silver service staff are specially trained to serve at banquets or high-end restaurants. They follow specific rules of service and it is a skilled job. They generally wear black and white with a long, white apron (extending from the waist to ankle). The head server is in charge of the waiting staff, and is also frequently responsible for assigning seating. The functions of a head server can overlap to some degree with that of the maître d'hôtel. Some restaurants employ busboys or busgirls, increasingly referred to as bussers, to clear dirty dishes, set tables, and otherwise assist the waiting staff.

Tipping

In the United States, United Kingdom, Canada, many other Western countries and parts of the Middle East, it is customary for customers to pay a tip to a server after a meal. 15% is considered standard in the U.S., with a possible range from

15% to 30% depending on the level and quality of service. In some situations, a tip or "service charge" will be included on the restaurant bill in the U.S. Also called a gratuity, a "service charge" will be automatically applied for situations where the restaurant management imposes this to ensure that the servers working in such situations earn their usual tip income. Such service charges are usually around 18%; an additional voluntary tip is sometimes given. There is some debate in the U.S. whether a "minimum tip" exists as a convention; some argue that 15% or 20% is a minimum tip or that it is extremely rude to not leave at least $1, even if the service was not up to standard. However, some people also believe that a "minimum tip" is a way for employers to shift the responsibility of paying employee wages onto the customer. These issues are regional, cultural, and very subjective.

In Germany and other Western countries, where minimum wages exist for servers and where tipping is not culturally entrenched, most tips take the form of rounding up to the nearest whole or half denomination of currency when the server is cashing a party out at their table. In the United Kingdom it is common practice to tip 10% cf the cost of the meal. By contrast, servers in Japan refuse tips because it isn't a Japanese custom.

Tipping is not customary in Asia, Australia and New Zealand and is not factored into wages of staff. However, tips may be appreciated, especially if the customer or party has been unusually difficult or has left a mess. For example, parents of small children may leave a small tip. In Taiwan, a 10% service fee is often added to meals in upscale restaurants. However, this fee does not go to the waitstaff-but is simply a surcharge that is added to the price of the meal.

2

Duties and Responsibilities of a Waiters and Waitresses

DUTIES AND RESPONSIBILITIES

Food service workers perform an important job that is always in demand. Waiters at restaurants have a responsibility to serve the customers' needs during the time they are in the restaurant. A waiter's salary is typically made up of a small hourly rate of pay and customer gratuity, so it is financially advantageous for a waiter to know how to properly serve customers.

Greeting Customers

In some restaurants, there is a host or hostess to greet customers and take them to their tables. Other restaurants, however, require the waiter to greet and seat guests before serving them.

Offering and Serving Beverages and Appetizers

Upon the arrival of a group of customers, the waiter should offer beverages and appetizers. The waiter should be knowledgeable about the various soft drinks, wines and spirits that the establishment offers, as well as the appetizers on the menu. The waiter places the orders and delivers the drinks and appetizers to the customers.

Taking and Serving Meal Orders: One of the waiter's main duties is taking and delivering food orders. The waiter must be able to discuss the daily specials as well as the restaurant's regular menu items. A waiter should be extremely familiar with the entire menu, including which entrees come with side dishes.

Continued Service: After the meal has been delivered, the waiter pays attention to the needs of the table, refilling drinks, taking away soiled dishes and offering napkins or other amenities offered by the establishment.

Delivering the Check and Accepting Payment: The waiter totals the guest check and takes it to the customer. He also accepts payment when it is not done by a cashier and must be aware of the accepted forms of payment. Waiters usually receive a tip of 18 percent to 20 percent of the total check. Whatever the tip may be, the waiter should accept it graciously.

What are the Side Work Duties as a Waiter in a Restaurant?

Although the specific duties will vary depending on the establishment, the one thing any waiter or waitress can count on is having to do side work—all the cleaning and stocking duties needed to keep the restaurant running smoothly.

Function: By assigning various tasks to specific servers, side work ensures that the restaurant will not run out of supplies during the night, while not requiring too much work of any individual.

Types: Side work includes such duties as stocking beverage glasses, brewing coffee, refilling to-go supplies, ensuring adequate condiments are available, checking salad preparation supplies and keeping soup pots stocked.

Features: In addition to running side work, which is performed continuously throughout the shift, a server may also have opening or closing side work, such as folding napkins or rolling silverware, which has to be performed only once per shift.

Considerations: Because side work is designed to divide tasks among the entire staff, if one or two individuals do not keep up with their duties, the rest of the staff will have to pick up the slack.

Warning: Side work is time-consuming and reduces the amount of time you can spend with customers. It can be difficult to balance side work with providing good service, potentially affecting your tips.

How to Get a Date with the Waitress or Waiter at a Breakfast Restaurant or Diner

With society's infatuation with taking the bartender home or getting the phone number of that cute waitress at TGI Fridays, your local breakfast restaurant remains an untapped resource. Having worked many years in the restaurant industry, and having met my wife in one, I have observed what it takes to find true love in the food service industry. I have a combined 10 years of experience as a bartender, resort waiter, steak house staff and I have never seen such an opportunity to pick up a waitress or waiter as I have seen in breakfast restaurants such as Bob Evans, IHOP, Denny's, Shoney's, Cracker Barrel or any morning diner.

Step 1: Even if a period of a slower economy, the breakfast restaurant provides an affordable place to pick up a date.

The first step is deciding which breakfast restaurant you want to become a regular. Find one that works best with your schedule. The slow time for breakfast restaurants is anywhere between 6 a.m. to 10 a.m. This is the ideal time to make your everyday breakfast calls. This may mean that you will have to choose a restaurant that is close to your home or you might see if you can arrive to your job a little later than usual. They key is to have a regular time that you can go eat breakfast, when the restaurant is not crowded. It is advised to do this Monday through Friday. The weekends are the busiest days for the breakfast restaurant industry. Lots of noise and people will hurt your efforts, as will be explained in the next step.

Step 2: Find your place at the counter. Once you have selected your restaurant and determined the usual time you will arrive at the restaurant, you want to find a seat at the counter. This is why it is important to always come in during the slower times, since you are guaranteed to have your seat of choice at the counter. Strive for a seat on the end. This way you have access to the waiter/waitress as they go to and from the service station to the dining room.

Step 3: Once the staff gets to know you, your conversation will move past courteous server-customer talk, and into something more casual and personal. After you found your place at the counter, you must then establish your place as a regular. If you don't drink coffee, you better start. Breakfast restaurants are known to never leave the customer's mug empty. If a waiter or waitress routinely comes around to fill your coffee, then you are provided with a frequent window to make small talk. Also, when the waiter or waitress passes by to go the dining room, make it a habit to make a humorous or witty comment as he/she passes by. Remember that breakfast restaurants and diners operate at a faster pace than dinner restaurants. Therefore, you will need every opportunity possible.

Step 4: If you work yourself into the wait staff's conversations, you become part of their social circle. After a few months of frequenting a restaurant, and making small talk with the staff, you should become more comfortable with striking up conversations. Become more flirtatious with your dialogue. Since your seat is on the end of the counter, and closer to the service station and places where servers will socialize, make it a habit to eavesdrop on conversations. You should listen to what the servers' interests are; what are their pet peeves; and what they do in their free time. Use this knowledge to help you converse with the wait staff.

Step 5: Become part of the staff's social group. Now it is time to make your move. Depending on your age, you may be asked to hangout with staff after work hours. Breakfast restaurants work really well, because the morning staff goes to work and leaves earlier than the usual late hours that dinner restaurant or bar staff work. Take this opportunity to become more acquainted with the staff. Do not ask for a phone number or date. Either wait to be invited to hangout or wait until ask you out. You do not want to appear as if you have a secret agenda to find love. You want to remain casual. Any wrong moves are sure are crucial to your success.

Step 6: Months of patience will finally pay off. Use the after hours socializing as a time to make a move. Once you have gotten to this stage, your foot is in the door. You are now part of the group and start dating within.

Tips & Warnings

- Always tip well. While $10 a day is all you really need it you order a standard 2 eggs, hash browns, toast and a coffee. Depending on your budget, it will payoff if you tip at least 5$ bill each time you come in. Remember, that good tips get you noticed.
- Don't make your move too quick and be prepared for the shutdown. If this happens, it can spoil months of hard work. You might have to find another breakfast restaurant and start all over.
- Always be brief with your visits. Don't spend more than 30 to 40 minutes, unless you are one who reads a paper. You don't want to appear creepy.

How to Win at Diner Dash: Hometown Hero

Diner Dash is the game you love to hate. With every incarnation, the temptation to play Flo the waitress hour after hour, serving the hungry patrons in each of her restaurants. Hometown Hero adds a few twists because now you are back in Flo's hometown. There are even competing waiters in some levels. Although a good amount of winning levels in Diner Dash is through trial and error, there are ways to get ahead in Hometown Hero.

Step 1: Know your customers. Some are more patient than others. Some absolutely hate sitting next to kids while others just have to yap on their cell phones. By knowing your customers instead of trying to pile them into whatever seat is open, you can maximize your points. Keep the families away from the business people. Put the teen boys and girls next to each other and they flirt, giving each other hearts. The construction guys are very patient but eat twice.

Step 2: Serve drinks and decorations often. Drinks add hearts and decorations add points. If you are only grabbing one dinner ticket, grab a drink. If you are carrying back a plate, grab another drink. Give the drinks to people with low patience or were forced to sit next to crying babies or cell phone users.

Step 3: Coordinate colours. It may seem tough to do at first, but seating according to the colours adds points quick, too. Every customer adds matching colours to the chairs. Just be patient enough to scroll around your customers and watch their eyes light up while sitting in their favourite seats.

Step 4: Pay attention to the end game clean up. You'll notice that in Hometown Hero you get bonus points for doing the same tasks in a row. It is difficult to keep up with during the open hours of the restaurant, but when it is closing time, Flo can get a lot of points by NOT cleaning up. Seat and serve the last of your customers, cleaning only the places where you need seating. Once you serve all the dishes, load the patrons up on drinks. When they are finished, collect the checks from all the patrons before their dishes. And then watch your points double and quadruple for every set of dishes you pick up in a row!

Tips & Warnings

Sit the Local Celebs in the middle of the restaurant but serve them first and quickly. They don't like crowds but everyone gets "starstruck" by them and gain hearts.

Free Diner Dash Games to Play

The experts at Play First created the Diner Dash series of restaurant games for time management game lovers. The story line of all four Diner Dash games follows Flo from her first dingy restaurant to a gourmet establishment that establishes her as the hometown hero. These games are available to download and play on Play First's website, but you'll have to look elsewhere on the Internet to play Diner Dash online for free.

Diner Dash: The original version of this fun waitress game can be played online for free on Shockwave's website. However, you can play Diner Dash only until you reach level 5 on Career mode. For longer play, opt for the Endless Shift mode, which lets you play as long as you can keep your customers happy. Or sign up for a free week-long trial Fun Pass on GameHouse.com and play Diner Dash (and any other game) free for a week. However, to continue playing after that week, you will have to buy the downloadable game or pay $19.99/ month for continued access to the online version on Game House.

Diner Dash 2: Restaurant Rescue

The second edition of this addictive game is even more fun than the first. Flo's outdoor patio restaurant may be much nicer, but the customers have less patience and there are more tables to serve. But Diner Dash 2 features fun upgrades like energy bars to make the waitress faster, fun restaurant decorations and a better stove to make the chef faster. Again, Shockwave offers a limited free online version that can be played only up to level 5 on Career mode, but longer on Endless Shift mode or by signing up for a Fun Pass at Game House.

Diner Dash 3: Flo on the Go

In the third installation of the Diner Dash games, Flo is headed on vacation with her best friend when she loses her suitcase and must wait tables to rescue her vacation. This edition of Diner Dash comes equipped with over 25 restaurant upgrades, hundreds of vacation outfits and more customers, tasks and surprises than any Diner Dash before it. To play up to level 5 on Story mode or as long as you can survive on Endless Shift, visit Gator Gamez. To play as long as you want for free for a week, get your trial Fun Pass at Game House.

Diner Dash 4: Hometown Hero

Diner Dash 4: Hometown Hero follows Flo and her Grandma Florence as they work to turn five restaurants into moneymaking gold mines. Hometown Hero features more customer types and features like reservations, six-person tables and colourful customers. Y8 games offers the standard limited five-level play on Story mode and unlimited Endless Shift play, but with the additional option of embedding this limited version of the game on your Web page. Game House also offers free week-long play of this version of Diner Dash with a trial Fun Pass.

Sponge Bob Square Pants Diner Dash

Following the popularity of the original Diner Dash series, Play First developed two versions of Sponge Bob Square Pants Diner Dash. Sponge Bob waits on characters from the popular cartoon at the Krabby Patty through 50 entertaining levels. And the second edition features a wider cast of characters, challenges and customizable restaurants. However, you can only play this edition of Diner Dash by downloading a free 1-hour trial version offered at Big Fish Games. System requirements are: Windows 2000/SP/Vista, minimum 600 MHz processor and 128 MB of RAM.

WHAT ARE THE RESPONSIBILITIES OF WAITER?

- Check patrons' identification in order to ensure that they meet minimum age requirements for consumption of alcoholic beverages.
- Collect payments from customers.
- Write patrons' food orders on order slips, memorize orders, or enter orders into computers for transmittal to kitchen staff.
- Take orders from patrons for food or beverages.
- Check with customers to ensure that they are enjoying their meals and take action to correct any problems.
- Serve food and/or beverages to patrons; prepare and serve specialty dishes at tables as required.
- Prepare checks that itemize and total meal costs and sales taxes.

- Remove dishes and glasses from tables or counters, and take them to kitchen for cleaning.
- Present menus to patrons and answer questions about menu items, making recommendations upon request.
- Inform customers of daily specials.
- Clean tables and/or counters after patrons have finished dining.
- Prepare hot, cold, and mixed drinks for patrons, and chill bottles of wine.
- Explain how various menu items are prepared, describing ingredients and cooking methods.
- Prepare tables for meals, including setting up items such as linens, silverware, and glassware.
- Perform food preparation duties such as preparing salads, appetizers, and cold dishes, portioning desserts, and brewing coffee.
- Stock service areas with supplies such as coffee, food, tableware, and linens.
- Garnish and decorate dishes in preparation for serving.
- Fill salt, pepper, sugar, cream, condiment, and napkin containers.
- Escort customers to their tables.
- Describe and recommend wines to customers.
- Bring wine selections to tables with appropriate glasses, and pour the wines for customers
- Make sure customer recieves the service needed.
- Always be in uniform while during working hours.

DUTIES OF A WAITER FOR FOOD AND BEVERAGE OPERATIONS

The duties to be carried out by the waiter before the service commences are many and varied according to the particular food & beverage service area concerned. In a regular dining hall where all the three meals are served and in coffee shops that operate round the clock, it is necessary that the dining area be ready for service. The dining hall has to be checked for the following aspects in an orderly manner:

1. All the doors and windows have to be opened, curtains to be withdrawn and lights turned on to the highest degree. The whole dining area has to be scrutinized on the following lines:
   i. Check for cobwebs.
   ii. Check for unpolished metal surfaces.
   iii. Check for stains on the carpets, curtains and tapestry.
   iv. Check for all the electrical gadgets like power points, bulbs, tubes, rechargeable batteries, trolleys for pasta, pastry and appetizers, display counters, microwave ovens, etc.
   v. Check for glass panes, fountains and other water bodies, artificial landscapes, etc.

vi. Check for damaged, broken furniture and fixtures.

vii. Check the traffic aisle for guests as well as those leading to the pantry.

viii. Check the front gate/door, the locks, etc.

2. After due scrutiny ensure that all areas are operational at the highest quality level as it should be in the restaurant. No task has to be kept for a later date since any form of negativities could arise due to unattended areas. The above mentioned preparation of the dining room and its general environment for the performance of the service is called as *"Mise-en-scene"*. The next part of the preparation is called "Mise-en-place" or "preparation for service" which encompasses all the duties that have to be carried out in order to have the room ready for service. Adaily Duty Rota showing the tasks and duties to be completed before service, and which member of staff is responsible, is drawn up.

The general tasks to be completed are as follows:

1) Check the booking diary for reservations
2) Make out the seating plan for the day to allocate guests accordingly.
3) Make out a plan of the various stations and the waiters working at each station.
4) Place all tables and chairs properly according to the restaurant layout.
5) Check that tables and chairs do not rattle or wobble.
6) Clean the bottom parts of the chairs and inner surfaces of the tables because guests tend to reach those parts more often.
7) Ensure that the under cloth on the table called the *Baize* or *Moulton* or silencer pad is fixed on the table.
8) Spread fresh table cloths, napkins and all other restaurant linen as and where required.
9) Place the covers on the table i.e. setting cutlery, crockery & glassware on the table. The place allocated for cutlery, crockery & glassware for one person is known as *"Cover"*

10) Wash, clean, wipe, sanitize, dry and polish all cutlery, crockery, glassware, china, stoneware, etc.
11) Remove all withered flowers, buds and other foliages to be replenished with fresh ones.
12) Scrape and clean all candle stands, wipe and polish them and fit in new candles.
13) Wash and wipe all kinds of sauce bottles and refill them.
14) Clean cruet sets by polishing and wiping them. Check for free flow by cleaning the perforations. Always fill the cruet sets upto 2/3rds only to ensure convenient shaking.
15) Check, count, cluster and tie the linen, make a bundle, exchange from linen room. Stack fresh linen in side board for recycling.
16) Carry the cutlery, crockery, crockery, glassware from back area and stack them in the side boards.
17) Switch on the hot plate and place the necessary crockery on the hot plates.

Where areas like coffee shops are concerned, most of these activities are carried out even though the restaurant is open for public.

POOR SERVICE IS A COLLECTIVE RESPONSIBILITY NOT JUST THE WAITER'S

Consider the lot of the frontline service professional. When consumers complain about poor service their venom is nearly always aimed at a person – the call centre agent, the waiter, the check out person – but on almost every occasion they are not the ones at fault. Responsibility for service delivery is a management issue and not one that can be delegated (or is that abdicated?). In a recent blog Tom Johansmeyer identified several characteristics of poor service. His points relate to the experience with the person not the situation. I don't particularly disagree with his thoughts but they are still all failings of management not the people.

Service companies can only invest a high degree of expectation in their frontline staff if they have given them the tools to the job – information and training (including attitude, civility etc.) are two important aspects but so is giving them that feeling of being supported, of having a team behind them, of having their manager's backing. By abdicating responsibility for service to an individual and expecting them to rescue every situation through charm alone you betray that individual and throw them to the lions – and let's face it customers are getting more and more confident in their right to complain. This situation is also true with senior management and the service department. The service a company provides is not the sole responsibility of the service department. They need to have the team behind them – abdicate the company's service strategy to the service department and you betray them and your brand.

One last semi related point. Isn't it sad that in a civilised society we need to have signs in customer service areas that say something to the effect that 'physical and verbal abuse of staff will not be tolerated and offenders will be prosecuted'. But the abuse happens: train staff are harangued for the failure of rolling stock; Jobcentre staff because of government policy; shop staff because the company has changed its returns policy. So another important message for managers – the failure to deliver the infrastructure and processes doesn't just damage your brand, sadly they also threaten your staff physically and emotionally.

Of course the responsibility for the abuse lies personally with the abuser and there is no excuse. Clearly there is something deeply unpleasant in the psyche of many complainers. Effectively it's a desire to bully rather than an emotional reaction to "poor service". I'm no sociologist but perhaps it is a vestige of our class system where new social aspirant thugs are taking the "right" to lord it up over "lower class" serving staff and treat them like punch bags. Who knows, but it is a disturbing trait and reflects the nation's low perception of customer service.

3

Instructions to Waiters and Waitresses

1. In the "demi-Russe' dinner here given, the joints or dishes are to be carved before placing before the person serving them.
2. The person serving fills plates according to the preference of each guest. The waiter then hands the plate, and if vegetables or sauce accompanies the dish, will a!so hand these to the guest at the same time he does the plate, unless a second waiter does this.
3. If waiter is asked for tea, coffee, or chocolate, he will furnish these from sideboard. If asked for water, he will take it from pitcher on table.
4. The waiter will see that the proper number of plates are placed before server for each separate dish of the course.
5. No plates are placed on the table for this style of dinner. Only a napkin With a roll or square of bread in it is placed where the plate would be. Also two knifes, one large, one small, and two forks and a spoon, also glass for water.
6. Furnish both ends of the table alike, and, in addition to the service placed for each guest, furnish a carving knife and fork, a fish slice and prong Also furnish a gravy spoon with each fresh dish placed at the ends of the table.

7. If two kinds of soup or in case where any two dishes are to be served, place one at each end of the table. If there are three or four entrees, place the two leading ones at ends of the table, and hand around the others.
8. Always hand the sauce for each particular dish to the guest partaking of that dish.
9. If asked for the pepper or anything else from the cruet or castor, hand the cruet or castor entire to the guests.
10. If asked for any condiment such as French mustard, olive, chow-chow, etc. etc., hand bottle, if in a bottle, or glass, if in a glass, to the guest, with the prong or fork, and let the guest serve himself, then place back where it was on the table.
11. Be on the alert, and in case of accident, hand your napkin to the guest, and if necessary remove his plate, remedy the trouble as soon as possible, lay down a mat on the soiled cloth, and replenish with knives and forks, napkin, etc., and procure the guest afresh supply of what he was eating.
12. When you place dessert on the table, place a dessert plate, dessert knife and fork also spoon, to each plate. Remember also the finder bowl.
13. If ice cream is served, serve it independent of the head of the table, as his work is through with the first courses. The usual form of ice cream now is bricks.
14. When dessert is half through, hand the menu, or bill of fare to each guest, calling his attention to the ice cream. Take his order and fill it.
15. If any guest has already ordered ice cream, do not offer the bill of fare to him.
16. If it is decided to have boquets, called a "boutonniere" for the guests, then place one in a glass or silver holder by the plate of each lady and gentleman, unless, as is sometimes the case, those for the gentlemen are placed on the napkins without a holder.

17. If salad accompanies any dish-a salad is always in order-hand it around to each guest
18. The host sits at the head of the table; the hostess opposite him at the other end of the table.
19. The soup is always placed before the hostess, and if the salad is placed on the table, that is also placed before her, and any portion of the dessert she may desire to serve, and is handed from her to the guests.
20. The waiter will remove each person's plate as soon as he has finished.
21. Be quick, yet do not appear in a hurry. Waiters should not speak to each other unless it is positively necessary.
22. The proper dress for a waiter is a dark dress coat and trowsers, white vest and necktie. A waitress should wear a dark dress with white apron and cap. Both should wear light slippers or boots, and make as little noise as possible.
23. If menus or bills of fare are used, place one at each plate.
24. If you have to lay a table for dinner a la Russe, the dessert is always placed on the table first, and should be placed tastefully around the centre of flowers. Note diagram for demi-Russe dinner; the dessert is placed round the edge of the table, that is if the hostess desires to have it thus placed. In a dinner a la Russe, the joints or dishes are brought in one at a time and carved by the host, and as he carves each plate, the waiter hands it on a silver tray. In the demi-Russe, the joints are carved before being placed before the server. In some dinners the joints or dishes are carved and handed to the guests for them to help themselves. In this case each guest must be furnished with a plate which of course must be placed-with napkin and roll on it-when the cloth is laid. The waiters should confer with the cook and the cook with the housekeeper or hostess, and have all these points settled beforehand. If there is a butler,

it devolves on him to see all these points settled and to instruct his assistants. Sometimes the host or hostess will direct each guest to his seat, sometimes the butler will do it, and sometimes the waiters.

INSTRUCTIONS TO WAITERS AT SUMMER BREAKFAST

First, air breakfast room well. See that everything has been dusted. Next lay cloth-white is the fashion now-and see that it is free from wrinkles and creases. See that all articles for table are perfectly clean. Place cruets, castors, sauces, salts, spoon, sugar, syrup, and everything that will not hurt to stand a while, in proper positions on table.

Then a few minutes before calling breakfast, add cake, sweet biscuit, muffins, etc. Just before guests begin to come, add flowers and salad. Note position of tea tray containing tea cups, also urns. Note also plate at head, which will show you what cutlery and plate to put near that plate. Place a glass for each plate for water. Place the plates bottom up with napkin on the top of each. At end of table where dishes are served, place plate, cutlery and glasses for other guests, also carver and carving fork and knife rest, also a fish trowel, also a few reserve plates.

In event of an accident they are handy. If any guest require bread, supply it from sideboard. A small roll should be placed in each guest's napkin. If this is not done, place two plates of rolls on table, or pass a dish of rolls. If any one requires a second roll, he asks for it In no case place napkins in glasses, but on plates, whether rolls are in them or not. As soon as guests are seated, ask if they prefer milk or water. If water, fill from the water jug. If milk, fill from the milk pitcher. Both jug and pitcher are kept on sideboard. It is necessary to have a waiter or some one at head to see that all table appointments are correct, and that other waiters discharge their duties, ft is also necessary to have some party outside breakfast room, to whom inside waiters may hand removes from table and from whom anything may be received for table. Waiters should be as quiet as possible and always should go to left of guest. There should be an understanding beforehand between cook, waiters and lady of the house, so that each may know what is coming next, and how to manage. It is the head waiter's place to see that salt is dry and free from lumps, that castors are in good condition, and that oil, mustard, and salad dressing are fresh, etc. For further instructions refer to diagram, and explanation of courses, and articles on dinners and breakfasts. It is best to place two or three extra cups and saucers in tray to use in an emergency. The sugar, milk and cream should be placed before hostess if she is to dispense them, or she may simply dispense tea and coffee, in which case the sugar and cream should be passed by waiters, or put within reach so that guests may help themselves. Chocolate will be served from sideboard, if at all, and sugar and cream handed with it for those who wish.

Remember the diagram is given only to show the lay of table, number of i dishes, also their nature, but these may be changed to suit. This does not show separate courses, but in case you wish to serve in courses, proceed as for dinner, observing the same rules. Lunches are similar to dinners; dishes are less in number, and not of a nature to require much carving. It is usual to have a larger variety of pastries, fruits, and confections than for dinner. In fact some lunches consist of sweets only. In winter lunch diagram two spaces are left to be filled in with anything choice in the way of preserved fruits, fruit jelly, etc. In summer lunch No. 13 14, 15, 16, are for same purpose, fruit being more plentiful then.

From the others it is easy to make up supper. These differ so, it is difficult to lay down a plan, as some make them a late dinner, some dinner and supper. To lay supper is an easy thing. The pages of this book tell how to provide a good supper whether for family or for party. In lunches the plan known as demi-Russe has been adopted, a compromise between the entire Russian, and the old fashioned English plan of placing every dish upon the table. The diagram calls for two carvers as servers, one at head and one at foot end of table, that is to say if dishes are carved by persons sitting at these places. Place the dishes before them whole, tastefully garnished. If dishes are first carved and then placed before them, they will simply serve them.

In either case place plates as shown in diagram, and as fast as each plate is supplied, let waiter hand to each guest, Carving knife and fork must be place! on table to serve with, to be ready in case carving is imperfectly done. In case cook or mistress wishes to display her skill in dishing up, garnishing dish, whatever it may be, waiter locates it in proper place on table, and while company are engaged in talking, quietly removes it to sideboard, and quickly and deftly carves it, garnishing as well as time will allow, then replace in its original place. Another plan is to carve, arrange nicely on the dish, and then garnish tastefully, and place before carver or server. If tea, coffee or chocolate are included in lunch, serve from sideboard. Waiters generally have less to do at lunch than at dinner because guests are under less constraint and oftener help each other.

HOW TO PROPOSE WITH THE HELP OF A WAITER AT A RESTAURANT

Proposing at a restaurant is a classic and traditional idea. Many girls dream of the day they will be eating dinner and then be caught off guard with a proposal. If you would like to propose in a restaurant with a waiter's help, follow these steps.

Instructions

1. Step 1: Decide whether it would be better to call ahead and speak to a waiter or wait until you arrive at the restaurant and pull the waiter aside. Sometimes, it is better and easier just to pull the waiter aside so that he or she will not have to remember the details for a lengthy amount of time. Waiters have such a hectic job that they may accidentally forget your request if it is made too far in advance.

2. Step 2: Decide what role you would like the waiter to play. Perhaps you want him or her to put the ring under a silver dome so that your girlfriend will think her entree has arrived. Or, maybe you would like the waiter to slip the ring onto the napkin in some way.
3. Step 3: If you have decided to ask for the waiter's assistance, you may want to write down the request and discreetly hand it to him or her as you excuse yourself from the table for a moment. If you are calling ahead of time, you may want to ask permission to send the waiter an email so he or she will have the request in writing.
4. Step 4: Be sure to let the waiter know exactly when you will need help.
5. Step 5: If you are going to give the ring to the waiter, you may want to enlist the help of a friend. Your friend can drop off the ring so that you will not give away the surprise.
6. Step 6: When the time for the proposal arrives, be ready with a few words to make the proposal official.

HOW TO BE A WAITER

Working in a restaurant environment can be tough work, especially when you have a nagging boss, complaining customers, limited time, and interesting co-workers. Yet, so many people are applying for this job, whether they know how to do it or not.

The restaurant business is stressful and competitive. Even if you have worked in it for a very long time, there is still more you can learn. When starting out, you're lucky to be training with someone who takes the time to show you the ropes. Perhaps you may be training with someone who doesn't want to teach you, or just doesn't know anything about the job. Alternatively, you might work in a good environment-but that doesn't mean we can't improve!

Steps

1. Always arrive at least 10 minutes before your scheduled shift.
2. Make sure you are presentable before you leave for work. Always be well-groomed and keep your clothes clean and wrinkle-free. Wear dress shoes and socks. Your hair should be neat and washed, your nails clean, your uniform/clothes clean and modest. Apply limited quantities of makeup and hold off on the perfume/cologne.
3. Approach your table with a smile and a greeting. Introduce yourself and say your name clearly. " Hello, nice to see you. My name's ___ Can I show you the menus and perhaps take a drink order?" Ask if they've been to the restaurant before, except watch out-if the answer is "yes, you served us last week"-the gambit fails!! Greet customers with a smile as they enter. Maintain balanced eye-contact, but avoid staring too much. As you seat them at their table, perhaps stir up small conversation as you proceed to take their drink orders.
4. Take drink orders clockwise starting at your left. If children are present ask for their beverages first, followed by ladies and then gentleman all following the left to right order.

   This is now the time to discuss the specials.
5. When you have served their drinks, ask if they have any questions about the menu. Don't rush them unless they are late and even then do it gently. If they are ready to order, take their order clockwise starting at the left and closest to you...if not, proceed to your next table.
6. Bring out orders in their entirety. Never bring one guest's food without the other's, unless specially instructed otherwise (this may happen if one or more

in the party plans to leave early). Normally, there shouldn't be any circumstance causing one part of an order be ready much later than another. If on occasion you foresee this happening and causing a problem, briefly explain the situation and ask how the customer would prefer handling this.

7. Don't overly badger the customers. Avoid going into eagle-hawk mode. Customers hate to be ogled at or constantly interrupted. How would you feel if someone was glaring at you as you ate your meal? If a table wants something they will glance around to look for you. If you stay alert and watch (not stare) your tables as you walk the floor most customers will make eye contact as a signal that they need you. This can give them the feeling like you're paying attention without hovering or badgering them. When their good food and conversation is over, they will start looking around at other diners or the walls. This can tell you when to clear plates, offer desserts or drop the check.

8. Clear any of the plates from the current course as soon as it is obvious the customer wants them to be removed. #Always clear plates from the previous course completely, before bringing plates from the next course to a table.

   Before clearing plates, be sure to ask politely. Use a manner and tone consistant with both the atmosphere and the customer. Generally, "May I clear?" is good. In most establishments, make no reference if they are still eating or more likely, the one who is doing the talking is still eating.

9. When the main course is served, always ask "May I get you anything else?" and give them a second to think about it. Check back again within five minutes, with "Are you enjoying everything?" with specific references about the hosts dish,..." How is your Steak?" at the very least. Listen to their response and more importantly

read their body language: Many people are shy to speak up about problems, and they may blame that on you come time to leave a tip.

10. When the main course is cleared ask.." Would you like to see the dessert menu?"
11. When they are finished with their meal, ask them "Is there anything else I can bring you?" If they say no, promptly give them their bill and wish them a good day. Don't assume the man will pay. If it becomes directly known to you during their visit which guest will be paying, you may leave the check at the end of the table by him or her. Otherwise, leave the check in the middle of the table. Check is always face down. If it is inside a check envelope, lay it flat on the table, don't stand it up.
12. Take their payment. Inform your guest that you will prepare the payment for them, i.e. change if cash or you will process their credit card for them. Never ask if they want change: Just break the bills and return quickly with the change/receipt.
13. When you return, thank them and say something like, " It's been nice to see you", "hope to see you again soon", OR if they seem to be lingering after their meal, just say "thank you", as they may need refills and such.

Tips

- After taking an order, repeat it back to the customers. This gives them confidence in you, and studies show can result in bigger tips.
- Learn proper table service manners: serve from the left, remove from the right; beverages poured from the right as the cups and glasses are always on the right; glasses never picked up when filling; bring fresh wine glasses with every new wine; and MANY others... Books written on this subject include "The Main Course on Table Service". Get one and read it. This knowledge is critical

for employment in an upscale restaurant, and "couldn't hoyt" in a diner.

- Learn the correct way to set a table: forks left, knives right, napkin left(usually). coffee/teacup handles at 5o'clock with teaspoons parallel to the handle... etc.
- When clearing a table do it quietly as not to disturb the diners at other tables.
- *If you have spare time: If two people are sitting at a table and one goes to the restroom or excuses her-or himself for a moment, and if the other person looks even slightly uncomfortable or awkward siting alone, go by and make small talk until the partner comes back or as long as you can before another table needs attention. (Do not fail to keep an eye on other tables while doing this.)*
- Even if not required in training, memorize the menu cover to cover ASAP. Talk to the kitchen to familiarize yourself with any specials. Taste sauces if possible.
- If you are not busy at the moment and notice a customer at another table is in need of something, assist them. If you help out your fellow waiters, they will be more likely to help you out as well. Good service (no matter who provides it) will ensure that customers will come back-that's keeping your paychecks coming.
- Striking up friendly chat is usually recommended, but keep it short and bear in mind that some customers desire privacy more than others and may become irritated by intrusions.
- Customers can boil up and become upset over the most minuscule things, such as the wrong drink order. When this happens, stay calm and correct the situation and apologize to the customer. You may find the LEADS policy helpful:
- Listen *to the customer's complaint.*
- Empathize *with the concern ("I know it can be frustrating when you get the wrong order...").*

- Apologize *personally for the problem, even if it isn't your fault.*
    - o *Do* what it takes to make it right with the customer, such as offering a free appetizer or other cheap item, or reducing the bill (check with your manager).
    - o *Stand* by your promise.
- Never tell a customer you will do something or "be right back" and not do it. Do not promise to do something, anything, and not do it.
- Interaction and cooperation among co-workers is crucial in the speed of the deliverance of food. Be kind to others, though they may be sour.
- Answering the phone may be part of the waiter's job. Clearly speak into the receiver to be understood, and make sure you understand what the customer wants. Always write down the customer's phone number.
- Use caution when writing down orders.
- Remember good drinks and quick service = good mood = good tips. Try your hardest to keep their water/tea glasses filled without being intrusive.
- Even when having pleasant conversation with co-workers, face your tables so you can see if they motion or start looking for something. If customers see you with your back turned, chitchatting with a friend, they are more likely to be annoyed and feel they are not receiving good service.
- Keep a spare shirt or tie at the restaurant. Accidents happen and a sloppy waiter is not good for the appetite.
- If someone forgot to make tea and there is only enough for half a glass or a little more, add more ice and fill the rest with water. Customers appreciate fast service more than anything. Go back and start the tea. If they notice the tea is weak (most won't), tell them you will start a fresh brew just for them.

- Don't give each table the same speech. It's much more personal that way.
- When serving couples, always take the woman's order first.
- Smile A LOT! Depending on the environment you work in, make jokes, small talk etc. to keep the mood light and friendly.
- If a customer complains, don't try to blame it on the cooks, hostess, or anyone else. Simply apologize and work to resolve the problem. Check with the manager before offering discounts, comped meals, etc...If the customer is still not satisfied, ask if they would like to speak to the manager.
- When you get busy, make sure to let new tables know you will be with them in just a minute. Don't get frantic, trust me, you'll start forgetting things.
- Never talk about how long of a day you've had or complain to customers or coworkers. No one wants to hear it. Leave your problems at the door and fake a smile if you have to.
- Be polite, call men Sir and women Ma'am or Miss.
- Interact with the kids. Parents love it. If children are becoming rowdy or irritable, offer to bring them crayons, paper, crackers, something to keep them busy. The parents will often be very grateful.
- Plates and silverware should always be brought before food arrives. You can to this when you greet the table, or after you have brought the drinks.
- Once you get into a routine, stick with it. Analyze it frequently to see if there's anything you can to more efficiently.
- Learn the menu, the ingredients and the cooking processes. Customers ask weird questions sometimes and if you don't know the answer, be sure to ask someone who does...most likely a manager.

- Be friendly with your co-workers, bartenders, cooks, busboys. If they like you, they'll help you out more and make you job so much easier.
- Stay alert for refills, customers trying to get your attention, frowns from guests, dropped silverware, spills, empty plates etc.
- If the restaurant you work at does not give free refills, but a customer asks for one, be sure to inform them and ask if they would like another anyway.

Warnings

- Working as a waiter, especially one in a very busy restaurant, can bring on a lot of stress.
- Don't let one mistake trip you up the whole night. If you let one bad thing get to you, you'll slip up more and more. Just shake it off, take a breather, and move on. Talk to someone you like or respect and get it off your chest-"I screwed up! I'm sorry" lightens the burden as does the honest reply "...You should have been here when I was doing your job!!"
- Never try to hide a mistake from management: You'll only make the problem worse. Acknowledge it promptly and let them help you resolve the situation.
- Keep it friendly...if people have a problem with you, or you with them, just keep some space between the two of you.
- Don't date your co-workers. This may bring trouble to the job site, particularly if you split up, as you still have to see them everyday, but who ever took this advice...
- When customers get nasty or rude, stay calm, listen, and communicate. If that doesn't work, grab the manager and let him/her deal with it.
- If your friends come to visit, keep conversations short and treat them as you would other clients. If they are not eating or ordering anything it is not looked good upon if they stay for more than just a couple minutes.

- Never go to a table smelling like smoke. If you are allowed a cigarette break, follow it by washing your hands, rinsing your mouth, and when possible, decontaminating your clothing by spritzing yourself with a twist of lemon.
- NEVER contaminate a customer's food or drink, no matter how rude and unreasonable they have been. It's unprofessional and could have serious consequences for you if you are caught.

5 TIPS FOR HANDLING A BAD WAITER

The number one complaint of restaurant diners is not the internal temperature of porterhouse, the crispness of fried calamari, or the martini's strength. Nor is it the soundtrack or banquettes colour. It has nothing to do with food or decor. The top gripe among those who eat out is service. As customers, how should we deal with poor service? (Hint: it has more to do with you than you think). Here are tips to dealing with that odd and mercurial species of restaurant employee known as The Server.

1. They're servers not servants. Smile. Be nice to them and they'll be nice to you. That's my number one tip for good service. You'd be amazed how terribly some customers treat servers. Anyone who has ever been a waiter or waitress (a job everyone should be forced to try at least once) knows how much a customer's attitude can dictate his dining experience. And if you've ever snapped your fingers, whistled, or yelled to get the attention of a waiter, shame on you.
2. Not everything that goes wrong in a restaurant is the server's fault. Remember, they're just one cog in the wheel. The long wait for the food is most likely the kitchen's responsibility. Perhaps the host sat too many tables at once, which would explain why drinks are taking so long. So before you start mouthing off, remembers someone else may be to blame. Having said

that, a good waiter will always apologize for delays and give you regular updates on the whereabouts of your food.

3. One way to avoid bad service is to eat at the bar, a favourite tactic of restaurant insiders. The server/bartender never leaves your sight, which makes it really hard for them to ignore you.
4. If you do get a waiter-from-hell there are a few courses to take. You can grin and bear it, take the abuse, and eventually show your displeasure where it hurts the server the most: the tip. (Some restaurants pool tips so just know your financial penalty might not have the effect you intend.) Another option is to pull the manager (or whoever looks like they are in charge) aside and let them know what's going on. Politely ask for another server. Management at any restaurant worth returning to will oblige. If they don't, leave and tell every person you know about the experience. No need to make a scene.
5. If all else fails, write the restaurant (or, more specifically, the owner) a letter explaining the situation. During a busy service even the best restaurants have a difficult time addressing specific problems and issues. If you really want to be heard and, with any luck, improve the future dining experiences of others, it's best to put pen to paper a few days after the incident when you've had a few days to reflect on the experience. If it's a restaurant that cares about its reputation, its employees, and its customers, you'll most definitely hear back from them.

4

Role of Waiter in Food and Beverage Service

Waiters serve food and drinks to guests in hotels, restaurants, clubs and similar establishments. Waiters greet patrons, present them with menus, make recommendations on available food and beverage choices and answer any questions they might have.

Duties and Tasks

A waiter may perform the following tasks:

- set tables with clean linen or place mats, cutlery, crockery and glasses
- welcome and seat customers and hand menus to them
- tell guests about the menu and drinks and appropriate combinations of food and drinks
- in some cases promote local produce and attractions to visitors from interstate and overseas
- take customers' orders and pass them to kitchen staff or bar attendants
- serve food and drinks
- carve meat
- make up bills and present them to customers
- handle money or credit cards
- take restaurant reservations
- clear tables and return dishes and cutlery to kitchens.

Work Conditions

It is busy, exciting work and requires someone with lots of energy and good communication and customer service skills. You will have to work nights and weekends, however, it gives you lots of opportunities to meet people and even to travel. Imagine the fun of working on a cruise ship or in a ski resort!

Waiters often work split shifts and in the evenings, weekends and public holidays. Uniforms may be supplied by employers. Waiters must be a minimum age of 18 years to serve alcohol. Waiters spend long periods on their feet, and may have to deal with difficult or dissatisfied customers.

Personal Requirements

- well presented
- good communication skills
- good memory
- polite and patient
- friendly, efficient and speedy
- enjoy working with people
- able to work as part of a team
- prepared to work weekends and evenings
- able to handle money
- stamina.

Education/Training

You can work as a waiter without formal qualifications. You will probably get some informal training on the job.

However, there are formal qualifications available, and these may assist you in gaining employment and advancing within the industry.

To be a qualified food and beverage attendant, you should have a Certificate II in Hospitality (Operations) as a minimum, although some places will let you start with no training as they offer training on the job. A Certificate III in Hospitality (Operations) is the qualification for a waiter or bar attendant.

You can specialise through electives in whatever best meets your job needs.

The Certificate II: Operations-is the entry-level qualification which provides the basic skills to work as a food and beverage attendant

The Certificate III: Operations-is the certificate for a qualified waiter, in both food and beverage

Other qualifications are available to help waiters to move into supervisory or more specialised roles:

The Certificate IV: Supervision-is designed to provide the supervisory skills to be a head waiter, sommelier or supervisor

The Diploma of Hospitality Management is designed to provide the management skills as well as the operational skills and knowledge needed to be a food and beverage manager

The Advanced Diploma of Hospitality Management provides the advanced management skills for those who are interested in managing a restaurant, heading up a large department or owning their own business. These qualifications can be completed in a number of ways. For more information on the main options, see the following pages:

- New Apprenticeships
- Find training.

Employment and Career Opportunities

There are many opportunities in a huge variety of places including hotels, motels, cafes, restaurants, clubs, recreation and convention centres and other entertainment venues. Most waiters are employed in cities, although many work in larger country centres, particularly those which are tourist resorts.

There are good job prospects. As turnover is high in this occupation there is usually a steady demand for replacement staff. As the tourism and hospitality industry continues to grow, with a growing number of hotels, cafes and restaurants, there are likely to be increased employment opportunities for skilled waiters.

Waiters who have undertaken appropriate training or who have suitable experience are highly regarded by employers. You can start as a waiter or bar attendant, and with experience and further training, progress to head waiter (maitre d'), supervisor or Food and Beverage Manager. If you are interested in wine, you can become a sommelier. Some waiters also specialise in silver service (serving food, using a fork and spoon, directly from platters on a the guest's plate at the table). Career paths are flexible and there are many associated jobs in areas such as training, marketing and events management.

BAR ATTENDANT

Bar attendants prepare, mix and serve drinks to customers in hotels, bars, cafes, restaurants and clubs.

Duties and Tasks

A bar attendant may perform the following tasks:

- serve alcoholic and non-alcoholic drinks
- draw beer from the tap or pour from bottles

- mix ingredients to make cocktails and slice fruit to garnish drinks
- prepare and serve a variety of coffees
- refill drink and cigarette dispensers
- collect glasses from tables and place them in glasswashing machines
- wipe down tables and empty ashtrays
- collect payment, operate cash registers and give change
- arrange bottles and glasses on shelves
- clean bar service area and polish glasses
- operate TAB and Keno or gaming machine terminals
- assist in the cellar
- assist in stock control
- make coffee using an espresso coffee machine or filter system
- observe workplace hygiene, occupational health and safety, and security procedures.

Bar attendants may also provide drinks to waiters or serve them to tables, depending on the type of business.

Work Conditions

Bar attendants generally do shift work, often in the evenings, weekends and public holidays. Many bar attendants are employed on a part-time or casual basis. Uniforms may be supplied by employers.

The work environment can be busy and noisy, and may be hot and stuffy, especially during peak periods. While legislation can vary between states, many licensed premises permit smoking, so it can also be smoky.

Bar attendants must be at least 18 years of age, and are required to comply with legislation on the responsible service of alcohol. Bar attendants spend long periods on their feet, and may have to deal with difficult or intoxicated customers.

Personal Requirements

- good interpersonal skills
- good memory
- efficient and speedy
- enjoy working with people
- prepared to work weekends and evenings
- good cash-handling skills
- able to stand for long periods.

Education/Training

You can work as a bar attendant without formal qualifications. You will probably get some informal training on the job. However, there are formal qualifications available, and these may assist you in gaining employment and advancing within the industry. To be a qualified bar attendant, you should have a Certificate II in Hospitality (Operations) as a minimum, although some places will let you start with no training as they offer training on the job. A Certificate III in Hospitality (Operations) is the qualification for a waiter or bar attendant. You can specialise through electives in whatever best meets your job needs.

The Certificate II in Hospitality (Operations) is the entry-level qualification which provides the basic skills to work as a bar attendant.

The Certificate III in Hospitality (Operations) is the certificate for a qualified waiter, in both food and beverage.

Other qualifications are available to help bar attendants to move into supervisory or more specialised roles:

The Certificate IV in Hospitality (Supervision) is designed to provide the supervisory skills to be a head waiter, sommelier or supervisor

The Diploma of Hospitality Management is designed to provide the management skills as well as the operational skills and knowledge needed to be a food and beverage manager

The Advanced Diploma of Hospitality Management provides the advanced management skills for those who are interested in managing a restaurant, heading up a large department or owning their own business.

These qualifications can be completed in a number of ways. For more information on the main options, see the following pages:

- New Apprenticeships
- Find training.

Career and Employment Opportunities

Bar attendants can work in hotels, bars, restaurants, cafes, clubs, recreation and convention centres, and other licensed entertainment venues. There are good job prospects. Most bar attendants are employed on a part-time or casual basis. As turnover is relatively high, there is generally a constant demand to replace those leaving the job. As the tourism and hospitality industry continues to grow, with a growing number of hotels, cafes and restaurants, there are likely to be increased employment opportunities for skilled bar staff. Bar attendants who have undertaken training or are experienced are highly regarded and sought by employers. Bar attendants with experience and additional training may progress to supervisory or management positions. Career paths are flexible and there are many associated jobs in other areas of the hospitality industry, as well as related areas such as training, marketing and events management.

THE FOOD SERVICE

Any business that prepares and serves meals, snacks, or beverages is part of the food service industry. The largest segment of the industry includes restaurants serving full menus and offering table service. The second-largest segment is limited-menu, or fast food, outlets. Although large fast food chains are a familiar sight all across the United States, more than seven out of ten eating and drinking places are single-unit, independent operations. Other segments of the food service industry include school and employee cafeterias, catering businesses, hotel restaurants, and vendors at sporting events and concerts. The food service industry in the United States is booming and appears to be immune from the weak economy of the twenty-first century's first decade. Sales have increased from about $43 billion in 1970 to $426 billion in 2003. The National Restaurant Association estimates that more than 54 billion meals were eaten in restaurants and school and work cafeterias in 2002.

Social scientists suggest that the boom is the result of people's busy schedules. They also point out that dual-income families have limited time for cooking. Although the rapid food service boom of the 1970s and 1980s may be slowing, the employment outlook is still very good. In 2002 the food service industry employed about 11.7 million workers, making it the largest U.S. employer besides the government. Food and beverage service employment is expected to reach 13.3 million by 2012.

Trends in Food Service

The growth of the take-out food market is a major trend in the food service industry. This market segment is called the "off-premises sector" because food is eaten away from the restaurant where it is cooked. It includes take-out, delivery, and drive-through restaurants. Many traditional restaurants that offer table service attempt to cash in on this expanding market by offering delivery service. Take-out and delivery accounted for 51 percent of total restaurant business in 2002. The Internet has also had a profound influence on the food service market; many workers now order their lunches online.

After rapid expansion in the 1980s the number of fast food restaurants remained stable through the 1990s. New restaurants are likely to be full-service restaurants, which cater more successfully to America's older population. In fact, the full-service sector is expected to be the fastest-growing sector in the industry. The number of Americans between the ages of fifteen and thirty-four-the age group that generally thrives on fast food-is decreasing, whereas the food service industry includes any business that prepares and serves meals, snacks, or beverages. Number of Americans age sixty-five or older is increasing. Many older diners have more time for a leisurely meal and do not seek out fast food.

Like any other business, fast food restaurants must adapt to changing times. Many fast-food chains are offering a wider range of choices and emphasizing low-fat items such as salads and grilled foods to appeal to health-conscious Americans. Another significant trend is the growth of the ethnic food sector. Whereas many Americans once limited their exploration of ethnic foods to Italian or Chinese cuisine, today they seek out traditional foods of Latin America, India, Africa, the Caribbean, and other cultures.

Food Service Workers

The people who work in the food service industry include food and beverage managers, restaurant managers, bartenders, chefs and cooks, bakers, dining room and cafeteria attendants, hostesses and hosts, waiters and waitresses, fast food franchise workers, caterers, stewards, dishwashers, and other kitchen workers.

The food service industry employs large numbers of relatively unskilled workers. Restaurants traditionally have depended on young people to fill these positions; however, low birthrates in the 1970s and 1980s limited the number of youths looking for employment in the 1990s. The food service industry was forced to attract workers from other age groups. It became common for food service businesses to offer more full-time employment, higher wages and bonuses, and more training for career advancement than before. The industry also began recruiting more women and minorities, as well as nontraditional workers such as seniors and mentally and physically challenged individuals.

FOOD AND BEVERAGE SERVING AND RELATED WORKERS

Nature of the Work

Food and beverage serving and related workers are the front line of customer service in restaurants, coffee shops, and other food service establishments. These workers greet customers, escort them to seats and hand them menus, take food and drink orders, and serve food and beverages. They also answer questions, explain menu items and specials, and keep tables and dining areas clean and set for new diners. Most work as part of a team, helping coworkers to improve workflow and customer service.

Waiters and waitresses, the largest group of these workers, take customers' orders, serve food and beverages, prepare itemized checks, and sometimes accept payment. Their specific duties vary considerably, depending on the establishment. In coffee shops serving routine, straightforward fare, such as salads, soups, and sandwiches, servers are expected to provide fast, efficient, and courteous service.

In fine dining restaurants, where more complicated meals are prepared and often served over several courses, waiters and waitresses provide more formal service emphasizing personal, attentive treatment and a more leisurely pace. They may recommend certain dishes and identify ingredients or explain how various items on the menu are prepared. Some prepare salads, desserts, or other menu items tableside.

Additionally, servers may meet with managers and chefs, before each shift to discuss the menu and any new items or specials, review ingredients for any potential food allergies, or talk about any food safety concerns, coordination between the kitchen and the dining room, and any customer service issues from the previous day or shift. Servers usually also check the identification of patrons to ensure they meet the minimum age requirement for the purchase of alcohol and tobacco products wherever those items are sold.

Waiters and waitresses sometimes perform the duties of other food and beverage service workers. These tasks may include escorting guests to tables, serving customers seated at counters, clearing and setting up tables, or operating a cash register. However, full-service restaurants frequently hire other staff, such as hosts and hostesses, cashiers, or dining room attendants, to perform these duties.

Bartenders fill drink orders either taken directly from patrons at the bar or through waiters and waitresses who place drink orders for dining room customers. Bartenders check the identification of customers seated at the bar to ensure they meet the minimum age requirement for the purchase of alcohol and tobacco products. They prepare mixed drinks, serve bottled or draught beer, and pour wine or other beverages. Bartenders must know a wide range of drink recipes and be able to mix drinks accurately, quickly, and without waste. Besides mixing and serving drinks, bartenders stock and prepare garnishes for drinks; maintain an adequate supply of ice, glasses, and other bar supplies; and keep the bar area clean for customers. They also may collect payment, operate the cash register, wash glassware and utensils, and serve food to customers who dine at the bar. Bartenders usually are responsible for ordering and maintaining an inventory of liquor, mixes, and other bar supplies. Most bartenders directly serve and interact with patrons. Bartenders should be friendly and at ease talking with customers. Bartenders at service bars, on the other hand, have less contact with customers. They work in small bars often located off the kitchen in restaurants, hotels, and clubs where only waiters and waitresses place drink orders. Some establishments, especially larger, higher volume ones, use equipment that automatically measures, pours, and mixes drinks at the push of a button. Bartenders who use this equipment, however, still must work quickly to handle a large volume of drink orders and be familiar with the ingredients for special drink requests. Much of a bartender's work still must be done by hand.

Hosts and hostesses welcome guests and maintain reservation or waiting lists. They may direct patrons to coatrooms, restrooms, or to a place to wait until their table is ready. Hosts and hostesses assign guests to tables suitable for the size of their group, escort patrons to their seats, and provide menus. They also schedule dining reservations, arrange parties, and organize any special services that are required. In some restaurants, they act as cashiers.

Dining room and cafeteria attendants and bartender helpers assist waiters, waitresses, and bartenders by cleaning tables, removing dirty dishes, and keeping serving areas stocked with supplies. Sometimes called backwaiters or runners, they bring meals out of the kitchen and assist waiters and waitresses by distributing dishes to individual diners. They also replenish the supply of clean linens, dishes, silverware, and glasses in the dining room and keep the bar stocked with glasses, liquor, ice, and drink garnishes.

Dining room attendants set tables with clean tablecloths, napkins, silverware, glasses, and dishes and serve ice water, rolls, and butter. At the conclusion of meals, they remove dirty dishes and soiled linens from tables. *Cafeteria attendants* stock serving tables with food, trays, dishes, and silverware and may carry trays to dining tables for patrons. Bartender helpers keep bar equipment clean and glasses washed. *Dishwashers* clean dishes, cutlery, and kitchen utensils and equipment.

Counter attendants take orders and serve food in cafeterias, coffee shops, and carryout eateries. In cafeterias, they serve food displayed on steam tables, carve meat, dish out vegetables, ladle sauces and soups, and fill beverage glasses. In lunchrooms and coffee shops, counter attendants take orders from customers seated at the counter, transmit orders to the kitchen, and pick up and serve food.

They also fill cups with coffee, soda, and other beverages and prepare fountain specialties, such as milkshakes and ice cream sundaes. Counter attendants also take carryout orders from diners and wrap or place items in containers. They clean counters, write itemized bills, and sometimes accept payment. Some counter attendants may prepare short-order items, such as sandwiches and salads.

Some food and beverage serving workers take orders from customers at counters or drive-through windows at fast-food restaurants. They assemble orders, hand them to customers, and accept payment. Many of these are *combined food preparation and serving workers* who also cook and package food, make coffee, and fill beverage cups using drink-dispensing machines.

Other workers serve food to patrons outside of a restaurant environment. They might deliver room service meals in hotels or meals to hospital rooms or act as carhops, bringing orders to parked cars.

Work environment. Food and beverage service workers are on their feet most of the time and often carry heavy trays of food, dishes, and glassware. During busy dining periods, they are under pressure to serve customers quickly and efficiently. The work is relatively safe, but care must be taken to avoid slips, falls, and burns.

Part-time work is more common among food and beverage serving and related workers than among workers in almost any other occupation. In 2006, those on part-time schedules included half of all waiters and waitresses and 39 percent of all bartenders.

Food service and drinking establishments typically maintain long dining hours and offer flexible and varied work opportunities. Many food and beverage serving and related workers work evenings, weekends, and holidays. Many students and teenagers seek part time or seasonal work as food and beverage serving and related workers as a first job to gain work experience or to earn spending money. More than one-fifth of all food and beverage serving and related workers were 16 to 19 years old—about five times the proportion for all workers.

Training, Other Qualifications, and Advancement

Most food and beverage service jobs require little or no previous experience and provide training on the job.

Education and training. There are no specific educational requirements for most food and beverage service jobs. Many employers prefer to hire high school graduates for waiter and waitress, bartender, and host and hostess positions, but completion of high school usually is not required for fast-food workers, counter attendants, dishwashers, and dining room attendants and bartender helpers. For many people, a job as a food and beverage service worker serves as a source of immediate income, rather than a career. Many entrants to these jobs are in their late teens or early twenties and have a high school education or less. Usually, they have little or no work experience. Many are full-time students or homemakers. Food and beverage service jobs are a major source of part-time employment for high school and college students.

All new employees receive some training from their employer. They learn safe food handling procedures and sanitation practices, for example. Some employers, particularly those in fast-food restaurants, teach new workers using self-study programs, on-line programs, audiovisual presentations, and instructional booklets that explain food preparation and service skills. But most food and beverage serving and related workers pick up their skills by observing and working with more experienced workers. Some full-service restaurants also provide new dining room employees with some form of classroom training that alternates with periods of on-the-job work experience. These training programs communicate the operating philosophy of the restaurant, help establish a personal rapport with other staff, teach formal serving techniques, and instill a desire to work as a team. They also provide an opportunity to discuss customer service situations and the proper ways of handling unpleasant circumstances or unruly patrons. Some food serving workers can acquire more skills by attending relevant classes offered by public or private vocational schools, restaurant associations, or large restaurant chains. Some bartenders also acquire their skills by attending a bartending or vocational and technical school. These programs often include instruction on State and local laws and regulations, cocktail recipes, proper attire and conduct, and stocking a bar. Some of these schools help their graduates find jobs. Although few employers require any minimum level of educational attainment, some specialized training is usually needed in food handling and legal issues surrounding serving alcoholic beverages. Employers are more likely to hire and promote based on people skills and personal qualities rather than education.

Other qualifications. Restaurants rely on good food and quality customer service to retain loyal customers and succeed in a competitive industry. Food and beverage serving and related workers who exhibit excellent personal qualities—such as a neat clean appearance, a well-spoken manner, an ability to work as a part of a team, and a pleasant way with patrons—will be highly sought after. All workers who serve alcoholic beverages must be at least 21 years of age in most jurisdictions and should be familiar with State and local laws concerning the sale of alcoholic beverages. For bartender jobs, many employers prefer to hire people who are 25 or older.

Waiters and waitresses need a good memory to avoid confusing customers' orders and to recall faces, names, and preferences of frequent patrons. These workers also should be comfortable using computers to place orders and generate customers' bills. Some may need to be quick at arithmetic so they can total bills manually. Knowledge of a foreign language is helpful to communicate with a diverse clientele and staff. Prior experience waiting on tables is preferred by restaurants and hotels that have rigid table service standards. Jobs at these establishments often offer higher wages and have greater income potential from tips, but they may also have stiffer employment requirements, such as prior table service experience or higher education than other establishments.

Advancement. Due to the relatively small size of most food-serving establishments, opportunities for promotion are limited. After gaining experience, some dining room and cafeteria attendants and bartender helpers advance to waiter, waitress, or bartender jobs. For waiters, waitresses, and bartenders, advancement usually is limited to finding a job in a busier or more expensive restaurant or bar where prospects for tip earnings are better. Some bartenders, hosts and hostesses, and waiters and waitresses advance to supervisory jobs, such as dining room supervisor, *maitre d'hotel*, assistant manager, or restaurant general manager. A few bartenders open their own businesses. In larger restaurant chains, food and beverage service workers who excel often are invited to enter the company's formal management training program. (For more information, see the section on food service managers elsewhere in the *Handbook*.)

Employment

Food and beverage serving and related workers held 7.4 million jobs in 2006. The distribution of jobs among the various food and beverage serving occupations was as follows:

Combined food preparation and serving workers, including fast food	2,503,000
Waiters and waitresses	2,361,000
Counter attendants, cafeteria, food concession, and coffee shop	533,000
Dishwashers	517,000
Bartenders	495,000
Dining room and cafeteria attendants and bartender helpers	416,000
Hosts and hostesses, restaurant, lounge, and coffee shop	351,000
Food servers, non restaurant	189,000
All other food preparation and serving related workers	56,000

The overwhelming majority of jobs for food and beverage serving and related workers were found in food services and drinking places, such as restaurants, sandwich shops, and catering or contract food service operators. Other jobs were in hotels, motels, and other traveller accommodation establishments; amusement, gambling, and recreation establishments; educational services; grocery stores; nursing care facilities; civic and social organizations; and hospitals.

Jobs are located throughout the country but are typically plentiful in large cities and tourist areas. Vacation resorts offer seasonal employment, and some workers alternate between summer and winter resorts.

Job Outlook

Average employment growth is expected, and job opportunities should be excellent for food and beverage serving and related workers, but job competition is often keen at upscale restaurants.

Employment Change. Overall employment of these workers is expected to increase by 13 percent over the 2006-16 decade, which is about as fast as the average for all occupations. Food and beverage serving and related workers are projected to have one of the largest numbers of new jobs arise, about 993,000, over this period. The popularity of eating out is expected to increase as the population expands and as customers seek the convenience of restaurants and other dining options. Projected employment growth varies somewhat by job type. Employment of combined food preparation and serving workers, which includes fast-food workers, is expected to increase faster than the average in response to the continuing fast-paced lifestyle of many Americans and the addition of healthier foods at many fast-food restaurants. Average employment growth is expected for waiters and waitresses, hosts and hostesses, and bartenders. Restaurants that offer table service, more varied menus, and an active bar scene are growing in number in response to consumer demands for convenience and to increases in disposable income, especially among families who frequent casual family-oriented restaurants; affluent young professionals, who patronize trendier, more upscale establishments; and retirees and others who dine out as a way to socialize. Employment of dishwashers, dining room and cafeteria attendants, and bartender helpers also will grow about as fast as average.

Job prospects. Job opportunities at most eating and drinking places will be excellent because many people in service sector occupations change jobs frequently and the number of food service outlets needing food service workers will continue to grow. Many of these workers, such as teens, those seeking part-time employment, or multiple jobholders, do so to satisfy short-term income needs before moving on to jobs in other occupations or leaving the workforce. Keen competition is expected, however, for jobs in popular restaurants and fine dining establishments, where potential earnings from tips are greatest.

Earnings

Food and beverage serving and related workers derive their earnings from a combination of hourly wages and customer tips. Earnings vary greatly, depending on the type of job and establishment. For example, fast-food workers and hosts and hostesses usually do not receive tips, so their wage rates may be higher than those of waiters and waitresses and bartenders in full-service restaurants but their overall earnings might be lower. In many full-service restaurants, tips are higher than wages. In some restaurants, workers contribute all or a portion of their tips to a tip pool, which is distributed among qualifying workers. Tip pools allow workers who don't usually receive tips directly from customers, such as dining room attendants, to feel a part of a team and to share in the rewards of good service.

In May 2006, median hourly wage-and-salary earnings (including tips) of waiters and waitresses were $7.14. The middle 50 percent earned between $6.42 and $9.14. The lowest 10 percent earned less than $5.78, and the highest 10 percent earned more than $12.46 an hour. For most waiters and waitresses, higher earnings are primarily the result of receiving more in tips rather than higher hourly wages. Tips usually average between 10 and 20 percent of guests' checks; waiters and waitresses working in busy, expensive restaurants earn the most.

Bartenders had median hourly wage-and-salary earnings (including tips) of $7.86. The middle 50 percent earned between $6.77 and $10.10. The lowest 10 percent earned less than $6.00, and the highest 10 percent earned more than $13.56 an hour. Like waiters and waitresses, bartenders employed in public bars may receive more than half of their earnings as tips. Service bartenders often are paid higher hourly wages to offset their lower tip earnings.

Median hourly wage-and-salary earnings (including tips) of dining room and cafeteria attendants and bartender helpers were $7.36. The middle 50 percent earned between $6.62 and $8.59. The lowest 10 percent earned less than $5.91, and the highest 10 percent earned more than $10.60 an hour. Most received over half of their earnings as wages; the rest of their income was a share of the proceeds from tip pools.

Median hourly wage-and-salary earnings of hosts and hostesses were $7.78. The middle 50 percent earned between $6.79 and $8.97. The lowest 10 percent earned less than $5.99, and the highest 10 percent earned more than $10.80 an hour. Wages comprised the majority of their earnings. In some cases, wages were supplemented by proceeds from tip pools.

Median hourly wage-and-salary earnings of combined food preparation and serving workers, including fast food, were $7.24. The middle 50 percent earned between $6.47 and $8.46. The lowest 10 percent earned less than $5.79, and the highest 10 percent earned more than $10.16 an hour. Although some combined food preparation and serving workers receive a part of their earnings as tips, fast-food workers usually do not.

Median hourly wage-and-salary earnings of counter attendants in cafeterias, food concessions, and coffee shops (including tips) were $7.76. The middle 50 percent earned between $6.85 and $9.00 an hour. The lowest 10 percent earned less than $6.11, and the highest 10 percent earned more than

$10.86 an hour. Median hourly wage-and-salary earnings of dishwashers were $7.57. The middle 50 percent earned between $6.78 and $8.62. The lowest 10 percent earned less than $6.01, and the highest 10 percent earned more than $10.00 an hour.

Median hourly wage-and-salary earnings of food servers outside of restaurants were $8.70. The middle 50 percent earned between $7.27 and $10.87. The lowest 10 percent earned less than $6.36, and the highest 10 percent earned more than $13.81 an hour.

Many beginning or inexperienced workers earn the Federal minimum wage of $5.85 an hour. However, a few States set minimum wages higher than the Federal minimum. Under Federal law, this wage will increase to $6.55 in the summer of 2008 and to $7.25 in the summer of 2009. Also, various minimum wage exceptions apply under specific circumstances to disabled workers, full-time students, youth under age 20 in their first 90 days of employment, tipped employees, and student-learners. Tipped employees are those who customarily and regularly receive more than $30 a month in tips. The employer may consider tips as part of wages, but the employer must pay at least $2.13 an hour in direct wages.

Many employers provide free meals and furnish uniforms, but some may deduct from wages the cost, or fair value, of any meals or lodging provided. Food and beverage service workers who work full time often receive typical benefits, but part-time workers usually do not. In some large restaurants and hotels, food and beverage serving and related workers belong to unions—principally the Unite HERE and the Service Employees International Union.

FOOD SERVICE, BARTENDING, AND WAITRESS CAREERS

Food Service, Bartending and Waitress Career Overview

In restaurants, coffee shops, and other food service establishments, food and beverage serving and related workers are important to first impressions of customer service. The responsibilities of these workers include: welcoming customers, showing them to their seats and providing them with menus, taking food and drink orders, and serving food and beverages. Additionally, they answer questions, clarify featured and normal menu items, and maintain the cleanliness of tables for new costumers. The majority work cooperatively as they assist coworkers throughout busy times to improve workflow and customer service.

Waiters and waitresses make up the largest group of these workers. They perform many responsibilities as they write down customers' orders, serve food and beverages, prepare detailed checks, and occasionally accept payment. Certain duties will differ with various restaurants. In coffee shops where similar items are always served, such as salads, soups, and sandwiches, it is expected of servers to provide quick, efficient, and well-mannered service. In nicer, up-scale restaurants who offer more complex meals and several different courses, waiters and waitresses take their time to give more proper service as they focus on personal and thoughtful treatment. Costumers may ask them for their opinions about certain dishes as well as how dishes are prepared. A few waiters and waitresses prepare items at the table, such as salads, desserts, or others. In addition, they may check identifications of some costumers ordering alcoholic beverages or tobacco products.

Sometimes waiters and waitresses do things that other food and beverage service workers do, such as taking guests to tables, waiting on customers seated at counters, cleaning and preparing tables, or using the cash register. Nevertheless, most restaurants who provide full service usually hire enough staff for various positions, such as hosts and hostesses, cashiers, or dining room attendants, to fulfil these responsibilities.

Bartenders prepare drink orders given by costumers at the bar or by waiters and waitresses who take dining room costumers' orders. To make sure costumers meet the minimum age requirement for the purchase of alcohol beverages and tobacco, bartenders check identification. Their responsibilities include: preparing mixed drinks, serving bottled or draught beer, and pouring wine or other beverages. Bartenders are expected to know several different drink recipes as well as quickly mixing drinks accurately and efficiently. Bartenders also stock and prepare drink garnishes; keep a supply of ice, glasses, and other bar materials; maintain the cleanliness of the bar and bar utensils; serve as a cashier, and serve food to those seated at the bar. Bartenders are in charge of inventory for the bar, maintaining enough liquor, mixes, and other bar supplies.

Most bartenders work directly with costumers. Bartenders should be sociable and like interacting with the public. Conversely, bartenders at service bars don't work closely with costumers because they work in confined bars located near the kitchens in restaurants, hotels, and clubs where only servers come to place orders. A few establishments, with higher volumes, use automatic appliances that mix and make drinks with just the push of a button. This still requires bartenders using this equipment to work fast in order to keep up with a lengthy list of drink orders and to know what certain ingredients different drinks call for. Also, many of the orders still require preparation by hand for specific requests of the costumers.

Hosts and hostesses greet guests and keep track of reservations and waiting lists. If the costumers must wait, a host or hostess can take them to a coat room, bathroom, or seating area until their table is ready. They must seat guests at tables appropriate for the number of people, walk them to their seats, and hand them menus. Further, they schedule dining reservations, organize parties, and arrange for any necessary special services. A few restaurants require hosts and hostesses to be cashiers as well.

Dining room and cafeteria attendants and bartender helpers clean tables, remove used and soiled dishes, and supply serving areas to assist waiters, waitresses and bartenders. They are also known as backwaiters or runners as they bring meals from the kitchen and help waiters and waitresses in passing out dishes to tables. Further responsibilities include: stocking up clean linens, dishes, silverware, and glasses in the dining room and keeping the bar supplied with glasses, liquor, ice, and garnishes for drinks. Dining room attendants are in charge of setting tables using clean tablecloths, napkins, silverware, glasses, and dishes; filling glasses with ice water; and supplying rolls and butter. When the costumers are done eating, attendants take away the dirtied dishes and linens. The responsibilities of cafeteria attendants include supplying serving tables with food, trays, dishes, and silverware and assisting dining patrons with their trays. The responsibilities of bartender helpers include maintaining clean bar equipment and glasses. Dishes, cutlery, and other bar equipment may also be cleaned by dishwashers.

Counter attendants work in cafeterias, coffee shops, and carryout eateries to take orders and serve food. Those who work in cafeterias serve food presented on steam tables, cut and carve meat, spoon out vegetables, scoop sauces and soups, and fill up drink glasses. Counter attendants who work in lunchrooms and coffee chops are responsible for waiting in costumers at the counter, taking orders to the kitchen, and transferring food from the kitchen to costumers. Additionally, they are in charge of beverages such as, coffee, soda, and other beverages; and make fountain specialties including milkshakes and ice cream sundaes. Counter attendants take to-go orders from diners, package these orders up, clean counters, write up detailed bills, and occasionally take payments. A few counter attendants may prepare sandwiches and salads or other short-menu items.

A few food and beverage serving workers at fast-food restaurants may take orders of costumers at counters or in drive-through. They put orders together, distribute the orders, and take payment. Several of these workers are combined food preparation and serving workers with duties of cooking and wrapping food, preparing coffee, and filling beverages from dispensing machines. Other workers may serve to costumers outside of a restaurant. For example, they may wait on people in hotel room, cars, etc.

Food Service, Bartending and Waitress Employment Information

In 2002, food and beverage serving workers and related employees occupied 6.5 million jobs. The following are numbers of the distribution of these jobs:

- Waiters and waitresses-2,097,000
- Combined food preparation and serving workers, including fast food-1,990,000
- Dishwashers-505,000
- Counter attendants, cafeteria, food concession, and coffee-467,000
- Bartenders-463,000
- Dining room and cafeteria attendants and bartender helpers-409,000
- Hosts and hostesses, restaurant, lounge, and coffee shop-298,000
- Food servers, nonrestaurant-195,000
- All other food preparation and serving related workers-117,000

By far most of the jobs for food and beverage serving and related workers were provided by food services and drinking places, including restaurants, coffee shops, and bars. Remaining jobs were mainly in hotels; pleasure, gambling, and leisure industries; school systems; grocery stores; nursing care facilities; civic and social organizations; and hospitals.

Typically jobs are found in big cities and where tourism is prominent; however, jobs are found throughout the country. Seasonal jobs are offered through resorts. Many employees go back and forth between summer and winter jobs instead of staying in one place year round.

Food Service, Bartending and Waitress Training and Job Qualifications

Food and beverage service jobs require no education. Several employers fill waiter and waitress, bartender, and host and hostess positions with those who have graduated from high school; however, it is not mandatory for fast-food workers, counter attendants, dishwashers, dining room attendants, and bartender helpers to graduate from high school. Food and beverage workers receive an hourly wage that is immediate, rather than a salary. Most individuals starting in these jobs are just out of high school (late teens or early twenties) and may not have a high school diploma. Many have no prior experience and are full-time students or homemakers. These jobs are popular for high school and college students looking for a part-time job.

Fine food and quality customer service are essential for acquiring loyal costumers and keeping up with intense competition among other restaurants. Highly desired qualities for food and service workers include: excellent personal skills, a clean appearance, good verbal abilities, cooperation, and a pleasant attitude toward costumers.

A keen memory is required for waiters and waitresses to keep orders straight and to remember common costumers' faces, names, and favourites. Additionally, these workers should be able to easily use a computer to process orders and produce customer checks. A few may need to add up bills mentally using good substantial math skills. A foreign language may be beneficial when communicating with diverse costumers and staff. Some restaurants may have strict expectations and therefore require prior experience waiting on tables. Because these jobs are higher paying and offer higher potential income from tips, they may have stricter requirements than other restaurants before being hired, such as furthered education or training. Typically, 21 year of age is the minimum age requirement for bartenders, but many restaurants prefer 25 year-olds. It is important for bartenders to be familiar with laws, both state and local, regarding the sale of alcohol.

The majority of workers in the food and beverage industry learn needed skills on-the-job as they observe and follow more experienced workers' examples. A few employers, especially fast-food establishments, train new employees certain food preparation and service skills through self-instruction programs with audiovisual productions and instructional pamphlets. A generalized curriculum for food service can be offered by a few public and private vocational schools, restaurant associations, and big restaurant chains.

A few bartenders learn their required skill as they attend a vocational and technical or bartending school. Through these programs, bartenders learn State and local guidelines, recipes for cocktails, what to wear and how to behave, and how to stock a bar. Graduates might be assisted in finding a job from a few of these schools. Even though formal training is not required for many food service positions, some employers require specialized training for handling food and dealing with legal issues that go along with serving alcoholic beverages and tobacco. Promotions and hiring may be based more upon personal qualities and people skills than schooling when employers evaluate candidates.

Because the majority of food-serving establishments are small, the chance to be promoted may be hard. After some experience is acquired, a few dining room and cafeteria attendants and bartender helpers become promoted to waiter, waitress, or bartender jobs. For waiters, waitresses, and bartenders, advancing to something better may be just to transfer to a job in a busier or more upscale restaurant or bar where the potential for tips is superior. Some bartenders choose to start their own bars. A few hosts and hostesses and waiters and waitresses become supervisors or related positions, such as maitre d'hotel, dining room supervisor, or the manager of a restaurant. Food and beverage service workers who perform extraordinarily may be asked to join the company's formal management training program in larger restaurant chains.

FOOD SERVICE, BARTENDING AND WAITRESS JOB AND EMPLOYMENT OPPORTUNITIES

Food and beverage serving and related workers should expect a surplus of job openings in their field. Over the 2002-12 period, general employment for workers is projected to grow about as fast as the average, due to an increasing population, higher personal earnings, and extra spare time. While many new positions will be created and filled, most of the openings will come from the high percentage of openings of individuals who leave the occupation each year.

Because requirements for training and education are few, there is considerable turnover in these occupations, and the large number of part-time jobs is appealing to those looking for temporary earnings rather than a career. Nevertheless, intense competition is estimated for bartender, waiter and waitress, and other food and beverage service jobs in well-known eating places and superior dining establishments, where earnings from tips can potentially be high.

Between 2002 and 2012, expected employment expansion varies by the kind of job. Due to the persisting fast-paced lifestyle in most of the United States plus the trend of more nutritious foods at several fast-food restaurants, employment of combined food preparation and serving workers, counting fast-food workers, is projected to grow faster than the average. A larger number of families and a richer 55-and-older population will push an increase in restaurants that offer table service and a big selection of menu items—resulting in average expansion for waiters and waitresses and hosts and hostesses. Dining room attendants and dishwashers' work will increase slower than other food and beverage serving and related workers due to the popularity of more casual dining spots, such as coffee bars and sandwich shops, as opposed to full-service restaurants who hire more of these workers. Employment of bartenders is expected to grow slower than the average.

Historical Earnings Information

Food and beverage serving and related workers make money through both hourly wages and customer tips. As a result, earnings are dissimilar and based upon various job types and restaurants. For example, fast-food workers and hosts and hostesses hardly ever get tips, so their base wage rates are probably higher than those of waiters and waitresses and bartenders in full-service restaurants, earning the majority of their income through tips. In a few restaurants, tips are sometimes combined in one large pool and then divided equally among all of the eligible workers. This practice permits those, such as dining room attendants, who don't usually receive tips from customers to benefit from the good service payments.

5

Different Types of Waiters or Waitresses

DUMB WAITERS

In buildings having the kitchen below the dining room, a dumb waiter is a necessity for serving the meals, and even where a dumb waiter is not needed from kitchen to dining room, it is a great convenience to have one running from cellar to kitchen or from laundry to upper floors.

A dumb waiter consists of a car enclosed in a shaft and suspended by ropes from a pulley, or pulleys above, so that it may be raised or lowered at will by means of a hand rope. The car itself is counterbalanced by iron weights, the extra weight due to the load being counter-balanced either by friction or resisted by a lock or grip. The car is steadied in its movement up and down by means of guide posts. The wheels and pulleys over which the ropes pass are made for this especial purpose, and are sold in sets under the name of Dumb Waiter Fittings. The car and guides may be made by the carpenter, who also usually furnishes the ropes and weights.

The size and shape of the car may be varied to suit the space available and the service required. The more common size for residences is 24 inches wide, 20 inches deep and 30 inches high, with two fixed shelves.

For tenement and apartment houses the car may be made

30 inches wide and 3 feet high, with one hinged shelf, so that a barrel may be set in it if desired.

The shaft should be at least 3 inches larger both ways than the car, and should be ceiled or plastered on the inside. If the weight runs between double guides, as shown, no extra space is required in the shaft, and the weight is readily accessible. For the style of dumb waiter, a square weight is used, running in a pocket behind or at one side of the shaft.

Dumb waiter fittings are a regular article of manufacture, and may either be bought separately or the complete apparatus, including car, ropes, runs, counterweight, etc., all ready to erect, may be purchased, the latter being usually the more satisfactory method.

The character and detail of the fittings vary with the manufacturer and with the size and capacity of the car and speed desired. Fixed shelves are placed at the top and bottom of the shaft for receiving the wheels, and the ropes pass through these shelves.

The rope by which the car is operated is fastened to the fixed upper shelf X, at I, and is carried down to and under the wheels E E on top of the car, up through the shelf and over the* wheel A, thence to the wheels at the bottom of the shaft and up to and over the wheels B and C, and there connected with the counter-balance by a pulley, the end of the rope being fastened to the top shelf close by where it started. A safety rope is attached to the top of the car, carried up through the fixed shelf over pulley D and connected with the counter balance so that should the operating rope break through long wear, the safety rope will keep the car from falling.

A brake grip, is attached to the under side of the shelf, so that the hand rope which elevates the car will pass through it. A cord attached to the grip passes over a small hooded pulley and down along side of the hand rope. To hold the car when loaded beyond its balance, it is only necessary to pull on the small cord, and by pulling on the hand rope the grip is released. It will be seen that all the working connections of this elevator are made with a single rope, so arranged that no matter how much it may stretch it will always be taut, the slack being taken up by the counter-balance, so that the slightest motion of the rope will start the car

The working mechanism of another type of dumb waiter, also very extensively used. In this style the hand rope merely turns the large wheel by friction, and hangs loose at the bottom. Attached to the axle of the large wheel is a smaller wheel, over which a rope passes, fastened at one end to the car and at the other to the counterweight. When the hand rope is pulled at one side or the other, the wheels are revolved and the car is raised or lowered according to the direction in which the wheels revolve. The lifting capacity of the waiter is regulated by the size of the hand wheel, which varies from 16 to 30 inches in diameter.

Dumb Waiters or Light Elevators

Dumb waiters or light elevators intended for buildings of several stories, are usually provided with a brake for the hand wheel, to which a check rope is attached, by means of which the speed of the car in descending may be regulated, the counterweight being adjusted so that the car will descend when the brake is released.

The fixtures for dumb waiters, not including ropes, weights or guide runs, nor the fixed platforms, cost about $15 for the smallest size, and about $25 for a medium size. With car and fittings all complete, the price varies from $30 to $40 for the smallest size, and up to $60 for larger sizes. For a run of more than 10 feet an additional price of from $5 to $10 per story is charged for the ropes, runs, etc.

Most dumb waiters may be made "double face," that is with openings on opposite sides for different stories; this involves, however, an additional charge of about $5 or $6, and more in some cases. A few styles can also be adapted to openings on adjacent sides, but this arrangement is not desirable if it can be avoided. The doors at the openings into the dumb waiter shaft are usually hung with cords and weights in the same manner as an ordinary window, and are provided with some form of spring catch which will hold the door either up or down.

WORK OF WAITER TRAY

A waiter's tray is similar to a waiter's stand or jack stand in the fact that it makes the serving process more efficient at an event. The waiter's tray is also used in restaurants and serves a couple of purposes:

- Ensures the waiter will not burn themselves on a hot plate
- Allows the waiter to serve the entire table at one time
- Allows for a more efficient cleanup
- Makes for a nice presentation of the food

A waiter's tray can be made of silver, glass, plastic or wood and usually is balanced on the palm of the waiter's hand. The tray is usually held at the waiter's head height and then rotated to chest level for serving. The waiter's tray is not meant to hold an abundance of plates because of the circumference of the tray itself, although this could vary. The stronger the waiter, the more plates that could probably be balanced on the tray especially during cleanup as plates could be stacked on top of one another.

Waiter trays that are used strictly for serving usually have a rubber surface covering that prevents plates and drinks from slipping around on the tray while it is being carried. Waiter trays can also be eaten off of which is more likely in a home setting or other small event. Waiter trays come in a variety of sizes and styles and can be very informal or formal in terms of design depending on the type of event. Waiter trays can also be obtained to match the design of the place setting as well. Waiter trays are great because they are usually stackable and store easily

Difficulties of the Waiter Job

Profession of the waiter has three compounds: rules of lying a table, rule and technical receptions of service of the visitors and basic rules. The waiters not only serve the visitors, serving tables according to the established standards, watching for cleanliness, condition and completeness of devices, utensils, cloths and napkins. They should well know the menu, basic and seasonal dishes and drinks, which offer to the visitors. The good waiter should manage to give explanations on each dish from the menu, to know, what products each dish is prepared from, what sauces can be offered to the chosen dish, to know and to offer fault to the order, having told thus to the client about a grade offered fault. Means, the waiter should have excellent memory.

One of the requirements to the waiter is perfect knowledge of assortment. Besides it is necessary to know a service: from what side to offer dishes, to watch for fullness of glasses, to be able to spread out the order from a general dish on personal plates, in time submit the bill.

Skill to communicate with the various people is integral skill for work by the waiter. The waiter within the framework of the competence can permit the problem which has arisen at the client. And main qualities, which should have the waiter, are mobility, politeness. It is simply necessary to the waiter to know bases of psychology, to understand subtleties of mood of the client. To establish contact to the visitors of restaurant is not simply skill to conduct professional dialogue. It and to a place the told joke, both having smile, and constrained manner to keep. The public catering is business based on personal dialogue. If you will manage to establish personal mutual relation, it will arrange the clients to your restaurant will help your institution to find the status "of the family friend", instead of it is simple place, where is possible to have a bite. Therefore, selecting the personnel, pay attention to; whether your future employee can support living conversation, instead of simply learn standard retorts and names of dishes.

Today restaurant business roughly develops and constantly requires the qualified staff. Therefore waiters are now very much claimed in the market of work.

Make More Waiter Tips

Many in the restaurant business will tell you that they heavily depend upon their waiter tips. This is the money that guests leave them for the quality of their service. In most instances the better service you provide the more money you are going to earn in this line of work. An extra dollar or two from each of the tables you serve will really add up at the end of the night.

To earn more waiter tips you need to be very sincere in your efforts. Your body language can say a great deal about how you feel in your role. It can be uncomfortable for the guests when they feel their waiter really doesn't want to be there. All of your efforts need to be sincere as well. Don't doubt that customers can pick up on fake enthusiasm as well.

It can take time for you to begin to earn more waiter tips but keep working on it. As you get more comfortable with your job you will learn ways to keep everyone happy. For example a nice greeting along with a smile when you first approach the table goes a long way. Being informed about specials and other menu choices is important as well. It will help you provide accurate information to your guests.

Pay attention to what is going on at their table as well. This way you can clear items out of their way, refill drinks before they are completely empty, and provide napkins and other items that will make their meal more enjoyable. Pampering each guest you serve is definitely going to result in more waiter tips coming your way.

If you do get any complaints from customers then listen to what is being said. You can learn additional skills this way too. For example some waiters are too quiet so they come across as being uninterested in those they serve. By working on opening up their communications though they will find they get more waiter tips. This type of job can be very convenient and fit well into any schedule. It is also an opportunity for you to make some money. In addition to your regular paycheck you will get waiter tips. It is up to you if they are going to be minimal or very good. Work hard to make sure you get the best possible tips from each table.

It is important to realize though that not everyone is a good tipper. You may provide excellent service and someone will only leave you a couple of dollars. Some people go by a set percentage of the price of their meals too. Keep in mind that customers don't have to leave tips. Some of them won't so to offset this you need to do your very best.

In general, most people that do go out to eat will base the amount of money they leave upon the quality of the service. So if you are doing very well you won't have any problem going home with a pocket full of waiter tips at the end of each shift.

RUDE WAITERS

Restaurants are now a flourishing, profitable and popular business in the country. Even celebrities have opened their restaurants. But I feel little attention is being paid to the recruitment of qualified, experienced and good waiters. By a good waiter I mean one who is smart, has a pleasing personality & good manners. Instead rude, argumentative and greedy waiters are being inflicted upon unsuspecting customers. I would like to share some of my experiences.

Experience 1: Our 1st year batch in hostel consisted of 17 girls and it was our first outing on our own after getting Freshers Welcome party. Just as we were entering a restaurant in Bhopal (thats where I did my B.E. from), a waiter came and started counting us like 1..2..3 !!!!!! As if we were some beggars lining up to eat at some temple to eat free food!!! We should have walked out but we didn't…God knows why! The service was horribly late and the food wasn't worth the price. (Shall I reveal the name of the restaurant to save any future customers?)

Experience 2: At a party with colleagues in a popular restaurant, one of my colleagues felt her glass has got mixed up with other glasses kept on table. So she asked the waiter to give a new one. But the waiter said pointing at a glass in front of her "This is a new one. I just filled it with water". Still this girl wanted a new one. He started shouting at her saying "I'm saying this is a new one. Why don't you drink from that one?" Till then we were quiet but after this I gave the waiter a piece of my mind (somehow the guys in our group are insipid and spineless lot) and said "How can you talk to a customer like that? Will a glass of water cost too much to the restaurant? Are we not paying?". Then I told him to stop looking after our table and we want to change our waiter. He went off grumbling in a huff. We complained to the owner but he didn't seem to care as if few less customers didn't make a difference to his booming business.

Experience 3: Yesterday again at a party with colleagues in another new and popular restaurant, we were sitting in the open air section when it started raining. Luckily our order hadn't arrived and we moved inside to another table. We were a group of 12 people. While I was placing the order (I m the official order-placer tip-decider waiter-handler in our group at every party..Sigh!) I'd just said the name of one dish when the waiter interrupted me saying "This wont be enough"!!!!!!!! As if I have never eaten at a restaurant before or we looked like bunch of 12 people who would eat only one dish !!! Come on nobody does that..not even the most miserly people. After I had completed he repeated same sentence again. I said "Don't worry, we will order again if there is a shortage." While waiting for dessert, lights went out and candles were lit & placed on upturned glasses!!!! Okay I understand they may not be familiar with the concept of candle sticks. At the end I left an adequate tip but the waiter said "Your group made us change tables. Atleast give some more tip." OMG!!!!! As if we had asked the rain to fall!! I mean since when did waiters start harassing customers for tip??? I gave him a stare and joined my group who had already gone outside.

There are still many incidents that I don't remember…consisting of ogling at the girls of any group, improperly dressed waiters with Salman Khan's Tere Naam hairstyle, overhearing talk and even commenting on it etc. etc.

The reasons for hiring such incompetent and ill mannered waiters may be any of these;

- Saving costs by keeping such amateur staff at low salaries.
- Unavailability of trained and experienced waiters.
- Ignorance of the employers regarding marketing strategies and thumb rules of a good service.
- The employer being of the same nature as that of the staff.
- The employer being indifferent towards the golden rule "Customer is the King" and being arrogant of huge profits.

Whatever maybe the reason, I feel the employers should learn a few things about the restaurant business and not run it like a grocery shop.

6

Job Descriptions and Training of Waiter or Waitress

WAITERS JOB DESCRIPTION

Definition and Nature of the Work

Waiters are the men and women who take orders and serve food in restaurants throughout the country. They are usually assigned to serve a certain number of tables (called a station) by the restaurant manager, the host or hostess, or the headwaiter. Waiters give a copy of the restaurant's menu to each customer and sometimes explain how the different meals on the menu are prepared.

They write down customers' orders so that the cooks can prepare each dish exactly as requested. When the food is ready, waiters carry it from the kitchen to the tables. Alert waiters remember what each person has ordered and can place the correct dish in front of the person who ordered it. This kind of service assures good tips and brings customers back to the restaurant. Waiters give constant attention to the guests.

They refill coffee cups and water glasses and ask if guests want to order anything else. They also record the food and drink prices on the guests' checks. When guests are ready to leave, waiters take the checks to the tables. In some restaurants waiters handle guests' payments for meals; in others guests take their checks directly to the cashier. There are many different kinds of restaurants, and the work of waiters varies accordingly.

In fine, elegant restaurants, waiters are supervised by a headwaiter and must serve food in special, formal ways. Many high-end restaurants offer a specific style of cooking—they may feature French, Greek, Italian, Japanese, or some other specialized cuisine. Quite often waiters in these restaurants speak the appropriate language when describing each dish. A completely different working atmosphere exists in other restaurants.

Some waiters work in cocktail lounges and nightclubs where alcoholic beverages are A waiter prepares a table before customers sit down. (© Steve Chenn/Corbis.) served. In small restaurants waiters are expected to perform many additional duties. They clean tables, clear dishes, and set the tables with clean tablecloths, napkins, silverware, glasses, and cups. Sometimes they do preparation work that includes filling salt, pepper, and sugar containers. They may also stock glasses and silverware where they can be reached easily during a rush period. In large restaurants dining room attendants usually perform these tasks. Because people often eat in restaurants during their leisure hours, waiters must be prepared to work evenings, weekends, and some holidays. The hours may be irregular, so many waiters work part time.

Education and Training Requirements

There are no formal education requirements for waiters; however, employers prefer to hire people who have a high school education. Basic skills in arithmetic are mandatory. A neat appearance and pleasant manner are also desirable. Some vocational schools offer training, but most waiters learn their skills on the job.

Fine restaurants like to hire people who have had experience or formal training. Candidates with little experience can accept jobs as dining room attendants and work toward a promotion. In certain restaurants waiters must have special skills, such as fluency in a foreign language or knowledge of formal table service. In restaurants that serve liquor, waiters must have reached the minimum drinking age in their state. Many states require that all waiters have health certificates stating they are free of communicable diseases.

Getting the Job

Interested individuals can find lists of job openings in newspaper want ads, on Internet job sites, or at their state employment office. Prospective waiters should also apply directly to restaurants in which they would like to work. Seasonal jobs are available in resort areas.

Advancement Possibilities and Employment Outlook

Waiters who do a good job may be promoted to a work shift that offers better opportunities for tips. Experienced waiters may look for jobs in restaurants that serve liquor, where tips are usually higher. They may become headwaiters or advance into the management end of the restaurant business. Americans are eating out more than ever, and new restaurants continue to open throughout the country.

The number of jobs for waiters through the year 2014 is expected to grow as fast as the average. More openings are available in less expensive restaurants because they have a high job turnover rate. Competition is highest for jobs in expensive restaurants, where wages and tips are higher. In some areas of the United States there are more openings than there are workers to fill them.

Working Conditions

Because restaurants serve the public, they are usually pleasant, comfortable places to work. However, the work can get hectic at times. Waiters must deal with many different personality types, handle any complaints from customers (or have the restaurant manager address them), and remain friendly and courteous even when extremely busy. This job is also physically demanding—it involves standing, walking, bending, and lifting heavy trays for hours at a time. Waiters can expect to work holidays, weekends, and evenings.

Full-time waiters usually work forty to forty-eight hours a week, and many belong to labour unions. Sometimes waiters work split shifts during which they work for a few hours, leave the restaurant, and return a few hours later. Many part-time jobs are available in this field. Some restaurants require waiters to wear uniforms. Employers may provide uniforms or an allowance for their purchase.

Earnings and Benefits

Wages for waiters vary greatly, depending on the type of restaurant in which they work and its location. According to the U.S. Bureau of Labour Statistics, full-time waiters earned a median wage of $6.75 per hour including tips in 2004.

Tips for waiters average from 10 to 20 percent of the guest check and are highest in the more expensive restaurants. Waiters usually earn more from tips than they do from wages. In some restaurants tips are placed into a tip pool that is shared by all waiters as well as other dining room staff.

JOB OF WAITERS AND WAITRESSES

The Job

WAITERS and WAITRESSES work in a lot of other places besides restaurants. You could work in hotel or motel dining rooms, coffee shops, diners, or other places where food and drinks are served.

To be a Waiter or Waitress you have to be able to think fast and have a good memory and be good at arithmetic. That's because in a lot of places the customers want their food right away, and you have to be able to remember their orders and write them down on the check correctly. You have to add up the items on the check without making a mistake and be able to figure out the tax.

In fancier places the customers are not in so much of a rush, but that also means they expect extra courtesy and better service. So, in these places you can relax a bit more, but you have to pay more attention to the customers.

They might want you to explain what goes into their meal and how it is cooked. You might recommend what wine they'd like to drink or you might prepare simple items like salads at the table.

Some smaller restaurants might have you doing things other types of workers are usually expected to do, like showing customers to their tables, or cleaning and setting up tables, or refilling salt and pepper shakers and making sure the mustard and ketchup bottles are full.

Working Conditions

Working conditions are generally nice. You work in clean, comfortable places, but there can be a lot of stress because you often have to work very fast under pressure during busy hours. Waiters and Waitresses have to do a lot of bending, carrying, lifting, reaching, standing, and stretching. The job has some dangers. It's possible to get burned by hot liquids or slip on food on the floor or to get hit by swinging doors.

Employment Outlook

The California Projections of Employment, published by the Labour Market Information Division of the Employment Development Department, estimates that the number of Waiters and Waitresses in California will reach 323,240 by 2005, an increase in new jobs of 109,830 over the number there was in 1993. There will also be an estimated 140,670 job openings due to people retiring or leaving the occupation.

Added to the 109,830 new jobs expected, this makes for an estimated total of 150,500 job opportunities through 2005. Over the next ten years, there will be more job opportunities for Waiters and Waitresses than for any other kind of job in California.

Wages, Hours, and Fringe Benefits

Although some very few are paid as much as $12.25 per hour, Waiters and Waitresses are usually paid minimum wage, plus tips. The amount of money you earn depends on the type of restaurant where you work. The bigger the restaurant the more tips you get; the more expensive the restaurant the bigger the tips you get. Waiters and Waitresses generally work a 40-hour, five-day workweek.

The employer usually provides one or two free meals per shift, depending on the length of the shift. Some employers provide life insurance and health and dental insurance. These benefits often are tied to and dependent upon the number of hours worked per week. In some work places, uniforms are provided for Waiters and Waitresses and sometimes the employer takes responsibility for uniform laundering. Some Waiters and Waitresses in California belong to the Hotel and Restaurant Employees and Bartenders International Union (AFL-CIO).

Entrance Requirements and Training

Waiters and Waitresses in restaurants that serve liquor must be at least 21 years old to serve alcohol. In some counties you have to pass a Food Handler course, which costs between $12.00 to $15.00, before being hired. Contact your county health department for a list of authorized schools that give the course. In some Mexican, Chinese, Vietnamese, etc., restaurants knowing how to speak the language is a plus and sometimes necessary.

Advancement

A few Waiters and Waitresses advance to supervisory jobs, like Head Waiter, Dining Room Supervisor, or Restaurant Manager.

TRAINING PROGRAMS FOR WAITERS

Training program for waiters is devoted to receiving of

qualitative education based on European and world standards, and allows to prepare certificated specialists who can work know-how on cruise vessels and in restaurants. Also this program is designed for perspective development of this sphere and increase of quantity of workplaces in it.

The goal of the Program: To provide theoretical and practical training in getting of waiter speciality, according to recognized European and world standards, preparation for innovations in cruise and restaurant industry just as in granting an opportunity to practice and apply this theoretical knowledge. The course gives students understanding about work of a waiter through an industrial practice, that enables students to apply the received knowledge and skills and also to expand further their skills.

Those knowledge is necessary for professional waiter for performance of duties in serving guests, reception and execution of orders, technique of serving courses and drinks, selection of wines to courses, maintenance of hygiene and sanitation level, maintenance of safety requirements and code of conduct. To engraft good taste and to bring up ethical behaviour and methods of work, ability to show skills and professionalism at all stages of work of professional wine steward. Basic methods of work of waiter with accent on European and basic world cruise and hotel standards, technical characteristics and exploitation of equipment.

Our personnel: Teachers have the richest work experience in the best hotels of Ukraine, Russia and are participants of various competitions, where they placed and have shown their high professionalism. They have passed accreditation in the Ministry of Education of the Crimea.

Studying of the Program

Training is carried out under three programs, destined for students with different level of vocational trading.

Level 1 is destined for students without waiter speciality and knowledge of English language, and who would like to receive a speciality and qualification of waiter. Duration of studying is 8 months.

There is five days per week training in our modern classrooms for theoretical classes and in training bars and restaurants. Classes are carried out by a form of introductory explanation of a theme with the further detailed studying of object of the lesson. Methods of work are explained and accompanied by demonstration of our teachers. The classes come to an end with comments of teachers and presentation of basic methods of work.

It is planned to visit constantly the best hotels of Yalta and cruise vessels where students can familiarize with methods and practical works and also the best wine factories located in Yalta. Periodically students will listen to lectures and attend master-classes, carried out by the best recognized specialists in this sphere. Students also have opportunity to practice in real conditions, demonstrating skills which they gained during theoretical and practical studying.

Received Knowledge during Studying the Program

During training students will get knowledge about work of waiter, flatware, utensil and rules of work with it, laying of tables, about classification of wines, about serving of wines, about decantation of wine, about temperature of submission of wine, technique of serving courses and drinks, on opening of bottles with a wine and shampagne, about different forms of serving, new forms of serving, about peculiarities of serving foreign tourists. Students will study methods of reception and execution of customers' orders, rules of serving courses and drinks, rules of serving sweet courses and ice-cream, rules of serving cheese, rules of serving receptions and banquettes. They will get knowledge on sanitation norms, safety and standards of hygiene, USPH requirements. Students will get attainments and skills of recommendation of wines to visitors according to the chosen courses; on granting wines to visitors of restaurant; on recommendations of various alcohol drinks.

The great attention will be paid to studying of English language-for 2-3 hours daily. It is basic requirement for work in international crews of cruise vessels.

Level 2 is destined for students without waiter speciality but with good knowledge of English language, and who would like to receive a speciality and qualification of waiter. Duration of studying is 3 months.

There is five days per week training in our modern classrooms for theoretical classes and in training bars and restaurants. Classes are carried out by a form of introductory explanation of a theme with the further detailed studying of object of the lesson. Methods of work are explained and accompanied by demonstration of our teachers. The classes come to an end with comments of teachers and presentation of basic methods of work.

It is planned to visit constantly the best hotels of Yalta and cruise vessels where students can familiarize with methods and practical works and also the best wine factories located in Yalta. Periodically students will listen to lectures and attend master-classes, carried out by the best recognized specialists in this sphere. Students also have opportunity to practice in real conditions, demonstrating skills which they gained during theoretical and practical studying.

Studying the Program

During training students will get knowledge about work of waiter, flatware, utensil and rules of work with it, laying of tables, about classification of wines, about serving of wines, about decantation of wine, about temperature of submission of wine, technique of serving courses and drinks, on opening of bottles with a wine and shampagne, about different forms of serving, new forms of serving, about peculiarities of serving foreign tourists. Students will study methods of reception and execution of customers' orders, rules of serving courses and drinks, rules of serving sweet courses and ice-cream, rules of serving cheese, rules of serving receptions and banquettes.

They will get knowledge on sanitation norms, safety and standards of hygiene, USPH requirements. Students will get attainments and skills of recommendation of wines to visitors according to the chosen courses; on granting wines to visitors of restaurant; on recommendations of various alcohol drinks. They will learn peculiarities and methods of work of waiter onboard of a cruise vessels, hotels and public catering enterprises.

Also there will be studying of English language but the main accent will be made on vocabulary and terminology of restaurant business and structure of a vessel.

During training students will receive knowledge of the menu and components in Russian and English languages. Students will get skills of work with drinks alcoholic and nonalcoholic. They will learn what is recherche cuisine, denomination and components of courses which lie in menu.

Level 3 is destined for students with waiter speciality and with good knowledge of English language and also work experience in restaurant industry and who would like to get employment on cruise vessels. Duration of studying is 1 month.

There is five days per week training in our modern classrooms for theoretical classes and in training bars and restaurants. Classes are carried out by a form of introductory explanation of a theme with the further detailed studying of object of the lesson. Methods of work are explained and accompanied by demonstration of our teachers. The classes come to an end with comments of teachers and presentation of basic methods of work.

It is planned to visit constantly the best hotels of Yalta and cruise vessels where students can familiarize with methods and practical works of waiter. Periodically students will listen to lectures and attend master-classes, carried out by the best recognized specialists in this sphere. Students also have opportunity to practice in real conditions, demonstrating skills which they were studying in theory.

Studying the Program

During training students will get an additional knowledge about work of wine steward. They will learn outstanding characteristics and methods of work of wine steward on cruise vessels and public catering enterprises. They will structure of crew on cruise vessel. They will learn what is cruise vessel and public catering enterprises. They will get knowledge on sanitation processing, safety and standards of hygiene, USPH requirements.

Also there will be studying of English language but the main accent will be made on culinary specialization, beverages and construction of a vessel.

7

Tipping of Waitresses and Waiters

WHY YOU NEED TO TIP YOUR WAITRESSES AND WAITERS

The hardest working, lowest paid, least appreciated worker has to be the server in your local restaurant. Waiters and waitresses are only paid $2.69 per hour in many places. The only workers in America that the government doesn't include in minimum wage laws, servers rely on tips from you to pay their bills and support their families. And many restaurants require servers to share their tips with bartenders, hostesses, and bus boys.

Now I'm not saying it's your job to support these workers. They're trying to do that themselves. On their feet for 8 hours a day—16 hours if they're lucky enough to pull a double shift—waiters and waitresses do an assortment of jobs in their work. They not only take your order and bring you your food, they clean, make food items such as salads, sundaes, and shakes, roll silverware, clean tables, refill salt and pepper shakers, ketchup and sauce bottles, sugar canisters, sweeteners, jelly, creamer, and napkin dispensers. They make coffee, refill drinks, pick up, vacuum, fill take-out orders, run the cash register, and clean bathrooms. They try to do all this with a smile and pleasant conversation for you and their other customers while following the rules of the establishment.

Servers try to anticipate their customers needs and wants and try to be available to fill needs and wants they haven't thought of. They converse with your children, bring over booster seats and high chairs, and offer suggestions from their own experiences to make your dining more pleasant. They know their earnings depend on how pleased you are with their service. At least, that's what they used to think.

These days are tough for everyone economically. Food prices are higher, so a couple or family going out to dinner may be presented with a bill that's higher than they expected. Rather than skipping dessert, ordering less expensive menu items, or passing on the appetizer and pre-dinner drink, most of these people are stiffing the servers.

Waitresses and waiters are expected to receive a tip that equals 15% of what the food costs. That's how restaurant owners report their wages to the IRS. One single mother that's been waitressing for ten years said, "I wish I made as much as I do on paper. I could afford to pay my rent and feed my son." Programs made available to lower income workers aren't available to waiters and waitresses in this situation. On paper, it looks like they make enough money to get by, so aren't eligible for help.

I'm not referring to incompetent servers. The waitress who

ignores her customers and doesn't even attempt to give them what they need, and the waiter who spends an hour on the phone haven't earned their 15%. But waiters and waitresses who have been praised by their customers and commended to their employers are going to clear their tables and finding a $4.00 tip for an $80.00 food bill. Even someone very bad in math should know that's not even close to 15%. And many people say, "Sorry, I didn't bring enough money," and don't leave anything. The server then has to pay taxes from their $2.69 an hour on the earnings they never received from their customers.

Why don't they quit and find something else?

I'm not sure what the job market is like where you live, but it's been very bad around here for over five years, and it's getting worse. Many servers don't have any options. Something, even if it's only $2.69 an hour, is better than nothing.

At least, it would be if it didn't cost more for gas to get to work than you make.

Remember that your server doesn't prepare the food. It's not their fault if it's not cooked the way you want it or doesn't taste as good as you expected. And it's not their fault that you wanted an alcoholic drink but forgot your identification. Stiffing a waitress or waiter because they can't break the law and the rules of their employers is not only grossly unfair, it shows a complete lack of class.

Look more kindly at the next waiter or waitress that serves you. Are they trying to make your dining experience pleasant? If so, you owe them at least 15% of what you paid for your food. Did they make your dining experience pleasant? Then you owe them more.

My income is lower than that of most people, and I still tip servers. I ask myself, did my server take my order and bring me my food and drink? If so, they'll get at least 15%. If they made pleasant conversation, checked to see how the food was and refilled drinks, they'll receive 20%. The more pleasant my experience is, the more my waitresses and waiters make. If I take care of the servers that take care of me, my next dining experience will be that much better.

Waiters and Waitresses Serve Food in Restaurants

Waiters and waitresses serve food in restaurants and other dining establishments.

Being a waiter or waitress is more than just asking, ¿You want fries with that?¿ You might say that it's the ultimate job in multitasking. The party at table one needs their waters refreshed, the entrees for the couple at table three are ready to be served, and the trio at table five need to be cashed out. This means that in a matter of minutes you can handle water pitchers, hot plates, and a credit card (or several if they split the check). So, if you are fast on your feet, quick-thinking, and can perform several tasks at once, working as a waiter or waitress can be a good choice for you.

Depending on the size and type of restaurant, waiters and waitresses have a variety of job duties. Waiters and waitresses take orders for food and drinks. They check customers' identification before serving alcoholic beverages. They describe daily specials and are sometimes asked to suggest an item on the menu or explain how an item is prepared. After writing down or memorizing orders, waiters and waitresses relay orders to the kitchen staff or enter them into computers. Waiters and waitresses serve beverages. If ordered, they serve appetizers, salads, or soups before the main course. When the main course is ready to be served, waiters or waitresses make sure the order is complete and may add garnishes to the plate. Sometimes waiters or waitresses carve meats or prepare special items at customers' tables.

Waiters and waitresses observe customers to make sure they have everything they need. They refill water glasses or other beverage items when needed. They also watch to determine when each course has been completed. Waiters and waitresses describe and take orders for dessert. They sometimes bring a tray containing a serving of each dessert special to customers' tables. When the meal is complete, waiters or waitresses remove the dishes and glasses from the table and take them to the kitchen. They compute the cost of the meal and prepare the check. They also accept payments or refer customers to the cashier.

After customers have left, waiters or waitresses may replace the tableware and linen. They refill salt, pepper, sugar, cream, and condiment containers. They also clean and arrange chairs, and table pieces. In more expensive restaurants, headwaiters may greet and direct customers to tables. Headwaiters also take reservations over the phone and supervise other staff.

Work Activities

The following list of occupational tasks is specific to this career.

- Check customers' identification before serving alcoholic beverages.
- Accept payments or refer customers to cashiers.
- Relay orders to the kitchen or enter orders into computers.
- Memorize or write down orders from customers.
- Take orders from customers.
- Observe customers to find out if anything else is needed. Determine when the meal and beverages have been finished.
- Serve meals to customers or direct customers to buffets.
- Compute the cost of meals and prepare checks.
- Remove dishes from tables or counters and take them to the kitchen.
- Give menus to customers, describe meals not on the menu, and answer questions regarding preparation.
- Inform customers of daily specials.
- Clean and arrange tables, including chairs, linen, silverware, and glassware.

- Prepare beverages for customers or serve wine.
- Explain how meals are prepared, describing ingredients and cooking methods.
- Help prepare food, such as salads, appetizers, and cold dishes.
- Stock shelves with supplies, such as coffee and linens.
- Help decorate dishes.
- Refill salt, pepper, sugar, cream, condiments, and napkin containers.
- Lead customers to their tables.
- Describe and recommend wines to customers.

People in this career perform the following list of tasks, but the tasks are common to many occupations.

- Work with the public.
- Establish and maintain relationships.
- Communicate with supervisors, peers, or subordinates.
- Handle and move objects.
- Identify objects, actions, and events.
- Get information needed to do the job.
- Judge the value of objects, services, or people.
- Perform activities that use the whole body.
- Make decisions and solve problems.
- Care for others.
- Monitor events, materials, and surroundings.
- Teach others.
- Coordinate the work and activities of others.
- Organize, plan, and prioritize work.
- Convince others to buy goods or change their minds or actions.
- Inspect equipment, structures, or materials.
- Resolve conflicts and negotiate with others.

Working Conditions

In a typical work setting, people in this career:

Interpersonal Relationships

- Have a high level of social interaction. They work closely with customers and coworkers.
- Often deal with unpleasant, angry, or discourteous customers.
- Are responsible for the health and safety of their coworkers and customers.
- Are responsible for work outcomes.
- Are often placed in conflict situations.
- Communicate with coworkers and customers daily in person.
- Work in a group or as part of a team.
- Communicate with coworkers and customers weekly by telephone.

Physical Work Conditions

- Work indoors most of the time, but may sometimes work in outdoor serving areas.
- Are often exposed to hazardous situations that may produce cuts or burns.
- Often wear a special uniform or dress according to a dress code.
- Work very near coworkers and customers. They often work within inches of other people.

Work Performance

- Must be exact in their work. This is to ensure that customers are satisfied.
- Must repeat the same physical activities, such as serving food.
- Make decisions on a weekly basis that affect customers.

They are able to make some decisions without talking to a supervisor.

- Are able to set some tasks for the day without talking to a supervisor.

Hours/Travel

- Generally have a set schedule each week.
- May work part time or full time, but most work less than 40 hours a week.
- May work weekends, evenings, and holidays.
- May work split shifts. For example, they might work from 6 a.m. to 10 a.m. and 3 p.m. to 7 p.m., with time off in between.

Physical Demands

In a typical work setting, people in this career: People in this career frequently:

- Stand and walk for long periods of time.
- Use their hands to handle, control, or feel objects, tools, or controls.
- Repeat the same movements.
- Bend or twist their body.

It is important for people in this career to be able to:

- Speak clearly so listeners can understand.
- Understand the speech of another person.
- Use stomach and lower back muscles to support the body for long periods without getting tired.
- Coordinate movement of several parts of the body, such as arms and legs, while the body is moving.
- Hold the arm and hand in one position or hold the hand steady while moving the arm.

It is not as important, but still necessary, for people in this career to be able to:

- Be physically active for long periods without getting tired or out of breath.
- See details of objects that are less than a few feet away.
- Use one or two hands to grasp, move, or assemble objects.
- Bend, stretch, twist, or reach out.
- Move arms and legs quickly.
- Move two or more limbs together (for example, two arms, two legs, or one leg and one arm) while remaining in place.
- Use muscles to lift, push, pull, or carry heavy objects.
- Focus on one source of sound and ignore others.

CAREERS SERIES: WAITRESS/WAITER/RESTAURANT SERVER

On the Job

Every restaurant or café is different when it comes to what it requires of it's servers. But there are some general tasks that you can expect to do. These are listed below.

- Bring wine selections to tables with appropriate glasses, and pour the wines for customers.
- Check patrons' identification to ensure that they meet minimum age requirements for consumption of alcoholic beverages.
- Check with customers to ensure that they are enjoying their meals and take action to correct any problems.
- Clean tables or counters after patrons have finished dining.
- Collect payments from customers.
- Describe and recommend wines/dishes to customers.
- Escort customers to their tables.
- Explain how various menu items are prepared, describing ingredients and cooking methods.

- Fill salt, pepper, sugar, cream, condiment, and napkin containers.
- Garnish and decorate dishes in preparation for serving.
- Inform customers of daily specials.
- Perform food preparation duties such as preparing salads, appetizers, and cold dishes, portioning desserts, and brewing coffee.
- Prepare checks that itemize and total meal costs and sales taxes.
- Prepare hot, cold, and mixed drinks for patrons, and chill bottles of wine.
- Prepare tables for meals, including setting up items such as linens, silverware, and glassware.
- Present menus to patrons and answer questions about menu items, making recommendations upon request.
- Remove dishes and glasses from tables or counters, and take them to kitchen for cleaning.
- Serve food or beverages to patrons, and prepare or serve specialty dishes at tables as required.
- Stock service areas with supplies such as coffee, food, tableware, and linens.
- Take orders from patrons for food or beverages.
- Write patrons' food orders on order slips, memorize orders, or enter orders into computers for transmittal to kitchen staff.

Benefits and Salary

$5.79 to $10.16 an hour. Although some combined food preparation and serving workers receive a part of their earnings as tips, fast-food workers usually do not. Tipped employees are those who customarily and regularly receive more than $30 a month in tips. The employer may consider tips as part of wages, but the employer must pay at least $2.13 an hour in direct wages.

Many employers provide free meals and furnish uniforms, but some may deduct from wages the cost, or fair value, of any meals or lodging provided. Food and beverage service workers who work full time often receive typical benefits, but part-time workers usually do not.

Daily Routine & Work Environment

Waiters and Waitresses are constantly moving around in a fast-paced environment. You'll have to weave in and out of tables and other coworkers, deliver food and drinks to your table in a timely manner. Food and beverage service workers are on their feet most of the time and often carry heavy trays of food, dishes, and glassware. During busy dining periods, they are under pressure to serve customers quickly and efficiently. The work is relatively safe, but care must be taken to avoid slips, falls, and burns. Food service and drinking establishments typically maintain long dining hours and offer flexible and varied work opportunities. Many food and beverage serving and related workers work evenings, weekends, and holidays.

Experience & Required Education

There are no specific educational requirements for most food and beverage service jobs. Many employers prefer to hire high school graduates for waiter and waitress, bartender, and host and hostess positions, but completion of high school usually is not required for fast-food workers, counter attendants, dishwashers, and dining room attendants and bartender helpers. For many people, a job as a food and beverage service worker serves as a source of immediate income, rather than a career. Many are full-time students or homemakers. Food and beverage service jobs are a major source of part-time employment for high school and college students. It also serves as a great way to gain customer service experience.

All new employees usually receive some training from their employer. They learn safe food handling procedures and sanitation practices, for example. Some employers, particularly those in fast-food restaurants, teach new workers using self-study programs, on-line programs, audiovisual presentations, and instructional booklets that explain food preparation and service skills. But most food and beverage serving and related workers pick up their skills by observing and working with more experienced workers. Some full-service restaurants also provide new dining room employees with some form of classroom training that alternates with periods of on-the-job work experience. These training programs communicate the operating philosophy of the restaurant, help establish a personal rapport with other staff, teach formal serving techniques, and instill a desire to work as a team. They also provide an opportunity to discuss customer service situations and the proper ways of handling unpleasant circumstances or unruly patrons.

Personality

Those likely to enjoy a job in waiting or as a server, you'll enjoy working directly with the public. You're constantly on your feet and on the go so this is a good job for someone who doesn't like to sit still during the day. Most times waiting staff develop relationships with "regulars" or customers who will visit daily or regularly. Sometimes when waiting you'll deal with some upset customers and can sometimes be high stress so individuals who can handle these types of situations calmly would be a good fit.

TIP (GRATUITY): EXTRA PAYMENT

A tip (also called a gratuity) is a voluntary extra payment made to certain service sector workers in addition to the advertised price of the transaction. Such payments and their size are a matter of social custom. Tipping varies among cultures and by service industry. Though by definition a tip is never legally required, and its amount is at the discretion of the patron being served, in some circumstances failing to give an adequate tip when one is expected may be considered very miserly, a violation of etiquette, or unethical. In some other cultures or situations, giving a tip is not expected and offering one would be considered condescending or demeaning. In some circumstances (such as tipping government workers), tipping is illegal.

Etymology

There are common inaccurate claims that "tip" (or "tips") is an acronym for a phrase such as "To Insure Prompt Service", "To Insure Proper Service", "To Improve Performance", or "To Insure Promptness." These false backronyms contradict the verifiable etymology, as follows.

According to the *Oxford English Dictionary*, the word *tip* originated as a slang term, and its etymology is unclear. The term in the sense of "to give a gratuity" first appeared in the 18th century. It derived from an earlier sense of *tip*, meaning "to give; to hand, pass", which originated in the rogues' cant in the 17th century. This sense may have derived from the 16th-century *tip* meaning "to strike or hit smartly but lightly" (which may have derived from the Low German *tippen*, "to tap"), but this derivation is "very uncertain".

Circumstances of Tipping

In countries where tipping is expected (the United States for example), complicated unofficial standards and customs have developed over the exact percentage to tip, and what should and should not be included in this calculation. In other cultures where tipping exists it is more flexible and no specific assumptions of the tip amount exist.

Some believe the custom of tipping helps to improve service, as workers may receive higher tips from satisfied customers. In the United States, some employers pay workers with the expectation that tips will make up the difference. The practice of tipping is controversial, with numerous criticisms. Some have criticized the inherent "social awkwardness" in transactions that involve tipping, the inconsistency of tipping for some services but not similar ones, and the irrationality of basing tips on price, rather than the amount and quality of service (a customer pays a larger tip to a server bringing him a lobster rather than a hamburger, for example).

A number of economists have suggested that tipping is economically inefficient. Ian Ayres, Fredrick E. Vars & Nasser Zakariya published a paper suggesting that tipping contributed to racial prejudice, since ethnic minorities would often be less able to pay a large tip. Another paper by Yoram Margalioth of Tel Aviv University argued that there was a negative externality associated with tipping, and that the practice facilitated tax evasion. Two other American studies have contributed to the thesis that tipping is racially discriminatory, finding that ethnic minority servers and taxicab drivers received lower tips on average than their white counterparts. In the study of the servers, an attempt by the author to isolate other possible contributing factors, such as poor service, found that "After controlling for these other variables ... the server race effect is comparable across customer race."

Others have criticised the belief that "Waiters know that they won't get paid if they don't do a good job," with one study from a Cornell University professor concluding that "consumers' assessments of the quality of service correlate weakly to the amount they tip," relying more on superficial factors such as the attractiveness of the server or how large the bill is.

Tipping is not expected when a fee is explicitly charged for the service. For example, a service charge for all patrons that is automatically added to the tab with no tipping is very common in Brazil, but it's never mandatory to pay this charge. Bribery and corruption are sometimes disguised as tipping. In some places, police officers and other civil servants openly solicit tips, gifts and dubious fees using a variety of local euphemisms. For example, a traffic policeman in Mexico might ask a commuter to buy him a "refresco" (soft drink), while a Nigerian officer might expect "a little something for the weekend."

TIPPING BY REGION

Asia

China

In China, traditionally there is no tipping. However, hotels that routinely serve foreign tourists may allow tipping. An example would be tour guides and associated drivers.

Taiwan

In Taiwan tipping is rare except when a customer uses a porter at an airport, which is usually 50 New Taiwan Dollars per luggage, or wants to show appreciation for exceptional service. Some restaurants and hotels already add 10% service charges. The service charge is generally applied at restaurants where the waiter is expected by the employer to pay a great deal of attention to the customer, or if the meal requires assistance from the wait staff (as in some barbecue restaurants).

Australia

Tipping is not a traditional practice in Australia, although in recent times it has become more prevalent in restaurants and hotels (particularly in larger cities) possibly due to more common exposure to American practices. Even in these places, it tends to be reserved for instances of particularly good service. Tipping staff of any other kind of business is very unusual. Casinos in Australia generally prohibit tipping of gaming staff, as it is considered bribery.

Central and South America

Argentina

Tipping is common in restaurants and bars, usually around 10% of the bill when happy with the service received. Leaving no tip when feeling unsatisfied is not an uncommon gesture, and it's interpreted as such. Many restaurants include a small service charge or *cubierto* of fixed value (typically no more than

5 Argentine pesos per customer), but even so a tip is expected. Tips are also usually given for food delivery services and luggage carrying and loading/unloading from buses. Taxicab drivers are not tipped.

Another local custom is to tip the ushers in theaters and opera houses when they're also in charge of handing out the *programmes* (one may request one without tipping, at the risk of being considered cheap).

Bolivia

Service charges are included with the bill. Still, a small tip, around 5% or so, is sometimes given, and is considered polite.

Brazil

Optional service charges of 10% are included at some restaurant bills, and additional tips are very rare. While tips can sometimes be given for some services, such as taxis, delivery or tourism, tips are very uncommon.

Colombia

Tipping is not very common in services like haircuts or taxi rides, therefore is not expected, the usual practice is to round up the total. nevertheless tips are highly appreciated.

In restaurants a 10% tip is commonly added to the bill, which can be paid or not depending on the guest's satisfaction.

Paraguay

Service charges are included with the bill, and tipping is uncommon.

Europe

In the European Union and elsewhere in Europe, tipping practices vary from region to region, although, in general, tipping is not considered obligatory.

In many European countries it is a legal requirement to quote prices including all taxes. The expectation when a price is advertised, is to pay that amount and no more. Restaurants post a menu outside including prices.

If a service charge is to be added, this is usually indicated on the menu. If an establishment attempts to charge more than was shown on a menu, for example by adding a service charge which was not clearly posted, or by adding a tip by default, this is likely to be seen as an attempt to overcharge the customer.

Iceland

In Iceland tipping is rare. Service charges are generally included in the bill.

Ireland

Tipping is not a general habit except in taxis, hairdressers/ barbers, and restaurants with table service. The same general rules apply as in the United Kingdom. For example, it is not customary to tip in bars or for any over-the-counter service, but waiters in pubs are usually tipped a token amount.

Although it has been cited that tipping for taxis is typical, it is not common in practice. Commonly people will roundup the fare to the nearest note to avoid fumbling for small change (for example, hand over €5.00 for a fare of €4.50)

In Ireland it is not customary to tip a percentage of the total bill, a few small coins is generally considered quite polite. Like most of Europe it is common to round up to the nearest note, (i.e. paying €30 for a bill of €26).

Romania

The tip is usually 10% of the bill and is expected in restaurants, coffee shops, taxi, hair dresser.

Slovenia

Tipping is not customary in Slovenia and traditionally it is almost never done. In recent times, however, high-tourist areas have begun to accept tips, which are welcomed but not obligatory. In such cases, the amount is typically 10 percent, but may range higher in exceptional circumstances.

Spain

Tipping ("propina") is not customary and not generally considered mandatory in Spain. In restaurants the amount of the tip, if any, depends mainly on the economic status of the customer and on the kind of locale, higher percentages being expected in upscale restaurants. In bars and small restaurants, Spaniards sometimes leave as a tip the small change left in their plate after paying a bill. Outside the restaurant business, some service providers, such as taxicab drivers, hairdressers and hotel personnel may expect a tipping an upscale setting. In 2007 the Minister of Economy Pedro Solbes put the blame on the excessive tipping for the increase of the inflation.

Switzerland

Tipping is expected, though not mandatory in Switzerland, but a tip of 10% would be considered "weird". For small amounts, round up to the next franc, in a restaurant a few francs at max (1-1.5%).

Turkey

In Turkey, tipping, or *bah°i°* is usually optional and not customary in many places. However, a tip of 5-10% is expected in restaurants, which is usually paid by "leaving the change". Cab drivers usually don't expect to be tipped, though, rounding the fare upward would be appreciated. In hotels, a small change as a tip would be enough make most porters happy. Tipping or "leaving the change" in shops or for fixed-price services is seen as an insult.

United Kingdom

Tipping throughout the UK is usually expected at restaurants (but not always given) and sometimes taxis. The practice is also relatively common for some other services, such as hairdressers.

It is not customary to tip for service at the bar in a U.K. pub. However bars (as distinct from pubs, for example cocktail bars) will often deliver change on a plate to a customer being served at the bar and expect some or all of it to be left as a tip. Tips are usual for table service in either pubs or bars.

It is a legal requirement to post prices including any taxes and other charges. Additional service charges at restaurants are unusual, although more common in London and other large cities than regional areas. Where these occur, it is legal to refuse to pay the service charge if you believe the service was inadequate.

Taxation in the U.K.

A tronc is an arrangement for the pooling and distribution to employees of tips, gratuities and/or service charges in the hotel and catering trade. The person who distributes monies from the tronc is known as the troncmaster. When a tronc exists in the UK, responsibility for operating PAYE on the distribution may lie with the troncmaster rather than the employer. (The word 'tronc' has its origins in the French for collecting box.) In June 2008, the Employment Appeals Tribunal ruled that income from a tronc cannot be counted when assessing whether a wage or salary meets the national minimum wage, although this decision is currently being appealed.

North America

Canada

Tipping in Canada is similar to that in the United States due to the close cultural nature of the two countries but tends to be somewhat lower due to better minimum wages and lower employee cost (e.g. universal medical care). Restaurant wait staff in Canada typically receive about 15% on the before-tax total, although anywhere from 10-20% is within the average range.

Quebec and Ontario allow employers to pay lower minimum wages to workers who would reasonably be expected to be receiving tips. In Ontario, the minimum wage is $9.50 per hour, with exceptions for: Students under 18 years old and employed for not more than 28 hours a week, who are paid $8.20 per hour; and liquor servers, who are paid $7.60 per hour.

Workers who receive tips are legally required to report the income to the Canada Revenue Agency and pay income tax on it. However, many workers have been known to report no income from tips at all or, perhaps more commonly, to "lowball" the figure. In response, the CRA has vowed that it will closely check the tax returns of individuals that it would reasonably expect to be receiving tips to ensure that the tips are reported, and that the amount reported on the returns is realistic.

United States

Tipping is a widely practiced social custom in the United States. Standards vary, but generally, gratuities are given for services rendered in the restaurant, bar, hotel, and taxi industries. For most of the 20th century it was considered inappropriate for the owner of an establishment to accept any tips, and while this is still considered the standard etiquette rule, the practice has mostly vanished as tipping has become ubiquitous for certain types of services. Tipping is done only by the host of a party. Guests should never leave tips as this breaches the host's hospitality. This etiquette applies to bar service at weddings and any other event where one is a guest as well. The host should provide appropriate tips to workers at the end of an event.

Tipping in the United States is so common and expected in some cases that in many service establishments, such as hair salons and restaurants, customers are actually asked by employees (verbally or with posted messages) to give a tip, or are verbally abused by staff for "stiffing" them, even though such behaviour on the part of the staff is considered completely contrary to proper etiquette and standard professional business practices.

Laws in the states of Alaska, California, Minnesota, Montana, Nevada, Oregon, and Washington require all employees to be paid at least minimum wage. However, it is still customary to give standard tips in those places. Elsewhere, wage laws allow employers to credit an amount of earned tips against the minimum wage, allowing them to pay tipped employees less than minimum wage. As of September 2009, this reduction can be as low as $1.45 per hour in West Virginia, or as high as 100% in Virginia, reducing potential wages to $5.80 or $0 per hour, respectively. Which employees may have their wages reduced varies as well. The Fair Labour Standards Act defines a tipped employee as anyone receiving more than $30 per month in tips, although several states set a lower $20 per month threshold.

Restaurants

Tipping is customary in restaurants offering traditional table service. While the amount of a tip is ultimately at the discretion of the patron, the customary tip until the 1980s was from 10 to 15 percent of the total bill before tax, for good to excellent service, and since then has risen to 15 to 20 percent before tax. Tipping percentages may fall when the economy is poor. Waiters, on average, fail to report at least 40 percent of their tips according to the IRS.

When a server has not adequately addressed issues a customer has with service, the patron may choose to speak with management to have the problems corrected before considering reducing the tip. In extreme cases of inferior service, the patron may choose not to leave a tip. Though not considered a standard business practice, some dissatisfied customers go so far as to leave a very small tip, such as one penny, as a personal insult.

For large groups, such as six or more, many restaurants add a standard predetermined service charge (~18%) in lieu of the gratuity. Reputable restaurants post their policy on a sign or the menu, or require servers to inform their patrons of such charges before they order. This charge can be verified by the customer on the bill to avoid tipping in addition to the service charge. A service charge is also taxed by the IRS. Customers have a right to negotiate, alter, or refuse charges which were hidden until the bill arrived. A customer may choose to include an extra tip for the server over and above the service charge, or, if service to a large party is poor, to negotiate an alternate service charge with management. While some advocate increasing tipping for the benefit of employees who lack direct customer contact, such as kitchen, bar, and bus staff, the funds may or may not be used for that purpose. Some service worker advocacy groups point out that some restaurants have agreements among the staff requiring servers to "tip out," *i.e.* give a portion of their tips to members of the support staff, while anti-tipping groups point out that some establishments already allocate a percent of the bill (such as 3%) directly to the support staff from the receipts rather than from tips. Many traditional restaurants offer carry-out ("pick-up," "take-out, or "curbside") service, and standards for tipping for such services vary. Tipping is not traditionally required for non-table services. Some advocate optional tipping in the case of exceptional service or difficult orders, while those working in the industry often promote 5-15% as appropriate.

Tipping at fast food restaurants and coffeehouses that do not offer table service is not necessary, despite the common proliferation of tip jars (*a.k.a.* guilt cans), which are considered inappropriate by many. Such tips may be divided amongst the on-shift staff (except for salaried management), whether or not such staff directly contributed to a patron's order.

Taxicabs

Most U.S. guides recommend 15% of the fare, more for extra services or heavy luggage.

Government employees

Under federal law it is considered bribery to tip federal government employees. However, they are permitted to receive unsolicited non-monetary gifts less than or equal to $20.00.

Other

Many retailers forbid their employees to accept tips, although this is illegal in some states, such as California, where the law states "tips are the property of whom they are given, and employers are not allowed to require employees to refuse, give, or share their tips with anyone."

Taxation

In some jurisdictions, tipped workers qualify for a lower statutory minimum wage from the employer, and therefore may supplement deficient pay with tips. For example, the United States Internal Revenue Service (IRS) requires restaurant employers to ensure that the total tip income (both cash and tips added to credit or debit card receipts) reported to them during any pay period is at least eight percent of their total receipts for that period. If the reported total is below eight percent, employers must allocate as income the difference between the actual tip income reported and eight percent of gross receipts. Legally, tips should be reported as income for tax purposes by the recipient. Form 4070 is provided by the IRS for daily tracking of tip income and reporting to employers by the 10th of the month for the previous month.

WHEN SHOULD YOU NOT TIP YOUR WAITER?

Generally, you should not tip your waiter when your are extremely unhappy with the service. Though the standard is to tip 15 percent of the total bill for good service at lunch and 20 percent of the total bill for good service at dinner, these are highly subjective. In other words, your tip should depend on what you think is appropriate, not what the social standards may be.

Sometimes, restaurants may offer exceptional service and the servers should be rewarded accordingly. If a server goes out of the way to correct an issue, or provides exemplary service in other ways, a 20 percent tip may balloon even higher, depending on your tipping style.

In some cases, to really send a message, it may be good to leave some sort of tip, even if tempted to not tip your waiter. Those who decide to not tip your waiter may be sending a mixed signal in some ways. For example many restaurants may allow tips to be left on a credit card. A waiter may not see this until the end of the night. In other cases, if you decide to not tip your waiter, he may think it was simply an oversight.

To truly send a message that is understood nearly universally by waiters, leaving a small tip, such as a US penny, if in the United States, is a good way to express your displeasure with the service. This sends the unmistakable signal that, yes, you meant to tip. However, a tip of any substantial value was not warranted.

For those who really want to offer some constructive criticism, leaving your reasons for not tipping would be a good idea. In this way, even if you decide to not tip your waiter with money, you can leave service tips in a very literal way. Of course, this may be redundant. In most cases, the waiter will know where things went wrong. It may be his or her fault, and he or she was having an off day. Or it may be the fault of the kitchen.

In general, if there is a problem with the service and you cannot figure out who is responsible, it is always good to ask what the problem is. It may be the kitchen, the server, or something beyond anyone's control. Determining what the problem is before deciding to not tip your waiter is always a good idea. That way, you make sure the wrong person is not punished.

GUIDE FOR WAITERS AND WAITRESSES TO MAXIMIZE TIP REVENUE

Waiting tables can be a tough and rewarding experience. Like most any endeavour in life, you get out of it what you put into it. However, as with the 80/20 rule (80% of the rewards are realized with just 20% of the effort), the attention to detail on the tips included in this book will maximize your tip income with very little extra effort. The tips included in this book will make stand out from ordinary waitstaff. You will become a wonderful server in the eyes of your patrons.

When John and Martha consider going out for dinner, you want them to first consider you. "Let's get that girl, Stacy to wait on us", Martha will say after they get going.

John replies, "Is she the girl that waited on us last time?"

"Yes."

"Yeah, I think she did a good job last time too."

"I think if we ask for her, they will seat us in her section." Says, Martha.

Remember the Golden Rule, "Do unto others as you would have them do unto you." Think about how you would like to be treated when you dine out and treat the people you are going to wait on that way too.

What follows are more specific tips of do's and don't's that I have gleaned over the years.

Finding the Right Job

First of all, you need to consider the potential for any job that you are or will be working at. Restaurant selection, available work shifts, and other factors can make a huge difference in your tips regardless of your abilities. Here are some things to consider:

Restaurant Selection

In general, the more upscale the restaurant, the better your opportunites will be for earning large tips. However, you can also make good tips working at more mainstream restaurants with high volume/turnover. If you don't already know where a restaurant stands in these terms, you can usually figure it out by checking these criteria:

Menu

What is the average cost per person for a typical meal? This will have a direct bearing on your tip potential as most patrons base tips on percentage of the total bill. While it is not unusual for wonderful servers to receive tips far in excess of 20% of the total bill, patrons of upscale restaurants are generally more inclined to reward good service. It is good to pick a restaurant where the menu prices are high.

Parking Lot

You do not want to see an empty parking lot with no cars in it. However, you also do not want to see people fighting for parking spots so they can go into the mall and check out the nearest sale. What you want to see, is people vying for parking spaces, so they can go in and eat (even waiting in a line if they have to). There should be cars parked neatly, and the building should be easy to get to from any location.

Appearance

When you get into the parking lot, be sure that it is clean too. By clean, I mean well kept. If it isn't clean, then you have a problem. Check for trash (you don't want to see any). Something I've found is that people give more money to waiters that work in nice places. Winding sidewalks from the parking lot, nice landscaping, interior decorating, lighting and furniture can all contribute to the ambiance for the dining experience.

Look for restaurants that pay attention to these details. If people don't like the food or their experience from beginning to end, they will not like giving you money either. You should also talk to the current waitstaff at the restaurant and see how much money they make on an average shift. Of course, this will not necessarily apply to you (you should make more than most of them with the tips you learn in this book), but it should give you an idea of the general potential.

Try to avoid restaurants offering buffets. Customers do not tip well when they serve themselves. Also try to avoid restaurants that have television sets in the dining areas. TVs distract diners and can cause people to sit at tables too long. Slow turnover cuts into your profit potential.

Work Shifts

The day of the week can have a huge impact on your tip potential. Generally, new waitstaff are given the worst work shifts and waitstaff with seniority are given the better work shifts, however, wonderful servers can earn their way into the prime time work shifts faster. So which shifts are "prime time"? Saturday night is the best shift to work if you get to pick your hours. This is when people feel the most generous, and when most people can get off and go out to eat together. Friday night is also very good. Comparatively speaking, Friday and Saturday nights are the two best work shifts of the week.

If you get your choice, the night shift will make more money for you for most restaurants. Dinner on most menus, is more expensive than lunch. The night shift is usually from 5 PM (or sometimes 4 PM) until whenever the place closes (typically 10 PM where I live). Monday night is the worst night shift, with money (tips) getting better as the week progresses.

The same goes for lunch. Except, remember to expect less money to begin with, during the lunch shift. Monday lunch shift really stinks, and Friday lunch shift is usually pretty good, comparatively speaking. Most people get off work for lunch between 11 AM and 12 PM, during the week, so that's when restaurants expect customers. The lunch hour is usually from 11 AM to 2 PM-just three busy hours with tip potential compared to 5-6 hours on a typical night shift.

Now... what does one do with that little space of time between 2 O'clock and 4 O'clock? Most places save that time for catching up after the lunch shift. People find themselves rolling silverware, and doing things that they didn't have time to do before. This is because there are no customers (usually) to be waited on and always other things to do.

Other Considerations

Weather

Weather conditions have much to do with how people eat

(and where and when.) For example, most people aren't going to want hot soup in the middle of June. And there are people out there who will be fighting for the same in January. Be sure that your menu offers attractive selection during all weather seasons. Try to schedule sunny weather shifts when given the opportunity over rainy weather shifts. Keep up with local weather forecasts prior to setting the shift schedule for the week. Restaurants are usually less busy when its raining outside.

Monthly Cycle

January through February is the slowest time of all. This is the time when waiting tables is not nearly as lucrative as it could be. People are usually broke from Christmas, so they don't have as much money for tips.

March, April and May are a little better. Spring is setting in and people are usually enjoying the season. June, July and August is the best time to start waiting tables. This is the hottest time of year, as well as the time when people love to dine out. Expect them to be freer with their wallets during the summer. Also, notice that many people will be on vacation during this time of year, and will give bigger tips than people who dine at the restaurant regularly. Starting in September, tip potential starts declining as most people start their Christmas shopping. Not to mention the fact that school starts and most families get into more of a routine eating at home.

Waiting Do's

Tip #1-Introduce Yourself the Right Way

Description: Always introduce yourself promptly when customers are seated in your section. When you are introducing yourself, always look at the people that are sitting at the table, in the eyes. If you hand the menus out, hand the child's menu(s) out first. While you are handing out the menus, make sure your customers have enough silverware, and that it is the appropriate kind they will be using. Also make sure enough napkins are provided.

Reason: Always make the customer feel as if they are cared about. This way, they will come back and ask for you. There is almost nothing worse than making a customer wait too long for anything. Prompt service is always appreciated. Maintaining eye contact with people when you are talking to them (or when they are talking to you) shows them that they have your undivided attention. It also shows that you are confident in what you are doing and this helps customers to view you in a favourable light.

Tip #2-Know the Menu

Description: You should know the menu inside and out. Are substitutions allowed? Does this dish contain any dairy ingredients? What's fresh? What is your favourite? Memorize the menu items. Know their ingredients and how they are prepared. Be clear on what you personally like and what is most popular with customers.

Reason: Not every customer that sits at your table knows what they want or can eat anything on the menu. When customers ask for suggestions, they will appreciate a confident and quick reply detailing what you like and what is popular with customers. Customers who are allergic to certain foods will almost always reward you if you help them avoid problem ingredients-especially if you can substitute an ingredient on a desired dish instead of forcing them to choose something else.

Customer: I'll have the Penne Puttanesca and a house salad please. I'd like a Balsamic vinaigrette dressing and no cheese on the salad.

Wonderful Server: OK. The chef usually puts Parmesan cheese on the Penne Puttanesca even though it is not mentioned on the menu. Would you like for me to instruct him to hold the cheese on the pasta too?

Customer: Yes, please.

Wonderful Server: Our toasted garlic bread also has Parmesan cheese. I'll get the chef to prepare some fresh toasted garlic bread for you without Parmesan cheese.

Customer: Excellent. Thank you.

Tip #3-Handling Drink Orders

Description: Take drink orders in any order. Pay attention to parents when kids are ordering.

If adults order alcoholic beverages, ask them if they would like some water as well. If your restaurant has a bar with happy hours, be sure to inform your adult customers about happy hour specials.

Learn how to open a bottle of wine.

Reason: Sometimes kids will order drinks with milk, sugar or caffeine that their parents do not want them to have. Wait for the parent to confirm (or at least afford them the opportunity to object/overrule) a child's drink order. The parents are payin the bill, so make sure they are happy!

Many adults who drink alcoholic beverages also like to have some water on hand to help balance the effects of alcohol on their palate, hydration and/or sobriety. Asking if they would like some water in addition to their drink order is a proactive step that shows you care about their dining experience.

Customers who order a bottle of wine appreciate it when you open the bottle in front of them at the table. Practice this skill so that you can do it without dropping cork crumbs in the bottle, spilling wine or looking like an amateur.

Wonderful Server: May I take your drink order?

Child: I want a Coke!

Mother: No way. No caffeine for you tonight.

Child: But Mom! ...

Wonderful Server: We are out of Coke tonight, but we do have some really good strawberry lemonade if you would rather have that.

Child: Awww.. OK. That would be fine.

Mother:

Tip #4-Understand the Tea Drinker

Description: Go the extra mile to accommodate the (iced) tea drinker. Ask if they want extra lemon (bring them a small plate of lemon wedges if they do). Keep an eye on level in the glass and try to refill it only when it is almost all gone (or bring them a new glass for every refill). Be sure to let them know you will try to refill it only when it is almost empty.

If your restaurant offers different types of tea (iced, hot, herbal), be sure to ask the customer which type of tea they want-don't assume!

Reason: Tea drinkers can be very finicky about getting it to taste just right-with the correct level of sweetener and lemon. If you refill a half-full glass, it dilutes their carefully prepared drink and can be hard for them to correct.

Important: The finicky customer can be a PITA (pain in the ass), but s/he can also be a great opportunity because the more finicky people are used to bad service and usually will recognize and reward good service.

Tip #5-Remember Orders-Don't Write Them Down

Description: Try to remember orders without having to write them down. Always repeat the complete order when everyone at the table has finished.

Reason: It impresses the people at your table if you can remember every little detail of their order without writing it down. It sends the message that you are paying attention to them and are focused on their needs.

Repeating the order after it has been decided serves two purposes-first is to assure the customers that you understood the order and did not miss anything, second is to help you remember the order. Most restaurants have computerized ordering systems these days and so it is important to "write in" the order in the computer as soon as it's been taken.

Customers with special orders (substitutions, etc.) are usually extra appreciative of wonderful servers who get their orders right.

Tip #6-Check the Food Before Bringing it to the Table

Description: Make sure that the food matches the order before you bring it to the table, especially if the customer made a special order (substitutions, food allergies, etc.). If the order isn't right, send it back and tell the customer about the snafu.

Reason: When food arrives at the table, the customer expects to be able to eat. The disappointment in seeing a wrong order is much worse than a little extra wait. Customers also appreciate that you are looking out for them and attentive to their needs.

Wonderful Server: I'm sorry, the cooks forgot to leave the cheese off of your Penne Puttanesca so I sent it back. They should have a fresh dish ready in just a few minutes.

Customer: OK. Thank you.

Tip #7-Remember Your Customers

Description: Always remember the people that you wait on. One idea is to write down their names (if they pay by credit card), what they look like, and what they had. This includes details like how they like their dish prepared-like how they prefer their steak cooked.

Reason: It's really great when you can remember a customer and their preferences and they take notice. This is especially true when the customer happens to return with friends. The customers appreciate the VIP treatment and it really makes them look good. This always means, a bigger tip for you.

Wonderful Server: Hi Mr. Smith, would you like your usual today-Penne Puttanesca with no cheese, garlic bread with no cheese and a house salad with no cheese and Balsamic vinaigrette dressing?

Customer: Yes, thank you. That's my favourite.

Wonderful Server: Would you care for a glass of wine to go with that this evening? We have a terrific new Merlot in from Italy...

Tip #8-Mind Your Appearance

Description: Many restaurants will request that their wait staff wear a uniform. Whether you wear a uniform or not, make sure that your clothes are clean, ironed, neat and new looking. Also, make sure you have shoes that tie (double knots are most helpful so you don't have to keep tying them), and NOT tennis shoes. Your socks should not be visible (unless one is wearing a skirt), and a tie is always helpful. In some places, it is required that a person wear suspenders, or a hand cloth draping over their pants. Make sure your clothes fit well. Note that open toed sandals are not good, as things may get dropped on your feet.

Always have clean, dry hair, and make sure it is styled. Long hair should be tied back in a ponytail holder or scarf. Girls should pay attention to their nails too. Other girls look at your nails and want to make sure that your cuticles are shaped well, that your nails are painted, etc.

It is a great idea to wear something extra that makes you stand out in the restaurant and be remembered (a pin or a patch or something).

Reason: At a minimum, you don't want to offend customers with your appearance. At best, you want diners to take notice of you and regard you in a positive light. When you pay attention to detail in your appearance, it sends a message to people that you care about yourself and your job.

For example, I used to work with a lady that only wore "Betty Boop" ties. When people came in to eat, they would ask for "Betty Boop".

Tip #9-Mind Your Manners

Description: Manners are very important to any wait staff. Just ask Miss Manners...or your grandmother. Pay attention to your posture-stand up straight, shoulders back. Grammar and diction are also very important in order to make a good impression.

Reason: A guest in a restaurant does NOT want to hear, "We ain't got none." The correct way to say it is, "We do not have any of that." The more a customer respects you, the easier it is for them to decide that you are worthy of a good tip.

Tip #10-Be Honest

Description: Always be honest with the customer. Especially when it comes to admitting any mistakes on your part. Don't try to blame others when you are at fault.

Reason: Don't assume that customers are too stupid or ignorant to figure out the truth. Taking responsibility for your mistakes breeds respect and even if the infraction is severe enough to ruin your tip for that particular dining experience, at least the customer will be willing to give you another chance the next time you wait on them.

Customers will never tip you well if they perceive you as being a weasel.

Tip #11-Anticipate Condiment Needs

Description: If you work at a restaurant that serves sandwiches, fried foods, etc. that are likely to be eaten with condiments such as ketchup, mustard, mayonnaise, etc., and those condiments are not already provided on the table, do not wait until the food is served to ask if the customer would like the condiments! Ask them when they place the order.

Reason: If you wait until the food is served, they will have to wait with their food sitting in front of them while you retrieve the condiments. Even if you are quick, the wait can be agonizing torture for someone who is hungry!

Tip #12-Always Carry an Extra Pen and Paper

Description: Always have an extra pen or two and a pad of paper handy for customers to borrow.

Reason: It is not uncommon for customers to think of things they need to write down while dining out.

When inspiration hits them, you want to be the hero that enables them to record their thoughts before the moment is lost.

Waiting Dont's

Tip #1-Don't Stare

Description: Avoid staring at customer's disabilities, cleavage or tattoos. Maintain eye contact when you engage a customer.

Reason: Many people take offense when people stare at them for whatever reason. The last thing you want to do is offend the customer.

Tip #2-Don't Refill Drinks Over the Table

Description: When you are going to refill a glass of water or tea, remove the customer's glass from the table and pour the drink while both the pitcher and glass are over the floor, away from the table.

Reason: You absolutely do not want to drip water or tea onto the table, or worse, into the customer's food. Customers also do not enjoy competing with your elbows for access to their food.

Tip #3-Don't Reach Across One Customer to Serve Another

Description: If you need to reach part of the table that is more than a foot away, move around the table until you are in front of the desired location. Do not reach across (or over) a customer to get/set items on the table.

Reason: It is rude to reach across the customers.

Tip #4-Don't Set Dangerous Objects Near Small Children

Description: When a parent and small child (with or without additional diners) is seated at a table, take care not to set dangerous objects (metal knives, forks, glassware, hot plates, etc.) down within reach of the small children.

Reason: Parents are especially sensitive to their children's safety. You can score lots of brownie points by being proactive in helping them keep baby safe.

Tip #5-Don't Neglect a Table

Description: Never neglect a table. Even if the kitchen is swamped and their order won't be ready for a while, always check in or be available in case the customers need more drinks or a status update.

Reason: Customers should never be ignored. It's your job to serve them and if you are not available (within reason), customers will get mad. This can ruin your tip faster than any other mistake.

Handling Special Circumstances

Tip #1-Splitting a Bill/Customer Fights Over the Bill

Description: When two or more people at a table request the bill and cannot agree on who is going to pay, try to set the bill in the middle of the table.

Reason: Try not to get involved in picking a winner in the tab paying lottery. You have more to lose when guessing wrong than to gain by guessing right. Stay neutral.

Tip #2-Vegetarians/Customers with Food Allergies

Description: Always be attentive to special food orders. If you know a little bit about vegetarianism or food allergies, talk to the customers about the subject and chances are that they will feel a lot more comfortable with you looking out for their order.

Reason: Vegetarians and people with food allergies are serious about their diets. They almost always appreciate a server who is sympathetic or knowledgeable about their dietary needs/choices.

Tip #3-Customers with Babies

Description: When you get a table that includes babies,

you should try to expedite the dining experience for that table (and always bring extra napkins). Ask if you can take the meal order with the drink order. Bring the check when they are done eating (before all the plates are cleared).

Reason: In general, babies have short attention spans and can get fussy in a hurry. Parents are usually very appreciative of prompt service that allows them to enjoy a meal without listening to their child crying the whole time.

Tip #4-Receiving Bad Tips

Description: Look at every bad tip as an opportunity to improve.

Reason: Most of the time, bad tips are given because people do not like the service they have received. If you get a bad tip, you should ask yourself the following:

- Was the service slow?
- Did I say something to upset someone at the table?
- Did I ignore a request?
- Did I flash an excess body part?

There are other times when people really do not have the money to spend on dinner out, and leave very small tips. If this is the case (and it's hard to tell), then the best course of action would be to stick the money in your pocket and wish the customers a good evening.

8

Menu Planning

So you want to open a restaurant? Many people come to me with their plans, and ideas after they have decided to build or open a restaurant. It is my responsibility to assist them in their planning process and determine how clearly they have thought their concept through. I ask them to show me a menu, and if their initial response is 'I haven't gotten that far in my planning process yet,' my response is "You haven't started the planning process yet".

A menu is the foundation of any restaurant; Guests will support or avoid a restaurant for its food. Starting with a preliminary menu is a simple and basic approach to restaurant development. Begin with a menu, and you are light years ahead in the restaurant development process. A menu will tell you and your Guest what you are trying to be as a business, and greatly enhance your chances for success.

I view a menu for content, image and pricing. Content (the actual items on the menu) will dictate service staffing needs, level of culinary experience and type of management required. Who will be doing the cooking, do they have experience in this type of food, and how much are you paying them?

Image is how the Guest will perceive the menu. Menu image helps define the targeted clientele and which other restaurants this operation would be competing with. Are the content and image of the menu appealing to your desired clientele? Pricing helps determine a potential restaurant's competitive placement. Is the pricing for the type of food offered competitive with other's in the market area, and does it permit the ability to manage a profitable food cost? Pricing sets the Guest's expectations in terms of food and service quality. This perception will, in turn, help define appropriate staffing levels. The budgeting process can now begin. Analysis of menu content, image and pricing will tell prospective restaurant operators whether their concept is appropriate for a certain market area.

With a preliminary menu in hand, a prospective operator can target a location that will be convenient and appropriate for their desired clientele. Once a site or facility is selected, sales volumes can be projected based on number of seats, menu pricing and the competitive business analysis. With projected sales volumes, how much an operator can spend to acquire, remodel or build a facility is determined. Leases and/or purchase agreements can now be negotiated.

With a clear menu, competitive analysis, sales forecast and development budget, financing can realistically be sought. A business plan can be derived which, if taken to potential investors will demonstrate what type of return they can anticipate on their investment.

Any restaurant business plan must begin with a menu. A proposed menu provides the basics for many questions that must be answered during the restaurant development process. It créates an image of the restaurant, identifies targeted clientele, and defines the proposed restaurant's competition. A preliminary menu allows a sound basis for business budgeting, tests potential profitability, and dictates the development dollars required for a facility. Most importantly, beginning the business planning process with a menu maintains the focus of ownership on the importance of food and the impact it has on the success of the restaurant.

INTRODUCTION TO MENU PLANNING

"Planning a menu" can mean several different things, depending on whom you're talking to. Some cooks think of menu planning as something that only occurs on special occasions, while others plan menus for several days or even weeks before shopping for the ingredients. Factors to consider in menu planning can range from whether the meal is nutritionally balanced to how a meal looks and tastes to how easy it is to serve to a crowd.

The first consideration, nutritional content and balance, is not something I'll address here. Later on I'll discuss the logistics of various types of meal service and menus, but for the most part, this class will concentrate on the gustatory elements of menu planning: how to design a meal that tastes good from beginning to end.

For me, menu planning starts with analyzing individual recipes or dishes in terms of flavour profiles and textural elements. Trying to combine dishes into a complete menu without understanding what each contributes to the whole is likely to result in a haphazard collection of food, rather than a progression of complementary dishes. And although there are plenty of times when my "menu planning" consists of opening the refrigerator and pulling out whatever lies within, I try not to inflict that process on my dinner guests.

Taste and texture

Some of the elements of taste to think about are

1. how strong the flavours are, and how complex;
2. whether one taste dominates or several blend together;
3. and which of the basic tastes (sweet, salty, sour, bitter and umami if you're inclined to treat that as a separate taste) are present.

This last part is crucial, because the basic tastes interact and influence your palate in very definite ways. Overt sweetness tends to dull the palate; acid tends to "wake it up." A little salt can whet the appetite, but too much is deadening. Likewise with bitter tastes — a little bitterness can be a great palate cleanser, but too much can overwhelm it. Aside from the basic tastes, you should keep in mind that very strong flavours — garlic, some herbs and spices, very ripe cheeses — can also overwhelm the palate, which can mean that too much of them too early in the menu will lessen your ability to appreciate what comes after.

Textural elements include

1. how rich the dish is;
2. the acid content (which plays a crucial role in the mouthfeel of the dish);
3. whether the dish is crunchy, smooth, chewy or crisp (to name just a few of the possible textures);
4. and a whole host of sensations known as "chemo-sensory irritations" — the burn of chiles, the heat of mustard or horseradish, the bite of mint and the tingle of carbonation (in drinks).

Probably the most important textural element is the balance of fat and acid, not necessarily within each dish, but within a menu. Fats and oils are wonderful ingredients — they carry flavour, provide a nice "mouthfeel" and give one a sense of satiety. But too much of this very good thing can be cloying and seem to coat your mouth most unpleasantly. Too much acid alone is likewise just nasty. But a touch of acid to cut through the fat (or a bit of fat to round out the acid) provides a balance that works. It's one of the reasons that a simple salad with a tangy vinaigrette is so often served (at least in France) between a heavy meat course and a rich cheese course.

Another element to consider when planning a menu is the complexity of each of the dishes. If you have a very complex main dish – either one with several elements or one with multiple layers of flavour, you might want to consider serving simpler starters or side dishes. For example, if I'm making chicken breasts with a reduction of vermouth and orange juice and finished with cherry tomatoes and capers, I probably don't want to serve it with a gratin of potatoes and cheese or a complicated risotto. If I really want to make the risotto or the gratin, I'll be better off going with a simpler roasted chicken.

Something you've probably noticed is that many of the "main" ingredients we work with as cooks are relatively neutral in taste and malleable in terms of possible textural elements. That is, chicken, beef, tofu, pasta or potatoes can be prepared in very different manners, which will give them different flavour profiles and different textures. Crispy fried chicken will thus suggest different accompaniments than will, say, Thai chicken curry or rolled, stuffed chicken breasts.

Once you've analyzed your individual dishes for these components, you can begin to combine them into a menu.

Balance, continuity and contrast

From a gustatory standpoint, a well-designed menu does two things:

- It stimulates the palate but doesn't confuse it.
- It provides a sense of continuity but keeps one's interest with contrasting elements.

Continuity is something that often seems to get lost in many American menus. We draw upon so many different ethnic cuisines that it can be difficult to stick to one (witness the disaster called fusion food). Consider the following menu:

First course: Thai-influenced chicken soup, made with coconut milk and garnished with peanuts

Second course: Salad of sliced tomatoes and fresh mozzarella topped with basil.

Third course: Lamb skewers with mint yogurt sauce

It's not that any of these dishes were bad on their own. But going from Thailand to Italy to the Middle East is a dizzying journey in the space of one dinner. Unless you have a very good reason, stick with one general cuisine type throughout the dinner.

Also for continuity's sake, it's best to stay with what's seasonal. This doesn't mean that I won't use tomatoes in the winter, but it does mean that I try to stick with dishes that "feel like" summer, or winter (or whatever season) or are at least neutral on that front. Following a spiced pumpkin soup with pasta primavera, for example, is disconcerting to the diner.

Before I started to pay much attention to this sort of thing, I served the following menu to some friends. I had fallen into a trap: I really, really wanted to try out a new idea for a salad; but at the same time I'd had a request from one of the guests to make one of my "signature" dishes, beef braised with onions and porter; and I tried to do both. So to start, I had an Italian salad with several types of peppers (including some with a little heat), cherry tomatoes, onion, and olives, garnished with basil. I then followed it with the beef, which I served with mashed root vegetables.

Thus, with one menu, I broke both of the continuity rules. The salad was summery and Mediterranean, while the beef dish (Belgian, incidentally) had a much more fall or winter feeling to it, as did the root vegetable mash. No one complained, but it struck me quite forcefully during the dinner that I'd made a big mistake.

It wouldn't have been tough to remedy. I could have kept the salad but switched to a more Mediterranean preparation for the beef — braised in wine with tomatoes and onions, perhaps. Or, as I've since done, I could have begun with a cabbage salad with carrot and apple, dressed with a warm caraway-studded vinaigrette and garnished with toasted pecans and crumpled crisp bacon.

Finally, think about the level of (for lack of a better word) sophistication of the dish. If you start out with foie gras on savory french toast or caviar and creme fraiche on new potatoes, it's probably better to stick with something on that level, rather than following with a country stew. Such a stark change can be an unwelcome break in the continuity of your meal. And it's just as true in reverse — if you start out with a more rustic dish, you don't want to follow it up with a lobster thermidor (if people actually make that anymore). The good news is that it's pretty easy to give minor tweaks to many dishes to move them up and down the sophistication scale.

Okay, so you want some elements of continuity in any menu. But, naturally, a menu that has no contrasting elements will fail just as miserably as one with no continuity. Of course you can provide contrast with flavour combinations. And textural components that involve the way food breaks against the teeth — whether it's crunchy or smooth, crispy or chewy — should provide plenty of contrast. No one wants a meal that's uniformly smooth and creamy, or so unrelentingly crunchy that it seems more like a dental exercise than a dinner.

But I think that the most crucial type of contrast in a menu is the balance between rich, creamy, fatty foods and acidic or bitter components. Let me illustrate the point with this menu:

First course: Cream of portobello mushroom soup garnished with a chevre/creme fraiche mixture.

Second: A caesar-type salad (no egg in the dressing, but very thick) with parmesan and croutons.

Third: "Pan roasted" chicken breasts with sauteed mixed mushrooms folded into a sherry cream sauce, served with polenta enriched with cheese and butter.

Dessert: an apple and cherry galette topped with cinnamon ice cream.

The main flaw with this menu is the sheer volume of rich dairy products. Too much, and too much the same: cream, cream and cheese in the first course; cheese in the second; cream and cheese again in the third and ice cream in the dessert. Not only is the menu incredibly filling, there's no break for the palate: it starts out with major rich and creamy elements and every course repeats them. Overall, even though the dishes themselves may taste fine, the menu is just like a hike across a not terribly scenic plateau: no ups and downs and no relief in sight.

Can it be fixed? It can certainly be improved with some modifications. If you really want the soup, fine, but maybe garnish it with herbs to refresh or some crisped prosciutto (which, yes, is rich, but not creamy, and which would at least add some texture). Then go on with a salad dressed with a tangy vinaigrette. Some bitter greens or maybe toasted walnuts would also help to refresh the palate after the soup. For the next course, well, if you were set on the mushrooms, then roast them and use them as a base for the chicken breasts (I'd ditch the cheese and cream in the polenta too). A pan sauce with a little sweetness and acid could make the dish much more interesting, and if you felt the need for some fat, you could still enrich it with a little butter without repeating the creamy mouthfeel of the soup.

Progression of Dishes

In most cuisine traditions, menus progress from subtler to more intense flavours, from light to heavy mouthfeel, and (often) from cold to hot dishes. The traditional French haute cuisine menu progression from fish to poultry to red meat may be cliché now, but there are valid reasons for it. As I mentioned previously, too many aggressive flavours can overwhelm the palate, lessening the impact of what comes after. Rich, heavy dishes early in the menu can satiate the diner too soon.

Also, think about this: you want your guests to stay interested in your dinner all the way to the end. If you start out with a showstopper, chances are that your next course will disappoint. Which is not to say that your hors d'oeuvre or first course can't be exquisite; it certainly can be. But it should function as does a good opening chapter in a novel: it draws you in, but leaves you wanting more.

Dinner Styles

Before planning your menu, you'll need to decide the format of your dinner: buffet, family style, serial courses, or some combination of the three. A buffet is, from a service standpoint, the easiest of the three to pull off for a large crowd. From a practical point of view, a buffet works well for a group with differing dietary needs. If your guests include some vegetarians, a cardiac patient, and an Atkins practitioner, a buffet with some dishes that each of them can eat could be your answer. The larger the group of guests, the harder it can be to plan a sequential dinner where the guests can all eat each of the courses.

The drawback to a buffet is that since your guests will be eating the various dishes all more or less at the same time, the progression of courses is all but non-existent. Thus you're going to want to prepare a menu of dishes that taste good together, or at the very least, don't clash with one another.

A family style dinner shares some of the elements of a buffet dinner in that your guests can take what they want and skip what they don't. They won't necessarily eat everything together, but the sequence of dishes is not guaranteed. A modified family style dinner can start out with a plated first course (soup, for instance, or a composed salad) and continue with the main course served family style. Such a dinner requires a bit more time for service than does a buffet, but not too much. It gives you some control over the sequence of dishes, but not absolute control.

A dinner with serial courses (usually plated) is the most labour intensive, from the standpoint of service. It also allows (or requires, depending on your viewpoint) you to plan the sequence of dishes with a great deal of control. It will put your guests in the position of not being able to skip any of the dishes without being obvious, so it can lead to some awkwardness if they have any dietary restrictions.

It also limits the time you will be able to spend with your guests, unless you have help serving. If you want to serve a serial multi-course dinner, think hard about the amount of last-minute preparation that each dish will require, and plan accordingly. Get as much done in advance as is humanly possible and write out a detailed timetable for the rest. To keep the pacing of your dinner smooth, it's great if at least one of the courses can be prepared entirely in advance.

The Practical Side of Menu Planning

So much for theory. Now, how do you take all that information and actually come up with a menu? You can start from any of several points: a type of cuisine (Italian, Thai, Mexican), a particular ingredient or ingredients, a particular recipe. Unless you're planning a tasting menu, it's probably easiest to begin with the idea for the main course and work from there, but you can begin with any of the courses. Whatever the dish you begin with, think about the season, the ethnicity of the dish, the flavour profile and the textural elements, and then think about what other dishes will complement it.

I think the best way to explain this is to give an example, so here are a couple of menus I prepared along with the planning processes by which I arrived at them.

Menu #1 (plated, sequential)

First: Sliced jicama, red and green peppers, and blanched carrots tossed with a lime and jalapeno dressing

Second: Rock shrimp quesadillas with guacamole

Third: Pan grilled salmon with a cumin-coriander rub, topped with an orange and chipotle salsa. Served with rice.

For this dinner, I started out with two ideas. I wanted a

Southwestern/Mexican menu, and there'd been some great salmon in my local market. Salmon, unlike some other fish, can stand up to some strong flavours, so I started thinking about a spice rub and some type of chile peppers. The orange and chipotle salsa, which also contains lime juice, red onion and cilantro, is something I'd made before and I thought it'd go well with the fish. Since the dish would be pretty complex, I decided on plain rice to accompany it.

I thought about starting with the quesadillas and then serving the vegetables, but the flavours in the dressing — lime, chiles, garlic — seemed too similar to the flavours in the salsa. And even though salmon is fairly rich, it still would have been an overload of acid.

So I began with the vegetables and kept the quesadillas pretty mild, flavour-wise. The richness of the cheese and guacamole provided a nice contrast to the sharp flavours and acid of both the dressing in the preceding course and the salsa in the last course.

Menu #2 (modified family style)

First: Trio of salads: Roasted eggplant and zucchini salad, Moroccan garbanzo bean salad, Tabbouleh

Second: Lamb curry served over couscous

For this menu, I began with the dietary concerns of my guests (one trying to watch calories, the other trying to increase his consumption of whole grains and vegetables).

For some reason, grains and vegetables suggested Middle Eastern or Mediterranean food to me, and I started playing around with some ideas for salads. I couldn't make up my mind about which of several to serve, so I finally decided to serve them all, as one course. The curry was made with yogurt, so it was relatively low in calories, yet it provided a creamy texture which, together with the richness of the lamb, balanced the acidity of the salads.

As you can see, neither one of these menus was particularly

complex. Your menus don't have to be either. Start out small—two or three courses. Plan family style or modified family style dinners if you find that easier. Remember, you don't have to plan eight-or ten-course tasting menus to rival the French Laundry's. But just putting a little thought into the dishes you prepare, their flavorings and accompaniments, and the order in which you serve them can turn a haphazard meal into a well designed dinner.

WEDDING PLANNER

What to Ask Your Caterer?

Most catering agencies have fixed menus to offer. Find out if they fulfil your requirements. You can 'mix & match' dishes to suit your liking. However, it would not be a bad idea to adhere to their format and select your preferred dishes from there. Find out about any extra charges so that you are not caught unawares at the time of payment. Seek their opinion since they have more experience than you do. It would be a good idea to put things down on paper as you will be able to compare notes of the various caterers you would have met,before making the final selection. Find out if there are any legal obligations that you may be required to fulfil, especially if you are planning to serve alcohol. The caterer might be able to guide you. Make it a point to have only one staff member of the catering agency attend to your enquiries Ask the person if he/she will be there at the function to ensure that all details are being taken care of. If no, then insist on discussing your plans with the person who will be in charge on the day of your function.

Menu Planing

It would help to have somebody who is well versed in the culinary arts to guide you while finalising the menu. It could be somebody in the family. Make it a point to discuss the final menu with the chef. It will make you feel all that more confident and the chef more involved in abiding by your suggestions.

Select items from your menu and ask your caterer for a food trial. This is especially so if you intend to serve either special dishes or a very traditional cuisine. Invite your core group to give their opinion of the food and to suggest any modifications. Take this opportunity to inspect the crockery, glassware, waiters and such like.

Winters & Summers

- Chilly winter wedding evening bring to mind hot steaming cups of coffee and piping hot soups Indulge your guests with a rich traditional cuisine. Ask your organiser to light a big cheery bonfire and make sure that there are enough coal braziers to light up the night! Hire a specialist bartender to do dustice to all those lovely bottles of Cointreau, Triple Sec. Creme de Mentheet al.
- A summer wedding? Avoid heavy, rich Indian curries. Opt for a variety of salads and fresh fruit delicacies. Serve light pasta dishes, fresh juices, mocktails, chaat-papri etc. Avoid milk and cream based preparations as they tend to go rancid in the heat have different flavours of ice-cream instead! Go ahead and hire the ice lolly vendor (chuskiwallah) it's a perennial hit with the young and old alike! For the bar, avoid heavy spirits; instead go in for beer, wines, nimbu-pani, spritzers and coolers! A cool refreshing fruit punch will have people raiding your bar counter and yes! do not run out of ice. Make sure that the venue is air-conditioned or has several pedestal fans and desert coolers.

Do Your Homework

Tell the caterer that you would like to attend a function organised by him, prior to your own visit the premises on that day to get a first hand idea of the decor, the waiters' attire etc. Observe whether there are enough of them to ensure a smooth service. Note the food display, cleanliness, hygiene, bins for collecting used plates etc. Check whether the food tastes as fresh as it looks. Take this opportunity to watch how well the car parking is being managed? Are there a sufficient number of attendants? Check the bathrooms for cleanliness. Are they manned? A word of caution, however. Since you are attending somebody else's function to do your survey, you should have your caterer accompany you. You could also try asking a few guests whether they are happy with the catering, are well attended to etc. Some catering agencies also take care of light arrangements and decor. If your agency does not, then you will find yourself handling the tent house-wallah, florists, musicians et al. In such a situation, you should have a joint meeting, wherein you discuss your various areas of responsibility. This way, you will know who's doing what exactly, and leave no scope for grey areas. Your catering agency could also be called in to cater to the large number of outstation relatives and friends who would have arrived some days prior to the function. You may do a package deal with the caterer. Remember, higher volumes ensure better rates.

Order Food in the Right Quantity

This depends on a lot of factors such as: is the day of your function a very busy date? If yes, you can expect a reduction in the number of guests you have to cater to. A lot of people arrive on the occasion, wish the bridal couple, have a drink or two but do not stay for dinner. Usually, catering agencies work on a guaranteed figure. Check with the caterer as to how much of a margin can he cater to should the number of your guests increase, and the amount of time he would take to make fresh preparations should the need arise. It is better to overestimate than understimate your numbers and save yourself undue embarrassment.

Buffets

There are different types of service but the most popular is the buffet system, being the most convenient. The wide variety of snacks are arranged attractively on platter, appear fresh, and are easily accessible to all. Having a 'live' counter where snacks are prepared in front of the guests, adds a lively charm to the event. Salads, main course and dessert are laid out on the buffet so that everyone can have exactly what they want and in quantities to their liking. An important aspect to be mentioned here is that most caterers charge clients on the basis of plates consumed, that is, a certain number of plates are laid out on the buffet counter and the host is charged according to the number of plates.

A good tip-have somebody from the family stand at the counter where the plates are being handed over to guests. It is a wonderful welcome feeling when a guest is handed his plate with a lovely smile from a member of the family. In fact, certain communities do adhere to a charming time tested tradition wherein members of the host's family serve the guests themselves. An advantage of 'plate control' is that the host does not get billed for what the musical band, florist and tent personnel ate.

BAR SERVICE

If you are serving alcohol, it is always advisable to have somebody from your core group handle the bar, making sure that the guests are never wanting. This way, unauthorised personnel will not gain access to your stock of bottles. Beer is a favourite with both men and women, so keep plenty of bottles chilled. Mocktails and ladies drinks such a sherry, gin and tonic etc. should also be kept available, besides the mandatory soft drinks. Remember to pile up on an endless supply of ice cubes.

Cocktails and all that's Yummmmmm.......

For Your Cocktail Function,

Where you invite fewer guests-friends and family really-try something different, Go spunky with exotic barbecued snacks for dinner or ask your caterer to do a Mongolian Barbecue bash, Have a That evening or invite your guests for a Mexican Treat with tequilas and fajitas, Keep it light, different and unforgettable!

The All-important Last-minute Check

For the function to be completely successful, it is absolutely necessary to check that the catering agency has followed your instructions and specifications to the tee.

- First of all, have all the dishes tasted. It is always better that you do not serve a badly made dish at all rather than have people remember your function with words like, "A splendid evening really, but the chillies in the curry made me cry"
- Check the waiters' uniform and gloves for stains.
- Ensure that all photographic equipment is ready and does not intrude into the gathering. You will not want your guests triping over loose wires, tripods etc. or have the cameramen impose over your guests. They should be as unobtrusive as ever.
- Nothing is as disgusting as having last evening's decorations and flowers hanging limply from their holdings. Check that your florist has removed all the old flowers and provided fresh ones.
- The carpet area should have been swept clean. Chairs must be clean and fans in good working order. Loose electric wires are both dangerous and ungainly to the sight.

BE THE PERFECT HOST

A good host will make his guests feel special from the time of their arrival at the entrance of the venue till the time of departure. Have your core group receive the guests, seat them and have the waiter attend to their refreshments. During dinner, while you have personally ensured that your wedding guests are being wellserved and are not in want of anything.

It is sad albeit true that the bridal couple often gets to eat leftovers from the buffet table, or worse, if nobody ask-does not eat at all. Food might be the last thing on their minds but eat they must. Close family members too might be surviving on excitement and happiness alone. A really good way to solve this dilemma is to have a semi formal sit down towards the end of the function, where the bridal couple, the host and the immediate family, sit down and enjoy a nice meal while recuperating from the evening's events. This is a great time to pop that lovely bottle of champagne and unwind. In the mean time, they must be kept supplied with a regular intake of soft drinks and hor d' oevres to keep their energies flowing.

PAYMENT

Do not forget to ask your caterer about the mode of payment. How much advance are you expected to pay? Will you be liable to pay the entire sum on the night of the function itself ? What are the procedures for cancellations ? Bargain all you can! More often than not, you can get away with a lot and save yourself some money.

Tipping

Speak to your caterer about tipping. Make it clear that you will not tolerate the catering staff soliciting you or your guests for 'baksheesh', or helping themselves to the goodies at the table. You will save yourself from such embarrassments if you deal with reputed caterers only.

Feedback From Guests

Seeking a feedback from your guests is the only way of gauging the success of your wedding arrangements. You will emerge all the more wiser too! While most guests will sing praises out of politeness, some may offer valuable insights.

Discuss the report you have gathered with your caterer at the time of final payment-in a frank, constructive and objective manner. Question the mishaps, if any, and give praise where due. It will help you build a long-lasting and mutually beneficial relationship with the caterer. As the axiom goes, a man doesn't change his 'naai' and 'halwai'!

MENU PLANNING IN FOOD & BEVERAGE OUTLET

A list of items served by a particular food & beverage outlet is called a 'menu' or a 'bill of fare'.

Origin

The early food comprised of BANQUETS of 2 courses. The courses would range with a variety of dishes from 10-40 in numbers. The first set of dishes would be placed before the guests entered-hence the word "entrée". When this set was over it would be removed or relieved by the 2nd set-hence the word "releves."

It is said that in the year 1541, Duke Henry of Brunswick was seen referring a long slip of paper. When asked what he was looking at, he said it was a form of programme of the dishes.

By this, he said that he could see what dishes were coming and accordingly reserve his appetite. We can presume that the menu could have developed from such an event. Thus the origin of the "menu"

Over the years, menu has undergone great changes. Today it is one of the most potential marketing tools employed in hotels.

The menu has also been reduced to a few numbers of items only, rather than the olden 10-40 items.

Menu Types: Menus can de divided into two major types:

- A la carte
- Table D'hote
- A la carte
- Means in the "Style of the Card"
- Offers a wide variety of dishes
- Each dish is priced separately
- Guest can choose what he wants to eat and pay for what he has eaten
- Dishes are semi-prepared and will take time to serve
- Only necessary Silver is laid. The remaining Silver will be laid according to the dishes ordered
- Suitable for ali types of catering
- It is economical as a complete meal
- Table D'hote
- Means " Table of the Host"
- The menu has a fixed number of courses
- The whole menu is priced together.

There is only a limited choice and the guest has to pay for the full menu, whether he eats it or not.

Food is normally in prepared forms and can be served immediately Silver for the whole menu is laid in advance as the menu is known. Suitable menu style for Groups, Institutional and Industrial Canteens and Hospitals.

It is more expensive if a similar meal is chosen.

Apart from the above mentioned types of menus, there exist some other forms of menu types:

Carte du Jour: Literally means "card of the day". It offers choices available for a particular day only. The chef's speciality for the day is a typical example of such a menu.

Cyclic Menu: This menu is a group of menus which are rotated on a set cycle. They are often used in the industrial and institutional sectors of the hospitality industry.

IMPORTANT POINTS FOR MENU PLANNING

Menu planning requires tremendous knowledge, experience and skill, depending upon the target group. From the managements point of view a menu should be designed in line with the goals and objectives of the hotels profitability, market value and goodwill.

The menu shouldn't overshoot the budget and should be calculated in view of long term standing in the market. Generally menu planning has to look into the following factors:

1) *Economic Level/target Market:* The food which is to be prescribed has to be designed keeping the targeted clientele in mind. They should be able to pay for the food and beverages as quoted by the menu card. Considering the menu is meant for the high class, the menu should be designed on the exotic levels. If the clientele is the middle class then more emphasis should be laid on nutritional aspects, calories and great value for money experience.
2) *Nutritional Requirements:* The nutritional requirements of target groups should be a major factor in menu planning. All the nutrients and calories must be balanced and enough for the dietary intake of the guests. Support food for variety of guests with various disorders should be planned. The focus should be on quality and not quantity. It is safer to calculate the total quantity, allowing 2400 calories per day per adult man, and using this unit to determine the amount required for women and children. The occupation and activity group one is catering to has to be considered too. Knowledge of the different constituents of food is required.
3) *Budget:* The following points must be considered while planning the menu:
   a) Money available for food.
   b) Cost of raw material.
   c) Proper ratio between high and low cost dishes.

4) *Type of Service:* Menus have to be planned in relation to the type of service. i.e. cafeteria, cruise liner, airline, etc. Depending on the above one should work out centralized and/or decentralized production units. What style of menu is going to be introduced also affects this factor.

5) *Availability and Seasonability of Raw Ingredients:* Certain foods are available only in certain seasons or places. Seasonal foods are, besides being economical, also better in quality. These must be studied and included. Both these factors have a huge weightage on menu planning.

6) *Menu Balance:* While designing a menu it should take into consideration the balance factors as follows:
   a) Light to heavy and back to light.
   b) Vary the sequence of preparation.
   c) Change seasoning, flavouring and presentation.
   d) Ensure that garnishes are in harmony with their main dishes.

7) *Equipments and Work Space:* Any meal must be compatible with cooking equipment available so that you can maintain a minimum standard of quality and method of cooking used. E.g. cooking Tandoori Chicken in an Oven-Toaster-Griller or microwave is an absurd option.

8) *Availability of Trained Manpower:* For any menu to be functional, available staff must have sufficient skill, dexterity and training to carry out the complete given operation. Therefore while considering personnel requirements it becomes important to analyze the following labour aspects:
   a) Skill and number of employees.
   b) Staff tasks and responsibilities
   c) Even distribution of the work load.
   d) Yield and portion control by staff.

9) *Product Presentation:* Food should be appealing to the eye before the palatability factor comes in the general

psychology of humans is that if a food looks great then it will taste the same too. To be able to entice the guests, the recipes have to be tried out and standardized before introducing it on the menu. Variety in colour, texture and flavour has to be worked out too. Accompaniments both traditional and innovative, garnishes used, etc. are the factors too are taken into account.

10) *Eating Habits and Traditions of the Customer:* It becomes very important depending on the type of catering establishment to realize the eating habits and traditions of the customers. Muslims don't eat Pork and pork products, Hindus don't eat Beef, Jews eat only Kosher meat, etc.

FRENCH CLASSICAL MENU

The French classical menu as the name suggests has its origin from France and much of the European nobility followed it for over a 100 years and more. Although the actual number of courses on a menu and dishes within each course, will depend on the size and class of the establishment. The classical format of a French Menu has to follow the order of service as mentioned below:

1) *Hors D'oeuvres:* The culture of hors d'oeuvres sprung gradually from Russia where traditionally in a banquet cold fish and similar items were served for the diners along with a glass of chilled vodka in a shot glass. The guest would eat the cold fish and gulp down the vodka and then proceed into the main banquet hall for the main meal. Hors d'oeuvres are basically small tit bits of food that are consumed to build up the appetite. Hence they are also called as Appetizers. Traditionally they were a selection of salads, fish and meat served either hot or cold. The cover set-up for the hors d'oeuvres will depend on what item is being served. Some of the common ones are:

   a) *Salads:* They could be plain salads like fish, meat, cucumber, potato, beetroot, etc. They can come as compound salads like Russian salad, Andalouse salad, Italienne salad, etc. Salads are also served as a course by it self.

b) *Fish:* Classical varieties of fish hors d'oeuvres are anchovies, lobster, mackerel and herring (marinated, smoked or fresh), smoked eel (filleted or sliced), caviar and prawns (plain, in cocktail sauce or in a mousse)

c) *Meats:* Includes items like pates, ham and salami of all sorts.

d) *Canapés:* These are small slices of bread minus the crust, cut into a variety of shapes, then toasted or fried in oil or butter and garnished. Garnishes can include smoked salmon, foie gras, cheese, and a whole load of food items left to ones creativity.

e) *Eggs:* They can be poached and coated in aspic or mayonnaise or hard boiled, cut into two and garnished or stuffed with various fillings blended with yolk.

f) *Fruits:* Like avocado, grape fruit, melon, papaya and passion fruit can be served accompanied by castor sugar, ginger powder and cherries.

2) *Potage (Soups):* The second course is the soup which acts as an appetizer in the absence of hors d'oeuvres. Soups can be classified into a number of categories like consommés, broths & bouillons, veloutes, cream soups, purees, bisques and international soups.

a) *Consommés:* These are clarified soups made from poultry, beef game or vegetable bouillon. Consommés take the name according to the garnish put into it. Consommé is usually served hot but can also be served jellied or cold.

b) *Veloutes, Creams and Purees:* These soups are thicker in consistency.

Normally thick soups are served with a soup spoon in a soup bowl with handles. Nowadays these soups are served with croutons unlike the traditional days where it was served only with Purees and Cream of Tomato Soup.

c) *Potages, Broths and Bisques:* These soups are usually eaten from a soup plate with a soup spoon. This is again of the thick consistency variety.

d) *International Soups:* These soups are the national soups of certain countries or are the speciality of a certain region. E.g. Mulligatawny (India), Minestrone (Italy), Cock-a-leekie (Scotland), etc.

3) *Oeufs (Egg dishes):* Egg dishes being served as a separate course has a debatable history. Omelettes have still managed to retain their popularity whereas classical egg dishes like Oeuf en cocotte are very rarely seen on menus nowadays.

4) *Farineux (Pasta & Rice):* These dishes are also referred to as farinaceous dishes and includes all types of pasta such as spaghetti, macaroni, ravioli, etc. the rice dishes also fall here such as pilaf, pulao, risotto, etc. For all spaghetti dishes, a joint fork should be laid on the right hand side of the cover and a dessert/all purpose spoons on the left. Grated Parmesan cheese is normally served with all these dishes.

5) *Poisson (Fish):* Fish is the first semi-solid food on the menu preparing the way for heavier meals to follow. The traditional practice of serving fish on a fish plate with fish knife and fork is still in vogue today. Fish in this course can be served hot or cold. If hot, then it can be accompanied by sauces or served plain. The other variations of fish preparations are:

a) *Fried fish which has been bread crumbed (an l'Anglaise)*

b) *Fried fish which has been dipped in batter (an l'Orly)*

c) *Cold poached fish dishes*

d) *Grilled herring served with mustard sauce.*

e) *Cold lobster (homard froid)*

6) *Entrée:* This is a French word meaning "entrance." It can be understood that the name perhaps

originated because the first meat course is introduced here. Meat here is cooked in simple methods like grilling, frying, etc. The quality of meat used is of best nature. Ajoint knife and fork is served along with the entrée pre-plated on a joint plate. Alternatively silver service can also be carried out. Generally they are small well garnished dishes and potatoes and vegetables can accompany them. Examples of this type of dish are tournedos, noisettes, sweetbreads, garnished cutlets and vol-au-vent cases.

7) *Sorbet:* This was a course that was traditionally served to give a pause within a meal, allowing the palate to be refreshed. They are lightly frozen water ices, often based on un-sweetened fruit juice and may be served with a spirit, liqueur or even Champagne poured over. Russian cigarettes are also to be offered at this stage of a meal.

8) *Releve:* This refers to main roasts or other larger joints of meat, which would be served together with potatoes and vegetables. This course and the next i.e. Roti are the high points in the French Classical Menu. The chef has to prove the best of their skills in the food being offered here in terms of flavour, taste, texture and presentation. This word Releve is used to relieve the course of entrée dishes.

9) *Roti (Roast):* This term traditionally refers to Roasted Game or Poultry dishes. Some of the most famous Roti items are as follows:

   a) *Roast beef served with Horseradish Sauce, mustard powder and Yorkshire pudding.*

   b) *Roast lamb served with mint sauce and redcurrant jelly.*

   c) *Roast mutton served with redcurrant jelly and white onion sauce.*

d) *Roast pork served with apple sauce and sage and onion stuffing.*

10) *Legumes (Vegetables):* Apart from the vegetables served with Releve or Roast courses, certain vegetables like asparagus and artichokes may be served as a separate course. They could also feature as starters.

11) *Salade (Salad):* Often refers to a small plate of salad that is taken after a main course (or courses) and acts as a meal enhancer. They can also be served as starters.

12) *Buffet Froid (Cold Buffet):* This course includes a variety of cold meats and fish, cheese and egg dishes together with a range of salads and dressings.

13) *Entremets (Sweets):* This course includes the service of sweet dishes hot or cold. On a menu if both, hot and cold are included then, hot is served first before the cold sweet. Some of the most common examples are puddings, soufflés, strudels, bavarois, pies, meringues, etc.

14) *Fromage (Cheese):* Includes a wide range of cheeses and various accompaniments like biscuits, breads, celery, grapes and apples. This course can also refer to cheese based dishes like cheese balls and soufflés. Cheeses are distinguished by flavour and categorized according to their texture. The recognized categories of cheese based on their texture are as follows:

   a) *Hard*

   b) *Semi-hard*

   c) *Fresh*

   d) *Soft*

   e) *Blue*

15) *Savoureaux (Savoury):* The savouries originated as part of the British culture.

   Sandwiches are the hallmark of this course. Pastries and soufflés with or without savoury stuffing's can feature here. They are of miniature size and sometimes served as starters too. Famous examples are Welsh

Rarebit, Angels On Horseback, Anchovies on Toast, Scotch Woodcock, Canapés, Buck Rarebit, etc.

16) *Dessert (Fruit):* Traditionally desserts meant only fresh fruits and nuts. Today the word dessert has become a bigger bracket encompassing Savouries and Entremets.

17) *Beverages:* Traditionally at the end of the French Classical Menu, the beverage coffee, was served, but nowadays a much wider range of beverages are served like tea, tisanes, chocolate and proprietary beverages. Although it is included in this sequence, it is not normally a part of the French Classical Menu. The idea of serving coffee originated because it acts as a very good digest if. Black coffee is the most preferred while some may choose to have with cream/milk. The general accompaniments with coffee are cigars, cognac or liqueurs with biscuits and liqueur chocolates. Proprietary beverages are Bournvita, Horlicks, Complan, etc.

9

Dining Table Services

1. A dining table service assembly for providing food to seated patrons comprising:
   a. a stationary dining table segment secured in place between seating positions and having a tongue extending longitudinally between said seating positions with a laterally expansive horizontal top terminating in contoured edges with subjacent surfaces for supporting a weight from above,
   b. a mobile serving cart carrying a table segment support having laterally spaced supporting members,
   c. a separate removable dining table segment having longitudinally extending arms with expansive horizontal upper surfaces terminating in edges formed in a contour to mate with the aforesaid contour of said edges of said tongue and spaced for lateral engagement with the aforesaid tongue to rest on and bear down against said subjacent surfaces, said removable table segment being positionable to removably engage said stationary table segment with the top of said tongue and the upper surfaces of said arms, lying in a common horizontal plane, and also being positionable to be removably supported on said table segment support separate from said stationary dining table segment.

2. The dining table service assembly of claim 1 wherein said stationary segment extends laterally outward in a pair of wings at one longitudinal extremity of said tongue to define longitudinally extending recesses in said stationary segment on either side of said tongue below the upper surface of said laterally expansive table top, and longitudinal appendages extend from each of the aforesaid arms of said removable table segment below said upper surfaces, and are receivable in said recesses.
3. The dining table service assembly of claim 2 further comprising a laterally disposed member spanning the underside of said removable segment between said arms.
4. The dining table service assembly of claim 2 further comprising a vertically aligned laterally extending panel to which said wings of said stationary segment are secured, and longitudinally aligned bench seats extend from said panel on either side of said stationary table segment, and a vertical pedestal supports said tongue of said stationary table segment remote from said wings.
5. The dining table service assembly of claim 1 wherein said mobile serving cart is mounted on casters and includes upright support means extending above and to the rear of said table segment support which is horizontally disposed and which abuts said upright support means, thereby providing a bearing surface which can be used to longitudinally force said removable table segment in a horizontal direction into engagement with said stationary segment.
6. The dining table service assembly of claim 5 wherein said mobile serving cart additionally includes a lower platform to which casters are fastened, and upright struts carry said table segment support above said lower platform, and said upright struts include height

adjustment mechanisms connected thereto between said lower platform and said table segment support.

7. The dining table service assembly of claim 6 further characterized in that a pedestal supports said tongue and a longitudinal guideway is defined in said lower platform, whereby said wheeled serving cart may be directed into position for said guideway to receive said pedestal to guide said removable table segment into engagement with said stationary table segment.
8. A dining table service assembly comprising:
   - a stationary table segment supported on an upright pedestal and having a horizontal surface terminating at a perimeter at least a portion of which forms a curved convex boundary having a subjacent support ledge extending outward therefrom;
   - a separate removable table segment having a flat horizontal upper surface the perimeter of which terminates in a concave boundary designed to removably fit with said convex boundary in mating fashion with vertical support for said removable table segment provided by said support ledge of said stationary table segment; and
   - a mobile serving cart for separately carrying said removable table segment in horizontal alignment at the level of said stationary table segment.
9. The dining table service assembly of claim 8 in which said serving cart includes laterally spaced support members extending longitudinally beneath said removable table segment in vertical alignment therewith when said removable table segment is carried on said serving cart.
10. The dining table service assembly of claim 8 in which said serving cart includes a guide mechanism for coacting with said pedestal to bring said removable table segment into juxtaposition relative to said stationary table segment.

Description

Field of Invention : The present invention relates to a dining table service assembly for bringing food and table settings to seated restaurant patrons in establishments seeking to provide efficiency of service.

Background of the Invention : The manner of serving meals to seated patrons in restaurants has remained substantially unchanged for many years. Traditionally, restaurant patrons are seated at a table or booth, usually facing each other. A waiter or waitress approaches the table with place settings and menus, or the place settings and menus may already be in position at the table. In either event, the waiter or waitress writes down the entree selection of each patron and then turns in the order for the entire table to the chef. The chef prepares the meal and places the meal and service dishes in a location accessible to the waiter or waitress. The service dishes are then manually carried, either on a tray or individually, to the table and placed before the patrons. When the restaurant patrons have finished their meal, the soiled dinnerware and leftovers are manually removed from the table and taken to the kitchen, either individually or on a tray. The table is then cleaned in preparation for subsequent patrons.

In this conventional manner of servicing restaurant tables a considerable amount of manual manipulation and handling of food and dishware at the tables is required on the part of the restarurant personnel. Food and dishes in the kitchen must be moved by the chef to an area accessible to the waiters and waitresses and in turn by them to a tray or directly to the table at which the patrons are seated. In clearing the table, dishes and leftovers must first be cleared from the table and placed in a busman's tray. The tray must then be carried to the kitchen. A dishwasher must lift the various dishes from the tray, dispose of scraps in the garbage, and carry dishware to be reused to a sink for cleaning. The many steps in the manual manipulation of the dishes and the food orders requires the services of many restaurant personnel.

Summary of the Invention : It is an object of the present invention to reduce the amount of manual manipulation of dishware and meal orders required in a restaurant. This reduction in labour requirement will allow the restaurant staff to concurrently serve a greater number of patrons with greater efficiency than is presently the case.

By reducing the restaurant staff requirement for the service of a particular volume of clientele, the number of restaurant staff members passing among the tables or booths is greatly reduced. This results in the achievement of another object of the invention which is to reduce the congestion and confusion that prevails among members of the restaurant staff in passing through areas crowded with restaurant staff members.

Another object of the invention is to alleviate the irritation of customers whose orders are needlessly delayed. Such delay frequently occurs when waiters or waitresses erroneously pick up orders for delivery to patrons when the orders where originally prepared for different restaurant patrons. In these instances, the patrons for whom the orders were intended are required to wait an inordinately long time for their selected entree to again be prepared.

A related object of the invention is to alleviate the confusion and embarrassment that occurs when orders for a particular table are incorrectly distributed among the patrons seated at that table. The customers in this situation are confused at receiving meals which they did not order, and the waiter or waitress is embarrased at having incorrectly recalled the orders placed by each person.

A further object of the invention is to reduce the amount of food and drink spilled on the floor in the customer serving area. With the present practice of extensive manual manipulation and handling of service plates and food orders, mishaps frequently occur and food is spilled either on customers or on the floor of the restaurant premises. Such mishaps are highly undesirable as they are quite irritating and frustrating to restaurant patrons, and result in excessive food spillage on the restaurant serving floor. This is a both unclean and hazardous to the restaurant patrons and personnel who walk rapidly through the dining area, as they must do in order to provide good service.

The achievement of these and other objects are accomplished by utilizing the apparatus of the present invention.

Detailed Description of the Invention : According to the invention the dining table service assembly 10 is provided with a stationary table segment 11 supported on a upright pedestal 12 and having a horizontal surface 13 terminating at a perimeter, a portion of which forms a curved convex boundary 14 having a subjacent support ledge 15 extending outward therefrom.

A removable table segment 16 is also provided and has a flat horizontal upper surface 17. The perimeter of which terminates in a concave boundary 18 designed to fit with the convex boundary 14 in mating fashion. Vertical support for the removable table segment 16 is provided by the support ledge 15 of the stationary segment 11. A mobile serving cart 19 is used to carry the removable table segment 16 in horizontal alignment at the level of the stationary table segment 11.

The stationary dining table segment 11 is secured in place between seating positions with a tongue 22 extending longitudinally between the bench seats 20 and 21. As previously indicated, the laterally expansive horizontal top 13 terminates in a contoured edge 14 while the ledges 15 form subjacent surfaces to support a weight from above. The stationary segment 11 extends laterally outward in a pair of wings 23 and 24 an one longitudinal extremity of the tongue 22. Longitudinally extending recesses 25 and 26 are defined in the stationary segment 11 at the wings 23 and 24 respectively on either side of the tongue 22 below the upper surface of the table top 13.

A vertically aligned laterally extending panel 27 is provided in a manner such that the wings 23 and 24 of the stationary segment 11 are secured to it. The longitudinally aligned bench seats 20 and 21 have backs 28 and 50 respectively associated therewith. The backs 28 and 50, along with the seats 20 and 21 extend from the panel 27 on either side of the stationary table segment 11. The vertical pedestal 12 supports the stationary table segment 11 at the tongue 22 remote from the wings 23 and 24.

At one longitudinal extremity of the removable table top segment 16 is an end 29 from which longitudinal arms 30 and 31 extend. The expansive horizontal upper surface 17 formed by the arms 30 and 31 and the end 29 is coplanar with the table top 13 of the stationary table segment 11 when the removable segment 16 is engaged with the stationary segment 11. Longitudinal appendages 32 and 33 extend from each of the arms 30 and 31 of the removable segment 16 below the upper surface 17. These appendages 32 and 33 are receivable in the recesses 26 and 25 respectively when the removable and stationary table segments are positioned together. In addition, a shallow U-shaped bracket 34 is provided on the underside of the removable table segments 16. This bracket 34 has longitudinally extending legs 35 and 36 which lie on either side of one end of the concave recess in the removable table top segment 16. A laterally disposed member 37 is fastened to the bracket 34 to span the underside of the removable segment 11 between the arms 30 and 31.

The stationary and removable segments 11 and 16 respectively are formed in a mating contour and are spaced so that the arms 30 and 31 of the removable segment 16 are laterally engaged with the tongue 22. When the removable segment 16 and stationary segment 11 are positioned, the appendages 32 and 33 extend into the recesses 26 and 25 respectively and the interior peripheries of the arms 30 and 31 rest on and bear down against the ledge 15. In this manner, the removable table top segment 16 is positionable to contact the periphery of the tongue 22 in engagement with the stationary table segment 11 so that the top 13 of the tongue and the upper surfaces 17 of the arms lie in a common horizontal plane. Alternatively, the removable table top segment 16 may be positioned to rest on the mobile serving cart 19. The mobile serving cart 19 carries a horizontally disposed table segment support 38 having laterally spaced supporting members 39 and 40. The support members 39 and 40 extend longitudinally beneath the removable table segment 16 so that the member 39 is in vertical alignment with the arm 30 and the member 40 is in vertical alignment with the arm 31 when the removable table segment 16 is carried on the serving cart 19.

The wheeled serving cart 19 also includes a lower platform 41 to which casters 42 are fastened. The axles of the casters 42 rotate in a horizontal plane, while the wheels mounted thereon are able to rotate in vertical planes about their axles. Upright struts 43 carry the table segment support 38 above the lower platform 41. Upright supports 44 and 45 extend above and to the rear of the table segment support 38 which is horizontally disposed and which abuts the upright supports 44 and 45. This arrangement provides a bearing surface which can be used to longitudinally force the removable table segment 16 in a horizontal direction into engagement with the stationary segment 11. That is, when the removable segment 16 rests on the table segment support 38, the end 29 of segment 16 bears against the upright supports 44 and 45 as the segment 16 is forced into engagement with the segment 11.

Upright struts 43 carry the table segment support above the lower platform 41. The upright struts 43 each include height adjustment mechanisms connected thereto between the lower platform 41 and the table segment support 38. Such a height adjustment mechanism is illustrat. The provision of such an adjustment arrangement allows minor adjustments in height to be made so that the removable support 16 may always be maintained in horizontal alignment with the stationary support 11 as indicat. The adjustment mechanisms include an upper pair of tightening nuts 46 which are engaged on a threaded bolt 47 on either side of a lower extremity 48 of each strut 43. The lower extremity 48 extends laterally from a crimp at the bottom of the strut 43, and is generally horizontally aligned. A second nut is engaged on the bolt 47 and acts with the head of bolt 47 to secure the bolt 47 to the lower platform 41. Thus, to adjust the height of the table segment 38, one of the nuts 46 need merely be backed off from the end 48 of the strut 43. The strut 43 may then be moved upward or downward as desired, and the other nut tightened to meet it. If upward adjustment is desired, the upper nut 46 is loosened, while if downward adjustment is desired the lower nut 46 is first loosened.

It may be advisable for the serving cart 19 to include a guide mechanism for coacting with the pedestal 12 that supports the tongue 22 of the stationary segment 11. This is useful is bringing the removable table segment 16 into juxtaposition relative to the stationary table segment 11. Such a guide mechanism is formed by a longitudinal guideway 50 in the lower platform 41. Thus, the wheeled surface cart 19 may be directed into positon for the guideway 51' to receive the pedestal 12 to guide the removable table segment 16 into engagement with the stationary table segment 11.

In the utilization of the present invention, restaurant patrons are first conducted to the bench seats 20 and 21 where they may easily be seated since the removable table segment 16 is not in position at that time. This facilitates seating of the patrons, since the only lateral obstruction to them in sitting down on the bench seats 20 and 21 is the width of the tongue 22, which is well out of their way. This feature of the invention allows the booth 10 to be of narrower width than conventional booths and thus allows more booths to be positioned within a given floor area. This increased utilization of available floor space does not result in discomfort to the patrons because of the ease of being seated without the removable segment 16 in position. The spacing of the seats 20 and 21 is limited only by the necessary knee room for the customers.

Once the patrons have been seated, the waitress or waiter attends them and takes their order. Returning to the kitchen, The waitress turns in the meal order to the chef who prepares the food and places the serving dishes in position on the arms 30 and 31 of the removable table segment 16. The order of placement is indicated on the order turned in by the waitress, so that there is no mistake in the positioning of the appropriate entrees on the arms 30 and 31.

At this time, the removable segment 16 is located in or adjacent to the kitchen. It may be positioned either on a serving cart 19, or if serving carts are not provided on a one to one ratio with respect to the number of booths 10, the table segment 16 may be otherwise supported at a convenient height. In either event, once the dishes have been placed on the arms 30 and 31 of the table segment 16, the table segment 16 is positioned on a serving cart 19 with the end 29 adjacent to the upright surfaces 44 and 45.

The serving cart 19 is then pushed to the appropriate table. The tables, may be numbered or colour coded, or include other indicia such as the design 51 which is emblazoned partially on the removable segment 16 and partially on the stationary segment 11. Any portion of the booth 10 and the removable segments 16 may be used for identifying marks so that the proper one of the removable segments 16 is brought to the appropriate booth 10 and engaged with the particular stationary segment 11 located therein. When brought to the booth 10, the cart 19 is pushed toward the vertical panel 27, thus forcing the appendages 32 and 33 into the recesses 26 and 25 and also capturing the end of the tongue 16 by the laterally disposed member 37. The cart 19 is then withdrawn leaving the removable segment 16 supported by the ledge 15 of the stationary segment 11. The pedestal 12 aids in bearing the load.

The patrons then proceed to dine. Once finished, a waiter, waitress, or busboy approaches the table with a cart 19. Again the cart 19 is moved toward the vertical panel 27 so that the longitudinal recess 51' engages the pedestal 12 to appropriately position the cart 19 relative to the removable segment 16. The attending restaurant staff member then grabs the outer edges of the arms 30 and 31 and pulls backward on them thereby drawing the removable segment 16 and the cart 19 away from the vertical panel 27, after first making sure that no dishware lies directly above the contoured edges 14 and 18. The removable segment 16 is then pushed on the cart to the kitchen where all soiled dinnerware and leftovers are removed. The segment 16 is cleaned in the kitchen, thereby avoiding food scraps, crumbs and debris from being unnecessarily spilled in the dining area. The removable segment 16 is then washed and is available for further use.

From the foregoing description of the embodiment of the invention illustrated, it is apparent that various other modifications of the invention may be employed. For example, the utility of the invention is not limited to tables use only in association with booths. To the contrary, a free standing stationary segment 11 supported by a pedestal 12 might be employed in the centre of a room. A removable segment 16 could be engaged with such a stationary segment 11 in the same manner as has been described herein. Undoubtedly, other modifications and variations of the invention will become readily apparent to those familiar with the operation and management of dining establishments and with the provisions of articles of manufacture for use in such establishments.

TABLE SERVICE

Table service is a form of service in restaurants, pubs, and bars where food or drinks are served to the customer's table. This is compared with counter service where service is provided at the counter. Table service is the norm in most restaurants, while for some fast food restaurants counter service is the common form. For pubs and bars, table service is the norm in the United States whereas counter service is the norm in the United Kingdom, in addition to most of the western world.

With table service, the customer generally pays just before leaving rather on the delivery of the food or drink. Various methods of table service can be provided. See, for instance, silver service.

LAYING A TABLE

Laying a table means setting the table with the appropriate cutlery, crockery, glassware, linen and accessories required on the table for the smooth service of food and beverage. They should be set on the table according to the number of covers. Laying the table should be according to the type of meal being served. Let us elaborate on each cover setup on the same lines.

Table Layout for Breakfast

The breakfast table layout or cover setup may be divided into two types. These are:

Full Breakfast Cover/English Cover

The full breakfast consists of a number of courses, usually three or four, with a choice of dishes within each course. The cover will therefore include some or all of the following:

1) Joint knife and fork.

2) Fish knife and fork.
3) Sweet spoon and fork.
4) Slop basin.
5) Sideplate/B&B plate with sideknife (B&B knife)
6) Tea or breakfast cup, saucer and teaspoon.
7) Tea strainer.
8) Sugar basin and tongs.
9) Underplates for teapot/coffee pot and hot water jug/ hot milk jug.
10) Salt and pepper cruet set.
11) Castor sugar in sugar dredger.
12) Ashtray (depending on smoking policy)
13) Napkin.

Continental Breakfast Cover

Continental breakfast is a small menu in comparison with the English breakfast. For a continental breakfast consisting of hot breads, butter, preserves, juices and coffee/tea, the cover setup would be as follows:

1) Sideplate/B&B plate with sideknife (B&B knife)
2) Tea or breakfast cup, saucer and teaspoon.
3) Sugar basin and tongs.
4) Underplates for teapot/coffee pot and hot water jug/ hot milk jug.
5) Salt and pepper cruet set.
6) Castor sugar in sugar dredger.
7) Ashtray (depending on smoking policy)
8) Napkin.
9) If tea is the beverage then the following additional items will be needed:
10) Slop basin and Tea strainer

The majority of the items listed above for the two types of breakfast are often placed on the table as part of the mise-en-place, before the guest is seated. A number of items, however, are then placed on the table when the guest is seated. These include:

1) Butter dish and butter with alternatives.
2) Preserve dish with preserve
3) Jug of cold milk
4) Toast rack with toast and/or bread basket with hot rolls
5) Teapot/coffee pot/hot water jug/hot milk.
6) Other items according to the guest's choice.

TABLE LAYOUT FOR AFTERNOON TEA SERVICE

The concept of afternoon tea service is based on old English traditions and the service time was at 4 o'clock. Nowadays, the trend is slowly being replaced, yet still, some places do serve afternoon teas. They can be classified into three types:

Full afternoon tea served in "A" class hotels and restaurants.

1) Sideplate/B&B plate with sideknife (B&B knife)
2) Pastry fork
3) Tea cup, saucer and teaspoon.
4) Tea strainer and slop basin
5) Sugar basin and tongs.
6) Underplates for teapot/coffee pot and hot water jug/hot milk jug.
7) Salt and pepper cruet set.
8) Ashtray (depending on smoking policy)
9) Napkin.
10) Jug of cold milk
11) Butter dish and butter with alternatives.
12) Preserve dish on an underplate with preserve spoon.

The last three items are to be brought to the table only after the guest is seated and are not part of the mise-en-place.

High tea served in popular outlets and café.

1) Joint knife and fork.
2) Slop basin and Tea strainer.
3) Sideplate/B&B plate with sideknife (B&B knife)
4) Tea or breakfast cup, saucer and teaspoon.
5) Sugar basin and tongs.
6) Underplates for teapot/coffee pot and hot water jug/ hot milk jug.
7) Salt, pepper and mustard powder cruet set with mustard spoon.
8) Ashtray (depending on smoking policy)
9) Napkin.
10) Jug of cold milk
11) Butter dish and butter with alternatives.
12) Preserve dish on an underplate with preserve spoon

The last three items are to be brought to the table only after the guest is seated and are not part of the mise-en-place.

Reception or Buffet Tea: These are offered at special functions, private parties and important conferences, conventions and meetings. As the name implies, it is served from the buffet table where the guests help themselves and not at their individual tables.

The buffet table should be well setup with table cloths and frills attached and placed in a prominent position in the dining area. When setting up the buffet it is necessary to ensure that there is ample space for customer circulation. The waiters should also be able to move easily and quickly to the kitchen and wash up areas without disturbing the guests. A number of tables and chairs can be laid out at occasional space with a clean table cloth on top and having a small vase and an ashtray.

TABLE LAYOUT FOR LUNCH/DINNER

The table layout for lunch and dinner is normally the same but will vary according to the type of menu being served. Based on this we can have two cover setups as follows:

A la Carte Layout: This cover follows the principle that the cutlery and crockery will be laid just before each course is served.

The traditional cover given below will therefore have the setup laid only for the first course i.e. Hors d'oeuvres. The cover will consist of the following:

1) Joint knife and fork
2) Dessert spoon and fork
3) Sideplate/B&B plate with sideknife (B&B knife)
4) Water goblet.
5) Salt and pepper cruet set
6) Ashtray (depending on smoking policy)
7) Bud vase.
8) Napkin.

Table d'hote Layout: This cover follows the principle that the cutlery, flatware and crockery for the whole meal/menu will be laid in advance. The cover will consist of the following:

1) Joint knife and fork
2) Fish knife and fork
3) Dessert spoon and fork
4) Soup spoon
5) Sideplate/B&B plate with sideknife (B&B knife)
6) Water goblet.
7) Salt and pepper cruet set
8) Ashtray (depending on smoking policy)
9) Bud vase.
10) Napkin.

General Rules for Laying the Table

Once the table cloth is laid on the tables start doing the setup according to the type of meal i.e. breakfast/lunch/dinner/afternoon tea. If an Ala carte/Table d'hote cover is being laid then the first item set on the table should be the dinner plate/joint plate on the centre of the cover.

This plate has to be removed once all the cutlery & flatware have been laid. After some months of practice, there would be no requirement of a dinner plate to assist you in laying the cutlery and flatware.

The purpose of initially placing a plate on the centre of the cover is to ensure that the covers are exactly opposite to each other and that the cutlery and flatware of each cover are the same distance apart.

Cutlery and flatware should be laid from a service salver/tray.

While laying a Table d'hote cover, the cutlery and flatware should be laid from inside to outside of the cover. This ensures even spacing of the cover.

After the above said covers have been laid, the table lay-up should be completed by the addition of "ABC" i.e. Ashtray, Bud vase, Cruet set.

All cutlery and flatware have to be laid 1.25 cm (1/2 inch) from the edge of the table

The water goblet has to be placed upside down at the top right-hand corner of the Cover In some restaurants extra items may be placed on the table like bread roll basket, butter dish with butter, etc.

Welcoming the Guest

The personal skills shown by the food and beverage staff go a long way towards selling an establishment and making the guests feel at home in a friendly and relaxed atmosphere. This aspect of service is very often neglected and all staff should be aware of the importance of healthy customer contact at regular intervals. A pleasant welcome to a guest can gain a sale; a poor welcome will lose a sale.

First Impressions Count: When the restaurant is thrown open to the guests, each and every staff should be seen at their strategic stations. The hostess should be available at the entrance at their counter with their table plans and booking register open. As soon as a guest or a group of guests arrive, they have to be warmly greeted according to the time of the day. It can be followed by a brief enquiry, if by chance they have booking, if so details thereof. In case of negative reply, enquire about number of persons by your personal assessment like "Table for Two or Four", check if you can possibly offer a table.

If the booking is heavy, you may not be able to offer a table immediately to guests without reservations. In such cases, suggest them something reasonable in a courteous manner like waiting at the bar and enjoying a drink or two so that when a table is vacated they could come over. The hostess will have to decide with the Restaurant Manager/Senior Captain if a table can be offered immediately when a non reserved guest walks in.

To arrive at such quick decisions the Manager/Sr. Captain should be able to use his experience & knowledge of human nature and the strategies of distribution of workload equally. Always escort the guests to the table and remember to address known guests by their names. Try to exchange some pleasantries and good humour in your conversation.

Ensure that the chairs are drawn out to seat the guests at all times for every guest, especially for the women guests. Parents should be helped in seating their on high chairs or on additional cushions placed on restaurant chairs. Any bags, wraps or parcels are to be checked at the appropriate place and the claim tag given to the guest. When the guests are comfortably seated, the menu has to be placed in front of each guest. Never wave or flourish the menu. The glasses of the guests have to be filled up with water of the guest's choice.

Rules for Waiting at the Table

1) After the guests are seated unfold each guest's napkin and place it on his/her lap.
2) Offer the menu card to each guest seated and stand away for a couple of minutes to let the guests decide what they want.
3) If there are extra covers on the table, ask the guest if any others are expected. If no then remove the extra covers immediately.
4) In a traditional Continental meal proceed with serving bread rolls to each guest and placing the butter dish on the table.
5) At the time of order taking excuse your self graciously by asking "May I please take your order Sir/Madam?" Always stand at the right of the guest and be ready to offer suggestions on the menu or translate any terms/ items if necessary.
6) Take the orders neatly on the waiter'spad. While taking the order one should not rest one's hand on the back of the chair or lean to close to the guest. Stand erect and bend forward slightly from the hips.
7) The waiter should be aware of the preparation times of all the dishes that are ordered by the guest. Do not mislead the guest on the timing. If the guest is in a hurry suggest some "ready to serve" item and never a "cooked to order item."
8) Always ask the guest how he/she would like the preparation to be e.g. less spicy, steaks cooked to rare, medium or well done, etc.
9) Place the order in the kitchen and bar/pantry and serve the drinks immediately.
10) Follow it up with any snacks/savories ordered. If the snacks are pre-plated serve from the right side and if not serve each guest at the table from the left side.

11) If wine is presented to the host, then present the bottle to the host, open it and let the host taste it. After his/her approval serves the ladies first, then the gents and finally the host. Remember that approximately six glasses of wine can be obtained from a bottle of wine. White wine should be served chilled and red wine at room temperature.
12) Serve the food in the correct sequence of the menu. Each course must be served with the appropriate cutlery and flatware and if wine is served as accompaniments the correct glasses should go with each course of menu.
13) All hot foods should be served piping hot and cold foods served cold
14) Check at regular intervals for replenishing the guests wine glasses and water goblets as well as the food on his/her plate.
15) After the main course is over clear all the items from the table except the ash tray, bud vase, the desert cutlery and the water goblet.

    The cruet has to be cleared after the main course compulsorily.
16) Offer finger bowls with all dishes at the end if the guest eats with his fingers.
17) Crumb the table and change the ashtray if required.
18) Offer the menu to the guest to choose a sweet dish/dessert. Take the order.
19) Lay the dessert covers and accompaniments.
20) Clear any wine glasses and bottles on the table.
21) Serve the dessert. Cold desserts are served before hot desserts.
22) Clear the dessert plates.
23) Take the coffee order and do the coffee service. Offer more coffee at the appropriate time.
24) Let the guests relax and obtain his/her permission for presenting the bill.

25) Always present the bill in a bill folder. Collect the bill, realize it and return back the bill folder with change if any, to the guest.
26) Always acknowledge all tips with polite thanks. If the guest does not give any tip, acknowledge it with thanks and a smile, which is a must.
27) See the guests out by helping draw out the chairs of ladies and escorting the guests till the entrance. Thank and wish them as appropriately.
28) Clear down the table. Re-lay if necessary and get ready for the next guest.
29) During the course of service if any mistakes occur at the guests table it is very important that one apologizes immediately followed by corrective action.
30) If a problem arises at the guests table do not enter into any sort of arguments with the guest. *"The guest is always right"* is one cardinal rule that the hotel industry follows. Attempt to solve the problem as courteously and tactfully as possible. If it is beyond ones handling capacity, immediately inform your senior.

STYLES OF SERVICE

Food service is a very important and skilled activity that requires organized managerial inputs because it concerns not only the service of food, but value addition by serving the same in different forms and styles. Some of the most important food service styles are as follows:

Silver Service/Platter to Plate Service

This type of service is the most elegant and time tested. It originated in the English tradition and today it is the most popular form of service. Here the highest skills of a waiter is demonstrated, not-withstanding the best skill of the chef which is on display over the platter. Here the food is decorated by the chef artistically on silver plated dishes.

The silver dish is placed on a clean and neatly folded waiter's cloth with glittering pair of service spoon and fork at the side of the silver dish.

The service is done at the table for each guest from the left hand side. The waiter will transfer food with great care on to the guest's plate in the most professional manner.

Silver Service Procedure

1) Place clean hot plates in front of the guests from the right from a stack carried in the left hand.
2) Hold the serving dish on a service cloth on the palm of your left hand balancing it at the centre.
3) Calculate the size of the portion allowed for each guest, and decide how it should be presented, considering the other items to be served.
4) As stated before, silver service takes place from the left of the guest but the beverages will be served from the right.
5) Hold the serving dish over the guest's plate, no more than 5 cm above it.
6) Place the main item of the course to the front of the guest's plate.
7) Place the vegetables around and behind the main item away from the guest in the pattern already decided for plate presentation.
8) Note that no items are placed on the rim of the plate.
9) Garnishes have to be placed to enhance the presentation.
10) Pick up food items from the silver dish using a service spoon and fork and serve by releasing the cutlery on the guest plate.
11) Move anti-clockwise round the table serving each guest in turn, with the host last.

Advantages

1) The chefs and waiters can display their demonstration

skills with respect to designing of the platter/silver dish and the service of food respectively.

2) It is a highly personalized form of service and the guests feels extremely cared for. Moreover it adds a luxurious ambience to the service setting. These factors add to the goodwill of the establishment.
3) It gives the guest the choice of selecting and quantifying the food served to him, therefore less embarrassment and wastage.
4) Unwanted accompaniments, garnishes and sauces are easily avoided.

Disadvantages

1) Very high expenses on training of staff and equipment costs.
2) Silver requires great attention and care. Maintenance is expensive.
3) Time consuming with regard to silver dish decoration in the kitchen as well as service of food in the restaurant.
4) At one time a maximum of 6 portions of the same item can be carried on a silver dish. For more of the same item, the waiter will have to go again to the kitchen.
5) When last portions are served, the dishes look scattered and possibly unappetizing.
6) Portions can be miscalculated, thereby ending up giving more or less portions to the last few due to uneven distribution.

AMERICAN SERVICE/PRE PLATED SERVICE

American service is a less formal style of service compared to the other. Most restaurants around the globe adopt this service for a quicker and casual meal experience. Food is normally decorated on individual plates of predetermined portions and kept warm.

In this type of service a waiter can carry about five plates fixing them in between two hands. Many restaurants use a plate trolley to carry more number of plates from the kitchen to the dining area. This form of service has become very popular but lacks the elegance and class of silver service. Service of food on plates and clearance are both done from the right hand side. This type of service can be found in fast food restaurants, coffee shops, discotheques, bars, etc.

Advantages

1) The service is quick and simple
2) The chances of spilling are less or nearly negligible
3) Less investment, less staff skills involved and reduced piling of dishes for washing.
4) No maintenance of silver items
5) Presentation on plate is decorated very beautifully and each guest can enjoy an individual plate experience.
6) Portion control can be strongly established thereby reducing wastage and helping set standards.
7) Less/reduced chances of guest complaints.

Disadvantages

1) Food service becomes a dull and lifeless affair.
2) Food gets rapidly cold, often may need reheating
3) More movements by waiters to and fro from the restaurant to the kitchen for fetching more plates.
4) Uninteresting, unnecessary garnishes cannot be avoided which may annoy the guest.
5) Large eaters may not be happy with the portion served and small eaters may end up with wastage on their plates.

English Service

English service is used occasionally for a special dinner occasion or for close family affairs. This style of service originated from the old English homes wherein two to three servants used to help the master of the house in service of food at the table. The food on platters and the heated plates are brought from the kitchen on a trolley and placed before the host at the head of the table.

Either the host or one of the waiters will carve the meat or dish up the entrée and vegetables on individual plates of the guests. The host may then hand the plates over to the waiter's to be distributed amongst his guests. The host normally offers the first portion to his wife as per authentic tradition, then the rest of the people. The waiters will have to take the platters/serving bowls around and do service for the second helping. Clearing is done in an informal fashion.

Advantages

1) This service involves a great deal of showmanship.
2) The host gets to carve and dish out portions as per his liking.

Disadvantages

1) The host may be required to do a lot of work with minimal assistance from the waiter.
2) Service can be time consuming.
3) Portions offered are to the hosts liking and could cause displeasure to certain guests.

French Service

This is a very formal type of service originated for European nobility in France and currently enjoyed by those who can afford the time and the expenses involved. In French service, the food is cooked or completed at a side table in front of the guest's. The food is brought from the kitchen to the dining room on heavy silver platters in a semi cooked condition and placed on a cart called a "Gueridon".

The gueridon is simply a trolley or side table that can be made of wood or metal alloys. By far this is the most exquisite and expensive method of food presentation and service. Asmall spirit stove called a "Rechaud" is used to keep the food warm.

The food is completed by cooking, deboning, slicing and garnishing as required and served to the guests on heated plates. Only those foods that can be cooked, assembled, or completed in a reasonably short time are prepared in front of the guests.

This type of service normally requires two waiters working together to serve the meal and may include a captain to seat the guests and a wine steward to serve the wine. Finger bowls are served on an underliner to the guests with all finger foods. Soiled dishes are cleared only when all guests have completed their meals.

Advantages

1. Since it is highly specialized form of service, the guest's receive a great deal of attention.
2. The service is extremely elegant.
3. Service with the aid of a Gueridon Trolley offers the guest an exhibition of the cooking and presentation skills in front of them.
4. Flambé items can be completed on the gueridon trolley with great flair.
5. The gueridon trolley acts as a great sales promoter in the restaurant.

Disadvantages

1. Only fewer guests' can be served at one time.
2. More space is necessary for service
3. Many highly professional waiters are required at one time.
4. Service is time consuming.
5. Safety while cooking at a gueridon trolley has to be of top most priority since cooking is done in front of the guest in the restaurant.
6. High cost of equipments and maintenance.
7. Shortage of inexperienced staff will render the service useless.

Russian Service

Russian service is very similar to French service in many respects. This too is a very formal and elegant dining experience and the guest is given great attention. Here also the use of heavy silverware is employed and the table setup is identical to that of French service. The differences between the French & Russian service are:

1. Only one waiter is required for service.
2. Food is fully prepared and attractively arranged on silver platters in the kitchen.
3. Gueridon trolley is not required.

To serve, the waiter takes a heated plate before each guest from the right side, going round the table clockwise. Then the waiter brings the platters of food to the dining room from the kitchen and presents them to the guests at the table. The waiter normally stands to the left of each guest and holding the platter of food in the left hand, the waiter shows each guest the food and then using a service spoon and fork, dishes up the desired portion on the guest's plate.

The waiter has to move anti-clockwise around the table and then return the unserved food to the kitchen. Finger bowls are served on an underliner to the guests with all finger foods. Soiled dishes are cleared only when all guests have completed their meals.

Advantages

1. Only one waiter is required
2. Service is very elegant, yet faster and less expensive
3. No extra space is required for special equipments, such as the gueridon.

Disadvantages

1. Large investment in the silverware and the number of plates needed, especially when every guest in a party orders a different selection.

2. This type of service is quite difficult in normal busy restaurants. Therefore it becomes ideal for banquet parties only.
3. Last guest served at the table will receive a scattered and less well displayed food.

BUFFET

The word buffet is of French origin. The literal English translation means self-service. With buffet service, guests select their meals from an attractive arrangement of food items, hot or cold. The food items displayed will have a number of dishes from a variety of courses.

The guest's either help themselves or are served by the waiters standing behind the buffet tables. Nowadays even the chefs stand behind the buffet counters and may also have a live display counter where food is cooked and presented to the guest on his plate. Awide range of dishes and the option of unlimited portions make the buffet style very popular. All buffets generally include a combination of the following:

1) A creative, innovative and centralized idea or theme.
2) Stylized preparation of food in volume.
3) Showmanship and flare.
4) Unusual table settings and configurations

The job of the waiter depends on the design of the buffet. There are many types of buffets in restaurant service. They could be described as follows:

Restaurant Buffet: These buffets are becoming increasingly popular in restaurants throughout the world. They are generally used to display cooked foods for breakfast, brunch, lunch, afternoon tea and dinners.

Fork Buffet: Also known as Buffet a la Fourchette or Standing Buffet. This buffet got its name because the guest's eat their food with the aid of Fork while standing. No chairs are offered for such buffets. In this style of buffet setup more guests can be accommodated because larger space is available.

Sit down Buffet or Formal Buffet: In this style tables and chairs are laid out with covers provided. The guests help themselves from the buffet counter and sir at the tables.

Finger Buffet: The finger buffet is one in which bite sized foods are offered for which no cutlery is required. The guests are provided with fancy cocktail sticks to pick the food and place in their paper napkin. The atmosphere is very informal. The foods served can be canapés, single piece dessert, sandwiches, vol au vents, etc. These buffets are mostly used for pre-lunch/dinner cocktail parties.

Advantages

1. Food can be displayed in a very attractive manner
2. A variety of themes and food ranges are possible
3. Large volumes of people can be catered to in very less time
4. Waiters can attend to many guests at one time.
5. Guests can choose their own dish and portion sizes.

Disadvantages

1. Food is displayed in large quantities; therefore care should be taken to keep the food fresh and complete.
2. Personalized level of service is not possible.
3. The guest's cannot choose a dish that is not on the buffet. They have a limited selection from the buffet itself.
4. Maintenance of large number of serving dishes and flatware's

CAFETARIA SERVICE

In cafeteria service guests collect their own meals as they select food items from a display counter. This type of service is generally found in schools, colleges, institutions and other organizations.

ROOM SERVICE

Room service is an essential feature of the food and beverage operation in a hotel. Room service is the service of food and beverages in guest's rooms in hotels or other accommodations. Room service offers the guest the facility and pleasure of having his meal at leisure in his own room. Most room service department has a single pantry located conveniently near the kitchen and the service lift. Room service catering can involve the delivery of everything from complimentary items and items for which no charge is made (such as ice buckets and glasses) through drinks or light snacks, to full a la carte with wine. The items available for service in rooms will normally be listed on a special room service menu. The service timings may also be mentioned on the menu to ensure transparency in operations e.g.:

- Breakfast: 6am to 11am
- All day dining: 11am to 11pm
- A la Carte: 7pm to 10.30 pm
- Night menu: 11pm to 6am

The pantry must be stocked with sufficient equipments to ensure that all orders can be met promptly even at the busiest times. Equipments generally used are:

1) Trays and trolleys
2) Cutlery, crockery, linen and glassware
3) Selected food and beverage items
4) Printed materials

Every item should have a par stock level.

BAR SERVICE

The proper service of alcoholic beverages is very important because many restaurants are merchandizing drinks to satisfy the demand of guests and to increase profits. The waiter's correct service of alcoholic beverages depends not only on knowing the procedure for serving but also on the knowledge of types of drinks, glassware, beverage temperature and garnishes.

A waiter should also know what beverages complement which foods on the menu and offer suggestions too. Beverages may be served as an individual item of service (e.g. in a bar or a lounge service), or their service may be carefully coordinated with the service of food, thereby enhancing the guests enjoyment of both. The style of beverage service offered will depend on the character of the establishment and the types of beverages being served.

Responsible Service of Alcohol: Every person engaged in the hotel industry is expected to have a responsible and professional approach to the serving of alcohol on licensed premises. The principles of responsible service of alcohol are:

1. No liquor should be served to minors
2. Drunken or disorderly behaved people should not be allowed on the premises.
3. No liquor should be served to already intoxicated people.
4. There should be no promotions that encourage binge drinking.

Beverage Selling: In a hotel alcoholic beverages can be sold at outlets like bars, restaurants, lounges, banquet halls, etc. provided they have a license. When selling beverages:

1) Do not force your personal preferences.
2) Offer a diversity of recommendations so that guests are prompted to choose what they personally prefer.
3) Suggest beverages that complement the occasion, but do not convey your displeasure if something "unsuitable" is chosen. Guests have the right to choose what they want. Your job is to make them feel comfortable and relaxed.

Taking Beverage Orders: Beverage orders should be taken as soon as the guests are comfortably settled. The following points have to be borne in mind while taking the order:

1) Make sure you understand the order given and record it properly on a Bar Order Ticket (BOT).
2) If there are many guests write the order down in the order of their seating. This will make things easy for the waiter during service of the same.
3) Avoid the use of abbreviations unless it is a coded practice in the hotel, else it will create confusion.
4) The order for the service of after dinner drinks like port, liqueur, etc. should be taken prior to the service of coffee, so that drinks can be served with the coffee.

Service: All glassware, whether clean or used, should be carried upright on a drinks tray, except that wine glasses may be carried upside down by their stems, held between the fingers of the left hand, before the arrival of guests.

A drinks tray is carried on a slightly cupped hand on the pads of the fingers. This allows the waiter to adjust the balance of the tray as glasses are removed or added to the tray. When serving drinks to seated guests from a tray hold the tray behind the guests head, and use your right hand to place the drink from the guests' right.

SUMMER BREAKFAST FOR TEN (TWO RESERVED PLATES.)

First Course, Melon-When Table Is Laid Guests Enter And Take Seats

Waiters place tea and coffee urns and bring melon. The gentleman serving asks each guest if he will be helped to melon. If the answer be yes, wait-er receives plate from server and hands to guest, exchanging plates and returning empty plate "to server, who places melon on it for another guest and so on. As soon as all are served, or have refused a second helping, the waiter removes the remains of the melon, and replaces it with dish for second course. The lady at the head of the table asks each guest to partake of tea, coffee, or chocolate. If any accept, waiter receives it and hands to guest. Asking guests to take tea etc., in first course, is a mere matter of form, as it is seldom taken until second course. Still the question must be asked, and waiter ready to serve it.

Second Course-In the place of melon, a dish of fish-fried perch, smelts, trout, or whatever is selected. Sauce Tartare is a proper accompaniment. Decorate dish of fish with shrimps or olives cut in half, or with little, bunches of parsley with shrimp placed on it.

Waiters also remove first set of dessert plates used for melon, and replace with a size larger, medium breakfast plates. The waiter then receives a supply of fish from the person who serves it, hand to the guests, receiving empty plates, and helping guests to what accompaniments they desire. Another waiter asks if guest will take coffee or tea, and supplies it from party serving it. Potatoes are handed round (with either meat or fish.) If two kinds, present one in each hand for guest to help himself.

Third Course-Young Chicken Sauced With Cream Gravy, Surrounded With Potatoes A La Neige

Waiter removes fish of second course, and replaces with young chicken, then attends to wants of guests as in second course, remembering to ask each if he will take tea or coffee; also asking each if he will take his tea or coffee warmer. Clean plates same size as for second course, must be supplied to each guest.

Fourth Course-Poached Eggs On Toast, Or Anchovy Toast

Waiter removes chicken and replaces it with dish of poached eggs, and furnishes clean plates. Party serving asks each guest if he can help him, and waiters serve as in the other cases. Lady dispensing tea or coffee asks guests if they will be helped to warmer tea or coffee. If any one accepts, waiter hands clean cup and saucer from the sideboard to lady serving and then hands it to the guest. If milk is asked for he procures from sideboard and hands to the guest. Waiter also watches the guests and supplies them with hot cakes, receiving a dish of hot ones for that purpose every five minutes, handing dish of cakes to guest who ' helps himself.

Fifth Course-Little Fillets Of Porter House Steak With Tomatoes A La Mayon-Naise

Waiter puts on steak in place of plate of poached eggs, and caters to wants of guests as before. While guests are eating this course, the waiters or an extra waiter, as quietly as possible relieve the table of the castor, pickles, sauces, dressing and butter. But not till the last moment must this be done, at the same time asking the guests if they require more.

The dessert or rather fruit, sixth course, is then brought in and placed where steak was; arrange as quickly as possible, the service remaining on the table in neat order, remove each guest's plate, and again furnish dessert plates, At a signal from lady at head of table, waiter hands around fruit to guests, each guest supplying himself, unless the person before serving the other dishes serves this, in which case waiter supplies each as before.

Waiter also supplies each guest with tea or coffee, and hands around cake, biscuit, etc., At this course a finger glass should be supplied to each guest.

Sixth Course-Peaches Quartered, Sweetened Or Half Frozen Or Any Fruit Decided Upon

Carry out the instructions given in the fifth course. In some breakfasts order is reversed, and fruit is served in first course only. In this case various fruits are placed on table, and allowed to remain till end of breakfast so that guests may partake at any time. In first diss breakfasts fruit forms the first and last course, but waiters should be instructed beforehand, which plan is to be followed.

WAITERS SERVING AND CLEARING TABLES

In a formal restaurant, there is a strict rule for how waiters and waitresses serve the food and then clear the tables. It's good to be aware of how these things happen.

First, the primary duty of a waiter or waitress is to be helpful, invisible and always present. As you can imagine, that can be a really rough thing to do! It is your duty as a patron to make it easy for the waiter/waitress to know when you are ready for another drink, when you are done with a plate. If you keep playing with your food, how should the waitress know to come and remove that plate?

First, the place should always be set when you sit down-that way the waiter/waitress does not need to bother you at all with moving around in front of you. They should bring you drinks quickly, and be available but not pushy in taking your order. It is up to you to choose what you want at whatever speed it takes you.

It is politeness to serve everybody at once. That means if someone orders a dish that takes a long time, everyone will wait until it is ready. You can't blame a waiter for this-this is proper etiquette. Once everything at that course level is ready, they should be brought out simultaneously. That means if a number of people ordered appetizers, they are all brought out together so that nobody is left "waiting for food" while others are eating. The dishes should be served from each guest's right side. The ancient theory here is that guests would carry their swords on their left side, so that the guest could always "face any danger" posed. It was least threatening for a waiter to be on the right.

There are two theories on then removing the plates. One is that it is polite not to interrupt the party at all until everyone is done eating. At that point, all plates should be removed-again from the diners' right hand side-simultaneously. Another theory says that some people eat slowly, while others eat quickly. Those who ate quickly don't mind sitting and talking, but they dislike staring at cold food remnants on their plate during that time. So in that sense, some restaurants remove those done plates as soon as they are done, to be polite to the early diners. There are of course proponents of both theories.

Finally, while a waiter should present a bill early so you can leave immediately if you wish to, the waiter should never press you to pay immediately. You can sit and talk if you wish. The waiter should both be ready to take payment if you are ready to pay-or be ready to offer refills if your aim is to sit and chat. While I usually find waiters that are happy to be patient, I also find waiters that suddenly forget to refill water glasses, ask about seconds on coffee or even ask about dessert once that final bill is brought. As long as you are in the restaurant, you are a patron, and potentially could still be hungry or thirsty. It is the waiter's job to be around in case you want to call him over for a change or addition to your bill.

SERVICE SEQUENCE

Formal Situation: Where there is a host, the first we should serve is the woman on the right of the host. Second, all women in clockwise direction from the host. Third, all men in clockwise direction from the host. The last is host.

Informal Situation: Actually we don't know the host. So we just nominate the host, the food is carried out in a clockwise direction from the host regardless sex/gender. We can serve from the most convenience focal point.

For beverage same as food we serve from the right handside, but the direction is anticlockwise. Food service has precedence over beverage service because hot food goes cold quickly.

What are two types of basic menu? Describe the characteristics of each menu. What are the elements that must be known in order to sell the menu?

To sell the menu we must know:

1. The availability of dishes
2. Alterations, additions and daily special

3. The ingredients, preparation method and presentation of each dishes on the menu
4. The vegetables served with each main course
5. Cooking order for beef & lamb
6. Cover and accompaniments for each menu items

4. What is a Table D'hote cover? What is the general rule for setting the cover? Describe the procedure for setting a Table D'hote cover with food items such as:
   a. Chicken Consommé
   b. Grilled Fillets of Bream
   c. Roast Loin of Lambs, Mint Jelly
   d. Poached Peaches with King Island Cream.

Table D'hote cover – cover that is used when the menu is known.

General Rule for Setting the Cover

Start from the inside toward to the outside, for setting. And for eating, start from the outside toward to the inside.

The procedures for setting a Table D'hote cover with following food items:

1. Mise en Place
   - Gather everything you need (table ware, equipment, etc.)
   - Make sure its clean
   - Fold your napkin
2. Place the centre guide (it could be folded napkin/dinner plate)
3. The MC knife placed to the right side of the centre guide app. 3 cm from the edge of the napkin and 1 cm from the edge of the table
4. The fish knife placed to the right side of the MC knife, app. 3 cm and 1 cm from the edge of the table

5. The fish fork placed to the left side of the MC fork, app. 3 cm and 1 cm from the edge of the table
6. Put Soup spoon app. 3 cm to the right side of the fish fork and 1 cm from the edge of the table
7. Put the side plate to the left of Fish fork app. 3 cm
8. Put the side knife to the right side on the side plate, leaving space for roll bread
9. Put Dessert fork on top of centre guide (the head of fork facing right) and Dessert spoon on top of Dessert spoon (the head of spoon facing left)
10. Put four suitable glasses in a diamond formation or arranged it depend on the space available on the table and house policy
11. Put the table décor (salt, pepper, ashtray, flower vase, ect)
12. All must be placed without double movement
13. Replaced centre guide with folded napkin
14. Check whether all are already uniform

Explain the difference between "Order Taking" and "Order Making". How do you know when a customer is ready to order? What are some of the signs that indicate a customer is ready to order? Describe the traditional sequence of Order Taking.

Order taking is simply writing down what the customers require in the correct abbreviations and sequence.

Order Making is the waiters do suggestive selling and encouraging extras to the customer and it can make the customer's day.

The differences: Order Making-the waiters do suggestive selling and encouraging extras to the customer while Order Taking doesn't do it.

We will know the customer is ready to order by their "Body language".

Some of the signs that indicate a customer are ready to order: A raise finger, a closed menu, a wave, an enquiring look, a fidget, a cough, a nod.

Traditional Sequence of Order Taking

1. Woman to the immediate right of the host.
2. All women in a clockwise direction from the host.
3. All men in a clockwise direction from the host.
4. Finally – the Host.

List the courses in a Traditional Menu and a Modern Menu. Explain why and how the Traditional Menu has evolved to become the Modern Menu?

Courses of Traditional Menu

1. Hors D'oeuvre
2. Soups/Potages
3. Poissons and Fish
4. Entrées
5. Releves
6. Sorbets
7. Rotis/Roast
8. Legumes/Vegetables
9. Entrimets/Sweets
10. Saroreaux
11. Dessert
12. Coffee

Courses of Modern Menu

1. Starting Courses
2. Main Courses
3. Sweet/Desserts

The Traditional Menu has evolved because there way due to economic pressures (wages & food cost) and to suit current eating trends & lifestyles we have been influenced by many different cultural experiences of the people who pioneered the hospitality industry.

What are the six commonly known styles of service? Describe the two most commonly used styles of service. What are the characteristics of these two styles that made them commonly used?

Styles of Service

- Plate Service – Buffet/Self Service – Silver Service
- Semi-silver Service – Room Service – Gueridon Service

Common Service:

Plate Service

The simplest form of service with all the food items being placed on the plate by the kitchen staff and the waiter delivers the meal in it's entirely to the customer.

Buffet Service

Where are rang e of food is presented on platters or in chafing dishes for the customer to make their own selection.

Characteristics – Cost Efficiency and Time Efficiency

Describe Suggestive Selling and Upselling. What are the common characteristic and the difference in these two styles of selling? Explain the benefits of using Suggestive and Upselling!

Suggestive Selling

The process attractively describing dishes on the menu (drinks & wines) to persuade the customer to buy a product of service which they may not have otherwise bought.

Up-Selling

Where you offer alternative to the customer to increase their average spending by recommending a higher priced dish to a lower priced one. We want customer spend more.

COMMON CHARACTERISTIC OF BOTH: PERSUASION

Difference: Value

Benefit

- The customer feels pampered, when you take time to describe or offering the alternatives
- Help the chef to get rid of "must move" items (avoid wasting food)
- Customer satisfaction and our self satisfaction
- Increase the profit

Describe the factors to consider when choosing a napkin fold. Two of these factors are directly related. Which are two factors and describe how they are related? Give one example of fold each for he most simple and the most complicated.

Factors to consider when choosing a napkin fold:

- Hygiene: hygiene napkin folds are those that are handled during folding we maintain the clean with handle it as fast as possible.
- Appearance: napkins are folded for specific effects, it must match/suitable decor.
- Time: minimum time is important, don't spend a lot of time just to fold napkin
- Storage Capabilities: when we fold a lot of napkins in spare time, make sure we have enough capacity/space to save it.

Two factors that are related: Time and Hygiene. As fast as we can fold the napkin, it will be more hygiene.

The most simple: Triangle

The most complicated: Opera House

In what type of operations you would want to use a No reservation system? Explain why! Reservation system is more suitable for what kind of operation? Explain he benefits of using a reservation system?

Reservation System

Restaurant with a high turnover of tables use a NO RESERVATION system; because in high turnover, all of table occupied at that time. And when the table finish, we direct clean it & use it again. Beside that, when we use reservation system we will miss the potential sale.

Reservation system is more suitable for restaurant/hotel with low turnover of tables.

Advantages of Reservation

- Planning table layout. Since the restaurant open, we're being able to plan table layout that going to use by customer.
- Setting staff level. We will know, how much the waiter & kitchen staff that you need to serves the customer.
- Staggering customer arrival time (giving time for customer to arrive). It's to avoid us overwhelmed when serve the customer that cause can't give the best service.
- Identifying busy periods. Allow the kitchen to order more economically and not run out of menu item.

In how many ways can customers make their reservations? What is a "walk-in"? Describe the procedures for taking telephone reservations?

The customers can make their reservation through the telephone, fax machine and when they do walk-in.

Walk-in – person who arrive without reservation in the hotel or restaurant.

Procedures to take telephone reservation:

1. Greeting the customer with a smile in your voice. Answer the call as promptly as possible; apologize for the delay if we take longer. Greet the customer with the "House Rule" and speak clearly & slowly.

2. Noting the important details. Listen carefully and note details directly into the reservation diary including number of cover, name of person making the booking, day, date, & time any special requirement that the customer may have & contact telephone number.
3. Concluding the call. Finish the call by summarizing the customers booking & repeating it back to them let the customer hang up first.

Explain the difference between Hors D'oeuvre and Canapés? Explain the difference between Sweets and Dessert courses in the Traditional Menu and where would you find the traditional Dessert items served nowadays? What was the purpose of Sorbet in the Traditional Menu?

Differences of Dessert and Sweets:

Dessert – consist of fruits, dried mustaches, and variety of nuts.

Sweets – consists of dish with sweets flavour (pudding with fla, etc.).

Now, the traditional dessert items are served with the cheese board.

The purposes of sorbet in traditional menu are to cleanse and refresh palate

What is the meaning of "Mise en Place"? Describe the categories of tableware. What is the meaning of the following: (Flatware, Holloware, Silver, and Sideboard)?

Mise en Place: All the pre-preparation jobs waiter have to do in the dining room and related areas which will allow service to flow smoothly & efficiently.

Categories of tableware

1. Linen: Collective terms for tablecloths and napkins
2. Crockery/Plateware/China: collective term for plates of all sizes and shapes which are used to serve the customer's meal.

3. Cutlery: was item for cutting. Now a collective term for eating utensils such as knives, forks, spoons etc.
4. Glassware: term for glass which used for drink.

Flatware: was term for forks and spoons.

Holloware: was term for teapots, milk jugs, and platters.

Silver: collective term for cutlery, flatware and holloware.

Sideboard: Piece of restaurant furniture in which items for immediate use are stored.

Describe the various formats of menu and how they are presented to the customer? What is the common sequence of menu presentation? In explaining daily specials, house specialties, and unavailable menu items, is it better to do it before or after the customer read menu and explain why?

Menus should be presented:

- To ladies first, then the gentlemen and lastly the host with the wine/drink list.
- Hold on to the menu at the top to leave the base free for the customer to grip.

It is better to explaining daily specials, house specialties, and unavailable menu items before the customer read menu, because it can make us (as the waiter) look as a professional waiter; it also can help the chef to cook the food (because special menu usually has been prepared); it also help customer to decide/order the menu, and wish they will order it, so it is increase the average spending and make more profit.

Explain why not all fish/shellfish dishes be eaten using Fish Knife & Fork, and what cutlery should be used instead? Explain why some soups are not eaten using soup spoon and give two examples and which cutlery is used for these soups?

Not all fish/shellfish dishes are eaten using Fish Knife & Fork, because sometimes for the shellfish, there are presented with their shell. So we need a MC knife to cut the flesh from the shell and also it must be included the MC fork.

Some soups are not eaten using soup spoon, because there may be served with a slice of bread topped with cheese and grilled or use another extra materials (topped).

The cutlery that is used for these soups are Dessert Spoon and Dessert Fork.

Plate Service

- The main item on the plate is the closest to the customer for ease of eating i.e. the main item (meat/fish) is at 6:00 o'clock on the plate.

Waiter's Duties & Responsibilities

- DUTIES
- Dining Room Preparation
- Greeting & Seating Customers
- Order Taking
- Selling the Menu/Drink List
- Service of Food and Beverage
- Presentation of Customer's Bill
- Collection of Payment
- Saying Good-bye to the Customer
- Cleaning Up and Resetting the Table
- RESPONSIBILITIES
- Personal Grooming
- Deportment
- Honesty
- Punctuality
- Loyalty to Employer
- Ability to Work within a Team
- Positive Attitude
- Components:

- Hair
- Face
- Uniform
- Hands
- Shoes
- Stance
- Movement

Waiter's Equipment

- Waiters friend (professional corkscrew)
- Ball point pen
- Handkerchief
- Note pad
- Matches/lighter
- Service cloth
- Service Fork & Spoon (where appropriate

Food service outlets are different due to the:

- Market/customers
- Type and size of operations
- Location
- Range and level of service offered
- Range of entertainment
- Hours of trading

Rosters and Time Sheets

- A roster shows when you are expected to work. It will list days on which you work, your starting, finishing and break times.
- Time sheets are the way in which the hours you work are recorded and consequently paid.

The Interviewer Judges You on:

- Eye Contact

- Voice Tone & Pitch
- Facial Expression
- Smile
- Posture
- Confidence
- Enthusiasm

LINEN

- A collective term for tablecloths and napkins.

Polishing Glassware

- Make sure is CLEAN
- Polish before used
- Hold over steaming water, fogged, remove and rub dry with clean cloth
- Never use customers napkins
- When clean, hold by the stem and place on the table
- Can be done directly from the glass washing machine while still hot

WHAT IS A SILVER SERVICE WAITER?

Referred to by the French as "English Service" or service anglais, silver service technique has all but died out in private homes (except perhaps for those of great wealth).

Silver service actually describes the process of serving diners from a "silver" service dish to the diners plate, rather than the more common practise of serving the plate to the diner.

Thus the silver service waiter or waitress must bring the food to the guests via a platter and must be well acquainted with the appropriate etiquette and technique.

Origins

Silver service waiting has it's origins in the manors, country seats and fine houses of the British middle and upper classes of previous centuries.

It has a sister term of "butler service" which emanates from the age old practise of giving the waiting staff Sunday evenings off-the butler, who presumably was not given the evening off-would serve the diners from a silver platter which he carried from person to person.

One can easily imagine that the food on the platter would be the re-presented meats etc. from a large Sunday lunch-perhaps the guests were still rather full?

Silver Service Etiquette

- Meals are served to the diners from platters carried to them, not by laying down plates of food on the table.
- The guest to the host's (hostesses) right is served first.
- Service is conducted in a clockwise direction.
- Food is always served from the left and cleared from the right.
- Glasses are served and cleared from the right
- Glasses are laid out to the right in a diagonal fashion with the water glass in front of the diner-ordered in sequence for the wines by course.

Is Silver Service Still Popular?

It is a convivial practise although not always particularly practical. This being said-many people really enjoy the sense of history and even grandeur that comes with this rare type of dining and in the right setting it can really add style to an event or function.

Where would I be Able to find a Silver Service Waiter?

Generally any quality hospitality staffing group or caterer should be able to offer you Silver Service for a dinner-and occasionally some restaurants too. Certain venues that you may choose for a special event, especially those with large private dining rooms should be able to provide you with appropriately trained staff.

WHAT ARE THE DIFFERENT WAITER JOBS?

A waiter is a restaurant employee who is responsible for taking orders and serving food to the customers. The waiter's job is to provide a pleasant dining experience by being available to answer questions about the menu, making sure the cook honors special meal requests, and promptly refilling drinks as needed. In some establishments, waiters may also be expected to help with tasks such as cleaning tables, stocking silverware, or filling salt and pepper shakers.

There are several reasons to consider working as a waiter. If you're friendly, outgoing, and enjoy interacting with lots of different people, waiter jobs will make great use of your natural talents. The flexible hours offered in most restaurants make this an excellent way for college students, stay-at-home parents, or people with full-time day jobs to earn some extra cash. Additionally, since you'll get your tips at the end of each shift, you won't need to worry about how to make ends meet until your next paycheck.

While waiter jobs do have many good points, it's important to keep in mind the work has its disadvantages as well. Working nights, weekends, and holidays on a regular basis can make it hard to maintain your own social life. The older you get, the more likely it is that you'll find long hours standing on your feet to be physically draining. Being expected to be polite to everyone, even people who treat you poorly, can also prove to be a challenge.

In most cases, waiters learn through on-the-job training. Smaller franchises and family style restaurants will often hire inexperienced people for waiter jobs if they show enthusiasm and good customer service skills. Hotel or motel dining rooms, diners, and coffee shops may also be willing to take a chance on less experienced applicants.

Once you've gained some experience in the field, you can begin to look for waiter jobs in mid-level restaurants. Waiters with one or two years experience can also try searching for employment at casinos, country clubs, or cruise ships. To increase your chances of being hired for a particular position, try to spend some time at the establishment before you apply. Notice the general atmosphere as well as any traits that the employees seem to have in common.

Fine dining establishments offer the most desirable employment opportunities for waiters, since the potential for tips is much higher. Special skills, such as fluency in a foreign language or knowledge of formal table service, can help you stand out from other applicants. Post-secondary coursework relating the restaurant and hospitality industry can be useful as well.

Since many restaurants believe on promoting from within, waiter jobs can sometimes lead to other opportunities. The best waiters may be promoted to a position as a headwaiter or host. Sometimes, waiters can even work their way up to a job as an assistant manager or manager.

WHAT DOES A WAITRESS DO?

Depending on the type and size of the eatery, a waitress may have any number of responsibilities during her shift. If there is no dedicated host or hostess on duty, for example, a waitress may greet incoming customers and seat them according to sections or smoking preferences. At this point, a waitress often fills drink orders while customers decide on their orders.

Once the customers make their decisions, the waitress fills out an order ticket, which could contain specifics such as table location, placement of each order, drink orders, server name and so on. All of this information is entered into a computer at a service station or a copy of the ticket may be sent directly to the kitchen. Once the kitchen receives the order, the waitress is free to take care of other duties.

One of those duties is known as a *table sweep*, which involves visiting every occupied table in an assigned section and replenishing beverages. During a table sweep, customers may also have specific needs, such as a change in their order or a new menu for an additional guest.

A waitress will often hover near her assigned section in order to anticipate customer requests. Once all of the tables have been swept and serviced, a waitress may check on the status of food orders, delivering any completed tickets from the kitchen's window to the customer's table. Once the food has been served, a waitress may be asked to bring additional condiments such as ketchup, mustard, mayonnaise or butter. At this point, the waitress could also refill beverages and ask customers if their orders are correct and prepared properly.

At this point in the meal service, a waitress may only make a minimal number of table sweeps, allowing customers enough privacy to enjoy their meals without interruption. The waitress often uses this time to clear dishes away from the customers who have finished dining. Some customers use this time to order desserts or after-dinner cocktails, so the waitress will place the appropriate orders with the kitchen or service bar. When customers are ready to leave, a waitress will prepare a final ticket and place it on their table.

If there is no dedicated cashier on duty, the waitress will take the customer's payment and process it at a designated cash stand. The customer receives a receipt for the meal purchase or change from a cash transaction. Any tipping would most likely be transacted at this time. Waitresses are often paid a minimal hourly wage by the restaurant, so customer tips help them earn at least the federal minimum wage per hour.

During a restaurant's slow periods, a waitress also performs a number of duties known as *side work*. Typical side work includes folding napkins, rolling silverware, replenishing beverage stations, restocking service areas, and cleaning assigned sections. Some waitresses work an entire shift until relieved by another server, but others may be asked to clock out or do side work after a rush period is over. A waitress' schedule and work hours are often determined by customer demand or a manager's need to reduce labour costs.

Some restaurants may hire cashiers, food runners, table bussers or hosts in order to provide waitresses the opportunity to concentrate on their main duties. Others may require waitresses to perform many different duties all at once, which can make the occupation of waitress both mentally and physically demanding.

WHAT IS FOOD SERVICE?

Food service is a large industry which deals with the preparation and service of food outside the home. Catering a wedding, establishing a restaurant, and running a cafeteria are all forms of food service. Many people take advantage of the range of options provided by this industry all over the world, ranging from stopping at a franchise to pick up a burger and fries to eating a prescription diet while in the hospital.

A number of goods and services fall under the umbrella of food service, such as companies which transport food and related products like kitchen equipment, silverware, and so forth. Restauranteurs, waiters, bussers, chefs, and dietitians are some examples of people who work in the food service industry, along with people like architects who design facilities where food is made and served, company representatives who travel the road selling products related to the service and sale of food, and consultants who help people coordinate events at which food will be served.

Some people in this industry receive special training so that they can work in food service. Some colleges and trade schools offer hospitality programs which can include things like restaurant management, and people can also receive special training in issues like nutrition for hospitalized patients or children in schools. Other people start from the ground up, driving trucks for food distributors, waiting tables at restaurants, and so forth, gaining an understanding of the industry by working from within it.

Work in the food service industry can be grueling and demanding, even for managers and executives. The hours are often long and irregular, and people tend to spend a lot of time on their feet, dealing with varied and complex situations. As with other facets of the hospitality industry, people must also be highly attuned to the need for customer satisfaction, whether they are developing menus for a college dining hall or providing service at four star French restaurants.

In some regions of the world, work in this industry is treated as demeaning or degrading. People may opt to work in food service while between jobs, or while struggling to make their way in the world. Wages are heavily based on tips from customers, and employees may have limited access to benefits and protections from the government such as minimum wage laws. In other areas, food service is an honourable profession, for everyone from waiters to the people who own famous restaurants.

WHAT IS A FOOD RUNNER?

A food runner is a specialized type of food server that may work in a very busy restaurant, especially during peak restaurant hours. In small restaurants, a waitperson typically takes orders from guests and delivers their food. In larger restaurants, some companies employ food runners who may be responsible for delivering meals ordered and for doing other things like getting drinks for guests. Food runners may also be called food attendants.

The work of the food runner helps free up the waitperson, so he or she can focus more on certain aspects of customer service. This could include discussing details of a menu, taking orders, and checking back with patrons to be sure their meal is enjoyable. A well-trained food runner may also perform a little of this work, especially if a delivered order is not correct. Food runners could replace incorrect orders with appropriate ones if this is part of their work.

Restaurants may differ on how many food runners, if any, they employ and the number of hours in which they employ them. During non-peak hours wait staff may both take orders and deliver food, but during extremely busy times, food runners can help serve diners more quickly. Improving efficiency of food delivery can help increase patron satisfaction and keep restaurants popular for years to come.

Most runners get an hourly wage and then a portion of the tips for any waitperson they work for. This team system of waiting can be extremely successful when the food runner is polite, efficient, and professional. Poorly performed jobs can diminish the tips of the waiters, which can create issues between runners and wait staff.

Since not all restaurants employ a food runner, this additional employee may sometimes confuse patrons. For instance, if a food order is incorrect, whom should the guest tell? There isn't total consensus on this issue but many advise that the food runner should be informed if a guest notices an immediate problem with a dish, like the fact that the guest ordered something else entirely.

On the other hand, if the problem with the food is more related to *how it is prepared,* the patron should speak to his/her waitperson, or a manager if necessary.

People also want to know if they should tip a food runner separately from the waiter. Generally the answer to this is that it is not necessary, unless the person wants to clearly recognize the skills of the food runner. Food runners make a percentage of the waiter's tips, usually about 20-30%, and will be compensated accordingly.

WHAT IS A GRATUITY?

A gratuity is a small monetary gift given to a service worker in acknowledgment for his or her service. Many people refer to a gratuity as a tip, especially in reference to food service workers. Gratuities show gratefulness and appreciation on the part of the customer, rewarding the employee for hard work and also ensuring excellent service in the future. Typically, the amount of a gratuity is a percentage of the total paid for services; this percentage varies, depending on the quality of the service and the industry.

Food service personnel and people who provide personal services such as haircuts, manicures, massage, and other body care are often offered gratuities.

One may also offer a tip to someone who carries luggage or supplies, or to someone who takes care of one's children. In some industries, tips are an important part of overall wages, with staff actively relying on the convention of tipping for good service. In these industries, failure to tip is considered a serious breach of etiquette.

In some regions of the world, gratuities are actually built into bills and tags. In Europe, for example, a bill may be labelled "service compris," meaning that a tip has already been included. If guests want to tip beyond this, they certainly may do so, although it is not required or expected. In other areas, tipping is not usually built into a bill, unless a party is extremely large; a restaurant may indicate that a service charge will be included for parties over a certain size.

In food service, a gratuity generally ranges between 15-20% of the bill after tax. In other industries, a gratuity may be much smaller, or it may include other forms of compensation such as gifts. If you have a long term relationship with a tattoo artist, hairdresser, or massage therapist, for example, you may offer a yearly gift during the holiday season to show appreciation for your service provider.

Although a gratuity is a kind thing to offer, it is by no means required. Some business owners unfortunately rely on tips to make up for poor wages; this is not your fault as a customer, and you should not feel obligated to tip. As a service worker, be aware that you are usually expected to claim tips on tax paperwork, although few people do so. In some industries, a base tipping rate will be calculated using the amount of goods you sold that year, and you must claim this as a minimum.

SHOULD I ALERT RESTAURANT STAFF TO MY FOOD ALLERGIES?

If you have food allergies, it is important to talk to the staff of a restaurant about them, to ensure that the food you are served is safe. Many restaurants use trace amounts of ingredients such as nuts, dairy, and shellfish in food which may not at first glance appear to have these substances. If the staff is aware of the issue, they can address it.

The restaurant does not want you to have an allergic reaction to their food any more than you do, and most establishments are happy to work with customers who have special dietary needs.

If you make reservations to eat somewhere, always tell the staff about special needs you may have, such as those related to food allergies. The staff can alert the kitchen ahead of time about your food allergies, and the chef can consider alternate dishes for you. This is especially important if you are attending a fixed dinner, where the restaurant is providing a limited fixed menu.

Making substitutions at the last minute can be difficult and costly, but if the kitchen knows about your food allergies ahead of time, they can make the evening run smoothly. Once you arrive at the restaurant on the evening of your reservation, remind the maitre d' about your situation, and make sure that your server knows as well.

If you are walking into a restaurant, you may find it useful to talk to staff about your food allergies before sitting down. A competent restaurant staff will check with the kitchen if they are unsure about anything on the menu, and should be able to give you several options for safe dining. If the staff thinks that they are unable to meet your needs, they can tell you this before you are seated.

When you talk to staff about your food allergies, remain polite. Many waiters and waitresses feel pressured because they have too many tables, or unexpected responsibilities. Let your waiter know that you would prefer that he or she check with the kitchen, rather than guessing about whether or not a dish is safe for you, and that you are happy to wait while the waitperson talks to the kitchen.

Make sure to clearly define your allergy as well; some people, for example, are allergic to dairy in any form, while others are merely lactose intolerant, and can eat dairy products such as aged cheeses which have a minimal lactose content. This is especially important with peanut and nut allergies, which are sometimes poorly defined.

In a high quality restaurant, the wait staff and kitchen will accommodate your food allergies and try to ensure the best evening possible for you.

In some establishments, food allergies are actually an excellent way to meet the chef, as he or she may come over to your table to see if the food is to your liking, especially if a dish has been customized for you. Never be ashamed to talk about your food allergies to staff in a dining establishment, because it is always better to be safe than sorry.

WHY DO WE TIP FOR SOME PROFESSIONS BUT NOT OTHERS?

In most countries, the practice of tipping remains more of a custom than a mandate. In fact, there are entire organizations dedicated to the complete eradication of tipping, which they say compels the public to compensate for the low wages paid by greedy or stingy employers. Nevertheless, tipping has become a very common practice when dealing with those in the service or hospitality trade. But why are we expected to tip certain professionals, such as waiters or valet parking attendants, but not others, such as desk clerks and chefs? There are a number of things to consider when it comes to the seemingly arbitrary practice of tipping.

One reason we tip certain service employees such as waiters or bellhops is to help compensate for a gap in wages. Employers are legally permitted to pay less than minimum wage to certain employees who routinely benefit from tipping. This means a waiter may only receive a few dollars an hour as a regular salary from the restaurant, so the difference must be made up in tips. A waiter may also be responsible for tipping other employees such as bussers and bartenders. Without regular tips, waiters and barmaids may not even earn the legal minimum wage.

However, other employees of the same restaurant are rarely tipped. Cooks, hosts and dishwashers are generally paid at least the minimum hourly wage for their services. Their job responsibilities are the same regardless of the volume of business.

Tipping a cook or dishwasher may seem counter-intuitive to most diners, since there is little personal interaction and those kitchen personnel appear to be properly compensated already. Waiters and waitresses may have to compete for part-time hours, while cooks and other kitchen staff are usually guaranteed full-time work or even overtime.

Tipping is also more likely to occur whenever the employee performs above and beyond the call of duty. A hotel desk clerk is only performing his or her duty during the check-in process, but a bellhop may carry several large suitcases directly to a customer's room and offer to fill the ice bucket or demonstrate the room's amenities. Many people equate the practice of tipping with rewarding good service. By tipping the bellhop or concierge well, the customer may receive even better treatment on a return visit.

Sometimes the decision between tipping and not tipping is a matter of perception. Some customers of a family-owned restaurant, for example, may not tip the owner of the establishment if he or she waits on their table, but will tip a hired waiter. The idea is that the owner of the restaurant is already well compensated through total sales, but the hired waiter still depends on tipping to earn a decent living wage. The owner of a hair salon may earn a decent salary through product sales and specialized services, but individual stylists who rent booths may rely more on tipping to earn a living wage.

Some experts speculate that tipping is also a form of social equalization, a means to share the wealth with a hardworking but underpaid service worker. The practice of tipping used to be connected to the perceived quality of services provided, but in modern times tipping has become almost ritualistic. Regardless of the actual quality of the service, many customers realize that service and hospitality workers do work extremely hard for relatively low wages. One reason we tip certain professions and not others is because of this perception. It simply makes us feel better knowing we can reward others for their service and attention.

10

How to Be a Great Host or Hostess in a Restaurant

The person who greets guests is a Host or Hostess. They welcome and escort our guests to their table. They set the mood for the restaurant.

Steps

1. Keep track of each station. Make a chart of each server's station, and what tables are in it (also learn the table layout by heart). Keep note of how many people are in a party and what table they are at. Also keep note of who is still there so that servers do not become overwhelmed.
2. Be aware as guests approach the restaurant. If you are busy with another guest, acknowledge the guest by saying, "I will be right with you," make eye contact, or a simple hand gesture also works.
3. Greet them with a smile and welcome them to the restaurant. Remember, you are the first chance for the restaurant to make a good impression, and set them at ease.
4. Find out how many people are dining. If there is a wait make sure to get everyone's name in right away so they do not feel ignored. Avoid giving them a specific time frame. Explain that we currently have a short wait, and

that there should be a table ready momentarily, or we are currently getting tables cleared and set. NEVER say 5-10 minutes. Guests are generally impatient, and will find somewhere else to dine.

5. After greeting the guests, look at the SIZE of the largest member of the party and assign the seating with that in mind. DON"T put them in a small booth! Also, a guest that has trouble walking should be given a seat as close to the hostess station as possible.
6. When figuring out where to seat them, rotate the stations. Distribute the tables evenly among the servers. But also keep in mind how many large parties they have or have had. Try not to seat any two parties too close together when it is not necessary.
7. When the guest sits down, place a menu for each of them by the place setting, or hand the menu to the guest. Don't just throw menus on the table and leave without saying anything.
8. Maintain supplies! If we are running low on any forms, highlighters, etc. ask the manager for the supplies you will need. (This should be done before the lunch or dinner rush.)
9. Make sure that there are complete place settings for each guest and that the table is clean. If not, get the napkins/silverware, or give the table a quick wipe down with a damp rag. If it is beyond that, seat them somewhere else and make sure the mess is dealt with.
10. Be prepared to get some things for guests, water refills, utensils, napkins, or carryout boxes. If a guest does ask for something else, inform the guest that you will let their server know.
11. Walk the floor! The only way to know the progression of tables is to see how many tables are on dessert, if they have paid their check, etc. If you need tables, let the servers know and see if they can expedite their meal. You are on the same team.

12. Help to clear and set tables when necessary. If there are customers waiting for tables, the more hands helping to make that happen, the better.

Tips

- You might want to do a quick coffee or water run if customers have a long wait and are starting to become unhappy.

Warnings

- If you're having a bad day, don't let that reflect in your service.
- Do not let grudges influence your seating. Don't give a server you hate the unwanted regulars who are a pain in the apron and don't tip, or purposely overwhelm a waitress, or leave someone else without any tables.
- Do not gossip with co-workers about other co-workers or guests. You are a neutral ambassador.
- It is your job to make sure that the restaurant runs smoothly and that all of the guests and servers are happy. How can you accomplish this? By bringing your level of professionalism up to its highest standards.
- Be aware of what is going on in the kitchen, in each of your servers' stations, and at the bar. As the shift progresses be aware how your actions impact the servers, bar and kitchen.
- When your guests leave, thank them sincerely, and genuinely tell them that you would like to see them return.

RESTAURANT DATA: HOW TO BE A SUCCESSFUL WAITER

The waiter (and waitress as well, but for convenience we are lumping everyone into one term) are the face of any food and beverage establishment. These men and women are on the front line any restaurant and the services they offer. One could argue that the services of a waiter are even more important (or at least as important) as the food that is served. As such, it the success of any food and beverage establishment is dependent on the quality services that its waiters provide.

Because waiters are an integral facet of the business operation of a food and beverage establishment, there duties in regards to guest service should be thoroughly detailed in a restaurant SOP (service operating policy). The restaurant SOP should cover the following points and much more.

A Successful Waiter Will...

- Be confident and friendly. Smile at guests and engage in useful conversation. Avoid personal talk, as guests are there to enjoy themselves and not help you through personal problems.
- Be accurate. Make sure you repeat everyone's order back to them to ensure that you have it right. Nothing frustrates a guest more than to have their order messed up and the delays that result.
- Ensure guest satisfaction. After you deliver food to guests, take a few moments before leaving to make sure that everything is to the guest's satisfaction. If drinks need to be refilled this is a good opportunity to do so. Also, check back in periodically to make sure that the guests have everything that they need.
- Not hover. While you want to make yourself available if the guest requires your services, once you have checked on them and they have everything they need, allow them to enjoy their meal.
- Keep an eye on guests. In connection with the last point, while you don't want to hover over guests, you do want to be within eye contact so that if they signal you or otherwise want to get your attention, you will be able to respond quickly.

- Rush guests. Do not give the impression that you are rushing guests by asking if they are ready of their check or asking if they are finished eating. Instead, allow guests to signal when they are done and ready to pay for their meal.
- In addition to following the above duties, waiters should have a few common characteristics that allow for consistent success:

Attributes of a Good Waiter

- A good waiter is tactful.
- A good waiter is responsible.
- A good waiter possesses round knowledge of an establishment's services and products.
- A good waiter pays attention to details.
- A good waiter is well dressed.

This is only a small sample of what the attributes and traits that comprise a good waiter or waitress that should be found in a restaurant SOP. For a restaurant manager, having personnel with these skills and characteristics is paramount for success. Much of this can be instilled with proper training. In addition to a restaurant SOP, every establishment should have a restaurant training guide that outlines procedures that allows food and beverage management to impart needed skills to personnel.

TEAMWORK SERVICE: AN IDEA WHOSE TIME HAS COME

Everyone complains about service in restaurants (including this column), but few seem to do much about it in specific terms. We urge more people to sound off or write in when they are especially well treated at a restaurant, so that we can emphasize positive aspects in the midst of what many see as a deplorable decline of courtesy in restaurants, hotels, and all types of businesses.

Two outstanding service systems on opposite sides of the country are worth bringing to public attention. One is in Santa Barbara, Calif., in a restaurant heavily frequented by members of the White House press corps whenever they are covering President Reagan at his nearby ranch. The other is in North Miami, Fla. Both examples show better service can be achieved when there is an innovative spirit from the top down and a willingness to carry through to help the customer.

Steven Ross Sponder was a budding 23-year-old entrepreneur when he opened The Palace Cafe at Santa Barbara's central Old Town district in 1985. Emphasizing Cajun-Creole cuisine, the upscale 48-seat place served only dinner from the first, with an average $25-per-person ticket. What's interesting is that Sponder launched a "teamwork service' system whereby a waiter or waitress would take the initial order and inform the customer that "any of our 12 waiters or waitresses can help you with whatever you want.'

Initially, Sponder recalls, his dining room staff viewed the system as a threat. "Waiters and waitresses were very protective of their own stations,' he says. But they gradually became believers—especially when their job satisfaction was enhanced in direct proportion to the appreciation of customers, who gave much higher tips than they had done before.

Now the system has been refined so that patrons, arriving for dinner, find pamphlets with this greeting on the tables: "Our staff works as a team in order to better serve you. You need not look for the person who initially took your order for additional service, just ask anyone! This system of service is designed to help you enjoy your time here by making everyone on our staff available to take care of your table.' Sponder is ecstatic about the morale-building results: virtually zero turnover in contrast to the shuttle service method of constant turnover that one sees at too many restaurants.

Top-and bottom-line results aren't bad either— an estimated $970,000 annual sales on just 48 seats and one meal period.

Kenneth Boxer, a chief waiter there, says he and the entire staff "vehemently take exception to always reading and hearing how the quality of service in America is slipping. At our restaurant gone are the days of ego-inflated waiters bringing you cold food from the food line when it should have arrived minutes earlier by someone else.'

The biggest challenge was training waiters who by habit wanted to stick to their individual territories or stations. But the problem was overcome by requiring dining room servers to pass an intense practical examination. "We're all a lot happier now,' says Boxer, "because the teamwork concept has turned out to be a far more efficient style, making jobs easier with better service and higher gratuities.'

It has become something of a crusade for Sponder and his dining room staff. W. R. Grace's Hola Amigos Mexican restaurant, also in Santa Barbara, recently invited the waiters and waitresses to visit and give a live demonstration of the system, which Hola now plans to adopt. The idea of teamwork service is not new. What's notable in this case is the way the dining room staff implements the teamwork so beautifully under Sponder's guiding hand.

A different twist on the teamwork idea may be seen at La Paloma in North Miami, Fla. Werner and Maria Staub, the European owners of this Swiss-Continental restaurant, have devised a system whereby the waiter or waitress takes the orders and gives them to the kitchen staff. But then speed "runners' bring the food to the tables, while waiters and waitresses answer customer questions. The result is far speedier and efficient service.

The waiters and waitresses in effect are public-relations people, or individual maitre d's. This requires a heavier investment but is more than worth it in customer satisfaction. Neither The Palace Cafe nor La Paloma is unique in its approach.

But their ability to implement true teamwork and harmony is a pleasant contrast with a number of other ego-driven restaurants where teamwork— and service—are almost nonexistent. A team pulling together can and will outperform individual stars each working only for his or her own gratification—especially when the owners show the employees that everyone plays on the same team and can win together.

RESTAURANT HOST OR HOSTESS

Restaurant hosts and hostesses serve as personal representatives of the restaurant for which they work. They are in charge of making reservations and greeting guests when they arrive at the restaurant.

They also seat the guests and make sure that they enjoy their meal. Hosts and hostesses try to give guests a good impression of the restaurant by greeting them in a warm, friendly manner. If guests have to wait to be seated, hosts and hostesses make them comfortable while they wait.

The guests are given an idea of how long they will have to wait and are seated in a waiting area. Sometimes hosts and hostesses suggest that the diners wait at the bar and have a drink. Hosts and hostesses locate a table that is the right size for the guests, take the guests to the table, and give them menus. They may also assist guests in seating small children, or fill their water glasses.

While greeting incoming guests, hosts and hostesses must take care of guests who are leaving. Some hosts and hostesses receive the money for the guests' food and make change. To do this they must know how to operate a cash register. Restaurants sometimes have a candy or cigarette counter. If guests want to buy these items, hosts and hostesses add their cost to the guests' checks. In some restaurants this work is done by a cashier.

At the end of their work shifts, hosts and hostesses record the transactions that have taken place and total all guest checks to determine how much money has been received. These records are used to balance the accounts at the end of the day. The records are then turned in to the restaurant manager for inspection. The host and hostess stand near the restaurant entrance so they can greet guests as they arrive and then seat them at tables.

Education and Training Requirements

Individuals interested in becoming a host or hostess should take courses in business, arithmetic, bookkeeping, family and consumer science, and public speaking. Hosts and hostesses should be friendly and outgoing people who can remain calm and courteous during rush periods.

They also must be neat and well groomed. Most restaurants prefer to hire people who have a high school education. Some vocational schools have programs in food service that can help prepare students for this kind of work; however, most restaurant hosts and hostesses are trained on the job.

Getting the Job

Prospective hosts and hostesses should apply directly to restaurants in which they would like to work. Newspaper want ads sometimes have listings for these positions, as do state employment offices. Previous restaurant experience is helpful in landing a hosting job.

Advancement Possibilities and Employment Outlook

Hosts and hostesses advance by transferring to more expensive restaurants that pay higher salaries. Experienced and responsible restaurant hosts and hostesses may become restaurant managers.

One big trend in the twenty-first century was an increase in the number of Americans dining out. With the restaurant business growing, the job outlook for hosts and hostesses is good, with positions expected to grow about as fast as the average through the year 2014.

Working Conditions

Because restaurants serve the public, they are usually attractive places in which to work. Expensive restaurants often provide elegant work surroundings. Hosts and hostesses are usually stationed near the restaurant entrance and are on their feet throughout their shifts. They must maintain a neat appearance and always be courteous to guests. Full-time hosts and hostesses work forty hours a week and may rotate shifts, but there are many part-time workers in this field as well. Hosts and hostesses must work their share of weekends, evenings, and holidays. Many of these workers belong to labour unions.

Earnings and Benefits

Earnings depend on the restaurant, with expensive restaurants generally paying higher salaries. According to the U.S. Bureau of Labour Statistics, hosts and hostesses earned a median wage of $7.52 per hour in 2004.

Their wages tend to be higher than that of waitpersons because they usually do not receive tips. (In some restaurants, however, they are included in a tip pool that gives them a small share of the day's tips.) Restaurants often offer full-time employees paid holidays and vacations, health insurance, and retirement plans. Most hosts and hostesses receive free meals when they are at work.

RESTAURANT SERVICE & WAITER TRAINING TIPS

Restaurant Service Consulting, by definition, is a review or evaluation of the restaurant dining room service system. This means, "how the dining room runs" which includes all of the service tools provided (or to be provided) by the management.

These tools include readable floor diagrams, seating coordination, menu descriptions, properly done staff schedules, sidework postings and a whole host of other things.

There are two main aspects to the Restaurant Service Consulting field:

1) On-site Restaurant Dining Service Operations Evaluation and Review
2) Waiter Training

After the dining room service system is organized properly, the waitstaff is now ready to be trained. The big mistake is to train the waitstaff without having understandable and coordinated systems in place.

If there are flaws in the service system, then even the most highly trained and experienced waitstaff will make errors translating into unnecessary headaches and lost revenue. It is plain common sense to train a staff according to that particular restaurant's procedures otherwise the balance and consistency of customer service will be thrown off.

At times, in my restaurant consulting experiences, I find that owners/operators can be very hesitant to let an outsider do the initial restaurant evaluation prior to waiter training for a score of reasons such as fear of embarrassment, dealing with egos being stepped on during the process, not wanting anyone to be very close to operations etc.

In truth, a restaurant and its dining room service cannot progress over time without experienced, objective, constructive criticism — whether it comes from the outside or within.

Restaurant service system flaws can continue on for years without being corrected costing time, money, and headaches. And just the same, waiter service technique flaws can go on for years as well.

Sometimes, it's not necessarily deep rooted flaws, but just a better, faster, more organized and streamlined way of going about procedures — no matter how small the solutions may seem to be. Time is money when it comes to the repetitive nature of dining room service and there are no two ways about it. To improve restaurant performance, you need to know what areas are in need of improvement. The Restaurant Manager should ask for feedback from experienced staff and repeat customers as well.

Once you know what you are doing right and what needs work, you can develop systems and documentation to improve your establishment. Many times, it's simply a matter of confusion as the "left hand" doesn't seem to know what the "right hand" is doing (or why). You'll find that clear communication between all staff members and management goes a long way in helping you achieve your restaurant performance goals.

11

Use of Napkins

Today, discriminating hosts and hostesses have a wide variety of napkin products from which to select. For formal dining, there is the cloth napkin, the paper napkin being reserved for more informal settings.

Cloth napkins come in several sizes, each size tailored to a specific use. A beverage napkin, used when serving drinks and hors d'oeuvres, like most cloth napkins, is square, about five inches to each side. A luncheon napkin is a couple of inches larger, and a dinner napkin larger still. The theory, evidently, is that the more food and drink that is served, the more potential there is for spillage, so the bigger the napkin must be to catch it.

Cloth napkins may be purchased in a rainbow of colours and a variety of fabrics, imprinted with custom designs and monograms, and can even come with matching tablecloths. However, a high-thread-count, white, linen or linen-cotton mix damask napkin is still considered the zenith of elegance.

Though a wedding reception should be considered a formal occasion, only the very wealthy can afford to have a catered meal for scores of guests, one that is served on fine place settings where cloth napkins have been set out. An acceptable cost-cutting compromise for big celebrations including weddings is to use a paper napkin whose size, heft, and finish resemble a cloth napkin. They can be ordered embossed with the bride and groom's monograms or otherwise tailored to the buyer's specifications.

NAPKIN ETIQUETTE

Whether the napkin is cloth or paper, when in polite company, a napkin is to be used with a measure of etiquette, so as not to offend other diners through a display of boorishness. (You're excused from these rules only when the napkin you are offered is one of those flimsy little paper things that pop out of tabletop dispensers – the kind of "napkin" you cannot place on your lap expecting it to not blow away within 20 seconds; even here, however, try to keep boorish behaviour in check.)

Rule 1: When you're given a napkin, use it. Don't let it sit beside your plate. It was given to you for wiping your face when you need to and to protect your lap from spills. Leaving it beside your plate marks you as a slob.

Rule 2: Wait for the host to pick up and unfold his napkin before you do the same with yours.

Rule 3: If the napkin is larger than your lap, fold it such that it just covers your lap.

Rule 4: In polite society, movements at the dinner table tend to be small, so don't make any ostentatious displays like wildly shaking the napkin to open it. Just unfold it. And when you wipe your mouth, don't use the napkin as you would a wash cloth during your morning shower; gently dab at your mouth.

Rule 5: Don't wait for the food to be served before you open your napkin. Should your napkin still be sitting on the table when the food arrives, the server may have to create space to set your plate.

Rule 6: Should you have to leave the table during the meal, leave the napkin, loosely folded, on your seat or on the table to the left of your plate. Also put the loosely folded napkin to the left of your plate when you're done eating, never on the plate.

Rule 7: The place for a napkin? In your lap. It is not tucked into your pants, nor does it belong tucked into your shirt collar. However, if you are in a milieu where that kind of behaviour is acceptable, don't be afraid to go along. For example, diners from Southern Italy (or southern New Jersey) have long known that a bowl of spaghetti topped with marinara sauce can be better enjoyed when you don't have to worry about the red stuff splattering on your shirt. Many Italian and Italian-American diners therefore tuck the napkin into their collars as a matter of course. Feel free to do the same. Live! Enjoy!

But what about that waiter who carries a napkin draped over one arm? In part, it's practicality. It's readily available to mop up any accidental spills or other messes at your table. But the practice dates back a couple of hundred years in France; that was how waiters carried the napkins they would distribute to diners. Napkins have been in use for thousands of years.

It's possible that cavemen at their wooly mammoth barbeques wiped the grease from their mouths using the animal's pelt... and then rubbed it in their hair to get that suave, slicked-back look. But we don't really know that. What we do know is that, by the Bronze Age, it's likely something like a napkin was in use in many parts of the world. The first recorded use of the napkin was by the Romans. When that hearty eater, Buffetus Allucaneatus, reached for his napkin at the Roman dinner table, he didn't find a cloth. What he used was some wadded up unbaked dough, which he pressed to his face. That removed whatever bits and morsels of food were sticking to it. Later, if he wished, he could bake and eat his napkin, morsels and all.

With the fall of Rome, Europe entered that slovenly, napkin-less period of the Dark Ages, with its uncouth barons and unwashed princesses wiping their hands on their tunics and mopping their faces with their shirttails and cuffs. We don't know how knights encased in steel armor managed to wipe off their mouths.

By the time of the Renaissance, the French had a single, large communal napkin about the size of a table cloth which everyone at the table used. It may have been the precursor of the table cloth. It got smaller and smaller over the years until everyone had his own napkin. By the 1700's, the French aristocracy had even promulgated rules of napkin etiquette, some of which we still use today throughout the Western world; e.g., we don't blow our nose into our napkin. Or anyone else's napkin, either.

RESTAURANT SERVICE PROCEDURE: SO SIMILAR TO NAVAL SHIP SERVICE PROCEDURE

This concept occurred to me after a restaurant service consulting session with the owner of a catering operation. His restaurant was in perfect order, incredibly neat and clean, better than I have seen in quite awhile.

In conversation, when I learned he was in the Navy for 4 years, it dawned on me that restaurant service procedure is very similar to naval ship service procedure — without the danger elements that exist on a ship, of course.

For example, on a ship, there are tight, crammed spaces that crew members have to quickly and orderly work through (same as in a restaurant). It is very important that the crew keeps the ship safe and sanitary (same as in a restaurant). Being on the frontline, the crew must have the ability to respectfully give orders and take orders (same as in a restaurant).

In a restaurant, the waiter takes beverage and food orders from the customers, and sends these orders to the bar and kitchen. The waiter may also give orders to the busboys, runners, and even the host to help coordinate dining room service. (And vice versa). At times, the waiter may have to receive orders or instructions from other staff and management.

In this case, the waiter must be listening attentively because it may be concerning the customer's needs.

The crew on a naval ship must be in excellent physical condition (as waiters must be) to perform the heavy duties necessary to keep the ship afloat — somewhat similar to the heavy duties required for keeping a restaurant afloat. More importantly, there is a mindset that all tasks are performed while keeping the ship and crew members in mind as a unit. In other words, "playing as a team." or "service for the good of the ship" (same as in a restaurant).

Even the phrases used by a ship's crew while moving amongst the tight spaces and each other are the exact same as the phrases used in a restaurant such as: "coming thru", "behind you," "make a path." Use of these phrases will prevent accidents.

There is also the story that it's bad luck to whistle on a ship which is the same as in a restaurant kitchen. On a ship, the human whistle can get confused with the ship's whistle which sounds out important messages to the crew at different times of the day.

The more you think about the similarities between restaurant service procedure and naval ship service procedure, the more concepts you can discover!

12

Roles of Workers

FAST FOOD FRANCHISE WORKER

Definition and Nature of the Work

Fast food franchise workers are employed by fast food restaurants throughout the country. The most popular restaurants of this type specialize in hamburgers, fried chicken, fried fish, roast beef sandwiches, and other easily prepared food items. Fast food franchise workers prepare and serve food, keep the restaurant clean, and make sure that the customers are satisfied with their service.

In many fast food restaurants the food is prepared in an assembly-line fashion. Workers in some franchises are trained to do all of the jobs in the restaurant; in others each worker learns a specific task.

In a typical fast food chain, a counter worker takes the orders and gives them to the cook, who prepares the food and places the order on a plate or packages it in a box or paper wrapper. The counter worker then completes the order with beverages and processes payment. Some fast food restaurants have one counter worker who works as the cashier and takes all of the orders and another who fills them. A counter worker may also prepare sundaes and other ice cream dishes, cook french fries, and toast buns.

Dining room attendants are in charge of clearing and wiping the tables, filling the salt and pepper shakers, stocking packets of ketchup, mustard, and other garnishes, and making sure the napkin and straw dispensers are filled. They also sweep and mop the floors. Sometimes counter workers assist the dining room attendants by cleaning kitchen equipment, sweeping, mopping up spills, and carrying out trash. All fast food franchise workers are supervised by a manager or an assistant manager.

Sometimes the owner of the franchise acts as the manager. Managers hire Fast food franchise counter workers take customers' orders, receive payment, and make change. They deliver the order to the cooks, who prepare the food in an assembly-line fashion and fire workers as necessary, oversee the running of the franchise, and make sure the customers are satisfied. The majority of fast food franchise workers are students who work part time. Managers must set up schedules that cover all work shifts.

Education and Training Requirements

There are no formal educational requirements for fast food franchise workers. Most skills are learned on the job. Counter workers, however, should speak proper English and be able to do simple arithmetic. Most counter workers use a cash register or a computerized system for taking orders, totalling the check, and making change. Fast food franchises provide training in the use of these machines. It is helpful but not necessary for cooks to have some cooking experience. Dining room attendants need no special training.

Most fast food franchises have their own training programs in which they teach workers what to say when customers reach the counter and exactly how each food-related task should be done. This is the company's way of making sure that customers get fast, courteous service. In these training programs, cooks gain experience preparing the foods served by the franchise, counter workers practice greeting customers, using the cash register, and making change, and dining room attendants learn how to work efficiently. Training programs may last from two days to two weeks. Counter workers must be able to get along with people and have a pleasant personality and a neat appearance. All positions require good health and physical stamina. State laws often require health certificates stating that workers are free from communicable diseases.

Getting the Job

Interested individuals should apply directly to fast food franchises in their area. Job listings often appear in newspaper want ads or on the windows or signs of franchises that are hiring. New restaurant openings are another source of job leads. The turnover rate for employees in the fast food business is very high, so potential workers are likely to find job openings.

Advancement Possibilities and Employment Outlook

Workers who show enough ability and enthusiasm can become assistant managers or managers. Some workers advance by taking other jobs in the food service industry. Jobs for fast food franchise employees are expected to grow as fast as the average through the year 2014 because the lifestyle of many Americans is increasingly fast paced and because healthier items are being added to the menus of many fast food restaurants.

Working Conditions

Fast food franchise employees must work quickly and efficiently. They rarely get a chance to rest, and they are always on their feet. The work can be monotonous. Job hazards include falls, cuts, and burns, although injuries are seldom serious. Fast food franchise workers typically have to work their share of weekends, evenings, and holidays. Students must arrange work schedules that allow them to attend classes. Most counter workers and dining room attendants work fewer than thirty hours per week. Cooks may work as many as forty-eight hours per week, although part-time work is available. Workers generally wear uniforms. Most employers provide uniforms or a uniform allowance, but some workers may have to purchase their own uniforms.

Earnings and Benefits

Earnings vary depending on the location of the franchise

and the experience of the worker. According to the 2004 Occupational Employment Statistics survey, fast food franchise workers earn a median salary of $7.06 per hour. A few workers also receive tips. Many receive free meals during work hours. Full-time workers generally receive paid vacation time and other benefits.

GAMING CAGE WORKER

Definition and Nature of the Work

Gaming cage workers or cage cashiers count the money at casinos and other gaming establishments. They work in a secure place, known as the cage, which is the central depository for money, gaming chips, and casino paperwork. Cage workers exchange real currency for playing chips used in dice, card, and roulette games. They also buy these tokens back from patrons for cash, verify credit references for patrons who want to open a credit account at the casino, and cash checks.

Because the gaming industry is highly regulated, the cage cashiers must keep precise records. Transactions involving large sums of money must be reported to the Internal Revenue Service for tax purposes. Gaming cage workers use computers to calculate and keep track of all transactions. They must balance their money drawers at the end of each shift.

Education and Training Requirements

There are no formal educational requirements for the job, although most employers require a high school diploma or the equivalent. Casinos usually provide on-the-job training to acquaint cage workers with the establishment's procedures. They also may offer classroom training in rules and regulations. Employers expect applicants to speak clear and proper English and to have excellent math skills. Some employers administer a math test to job applicants. Experience in handling money or other employment in gaming establishments is helpful in getting a job as a gaming cage worker.

Gaming cage workers must be well organized, detail oriented, discreet, and trustworthy. They often handle confidential material. Good customer service skills are essential. Gaming cage workers, like all casino employees, must have a license issued by a regulatory agency such as a state gaming control board or commission. To get this license applicants must show photo identification, provide proof of residency in the state in which they plan to work, and pay a fee. The fee may vary by geographical area. Age requirements for the job may vary by state as well. All gaming job applicants should expect a background check.

Getting the Job

People interested in casino work should contact the personnel offices of casinos directly for information on openings and entry-level requirements. Working part time or as a seasonal employee during major tourist seasons is a good way to move into full-time employment.

Advancement Possibilities and Employment Outlook

Gaming cage cashiers can advance to supervisory roles by maintaining spotless work records and by demonstrating professionalism and good customer relations skills. Additional education and training may be required for advancement.

The job outlook for gaming cage workers is only moderate through the year 2014, partly because of technology. All gaming establishments are finding ways to reduce the amount of cash handled by employees. Cash-out machines, change machines, and automated teller machines (ATMs) are common. Some slot machines make payouts in tickets instead of coins. The tickets can be read by other slot machines and the amount on the ticket transferred to a new machine. By reducing the amount of cash needed to play, fewer workers are needed in the cage. Gambling is legal in eleven states and the number of gaming establishments is growing. The largest growth will probably be in Native American-owned casinos and in racetracks that offer casino games. A fair number of openings for gaming cage workers should result from the continuous turnover in this occupation, which is usually due to the high level of scrutiny these employees receive.

Working Conditions

Most gaming cage cashiers work eight-hour shifts five days per week. Because casinos are typically open twenty-four hours a day, shifts are usually staggered, and cage workers are expected to work some nights, weekends, and holidays.

Cage workers are on their feet throughout their shifts but are usually given two short breaks and a mealtime break. They must work quickly and be able to concentrate for long periods in a noisy and hectic environment.

Stress is particularly high for gaming cage workers because they are always being observed by supervisory and surveillance personnel. Cage workers must be tactful when dealing with unruly and frustrated patrons. In establishments that are not smoke free, they must also deal with exposure to cigarette, cigar, and pipe smoke. They are sometimes expected to lift and carry heavy bags of money.

Earnings and Benefits

Wages for gaming cage workers vary according to their level of experience, training, location, and the size of the gaming establishment that employs them. According to the U.S. Bureau of Labour Statistics, the median hourly salary of gaming cage workers was $10.74 in May of 2004.

GAMING DEALER

Definition and Nature of the Work

The most high-profile workers in casinos and other gaming establishments are the dealers, or croupiers, who run the games of chance.

Dealers explain and enforce the rules and wagering guidelines for games, ask patrons to place their bets, conduct the games, make payoffs to the winners, and collect losing bets. Some games, such as dice, craps, baccarat, and roulette, require more than one dealer to run. Dealers are frequently moved from one gaming table to another during a shift and often switch between two or more games per day.

Education and Training Requirements

There are no formal education requirements for dealers, although employers do prefer to hire people with high school diplomas or the equivalent. They expect dealers to speak clear and correct English and to have strong mathematical skills. Some employers administer a math test to job applicants.

Gaming dealers are required to have a certificate or appropriate training from a dealer school. Some technical schools offer classes to train workers in specific games and skills. Other schools offer a Professional Casino Croupier certificate to students who have learned to run all of the games. Some colleges offer programs that include formal training for the casino industry. Casinos may provide dealer training, especially for employees who wish to change jobs.

Dealers, like all casino employees, must have a license issued by a regulatory agency such as a state gaming control board or commission. To get this license applicants must show photo identification, provide proof of residency in the state in which they plan to work, and pay a fee.

The fee varies by geographical area. Age requirements for the job may vary by state as well. All gaming job applicants should expect a thorough background check.

Getting the Job

Individuals interested in working as dealers should contact the personnel offices of casinos directly for information on openings and entry-level requirements. Working part time or as a seasonal employee during major tourist seasons is a good way to move into full-time employment.

Advancement Possibilities and Employment Outlook

Dealers can advance by maintaining clean work records and by demonstrating professionalism and good customer relations skills. Dealers may be promoted to a higher wage table or to a more desirable work shift. With additional education and training, they may become supervisors.

The employment outlook for casino dealers is good, with jobs expected to grow faster than the average through the year 2014. As more states are legalizing casino gambling, more casinos are being planned and built, which will increase the number of dealer jobs. The largest future growth will probably be in Native American-owned casinos and in racinos, which are racetracks that offer some casino games. Part-time and seasonal positions will be most readily available.

Gaming dealers must work quickly and remain alert for long periods of time.

Working Conditions

Casino dealers usually work eight-hour shifts five days per week. Because most casinos are open twenty-four hours a day, shifts are usually staggered, and dealers are expected to work some nights, weekends, and holidays. Dealers are on their feet throughout their shifts but are usually given two short breaks and a mealtime break.

Casino dealing is a high-pressure job. Dealers must work quickly in a noisy, hectic environment; knowing that they are being observed by supervisory and surveillance personnel adds to their stress level. Dealers must be tactful when dealing with unruly and frustrated patrons and those who do not know when to stop gambling. They may be exposed to cigarette, cigar, and pipe smoke.

Earnings and Benefits

Casinos pay dealers a base salary that usually begins at minimum wage. According to the U.S. Bureau of Labour Statistics, the median wage for dealers in 2004 was $14,340 per year; however, dealers earn a substantial portion of their income from tips. Gaming dealers generally prefer weekend, evening, and holiday shifts because those are the busiest times and often bring in the most tips. In some casinos dealers keep the tips they get; in others the tips are shared by all dealers. Casinos usually provide full-time workers with benefits that include health insurance, retirement plans, vacation time, paid sick days, and extra pay for working on holidays.

ROLE OF DINING ROOM ATTENDANT

Definition and Nature of the Work

Dining room attendants, formerly called busboys or bussers, work in restaurants, cafeterias, and hotel dining rooms. Attendants clear tables and unload their trays in the kitchen, separating the dishes, silverware, and linen. Then they reset the tables, laying tablecloths, arranging the silverware perfectly, lighting candles if appropriate, and filling flower vases. Dining room attendants may have to arrange tables and chairs to make room for large groups. They are responsible for seeing that the dining room is well stocked with utensils, napkins, glasses, tablecloths, table decorations, and foods such as butter and crackers or bread.

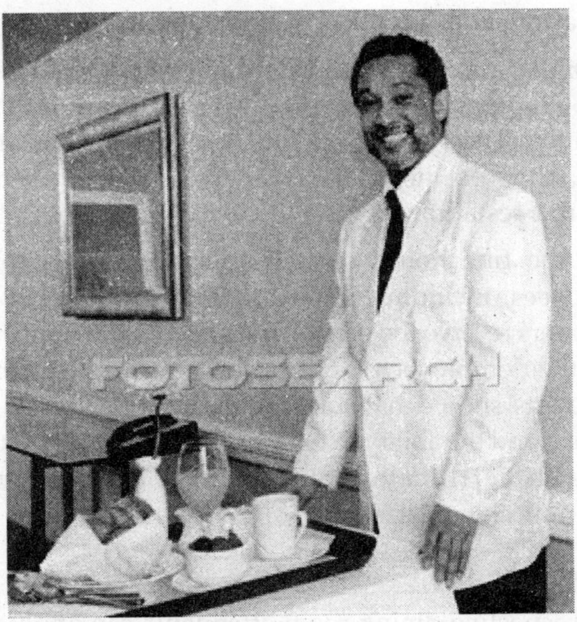

Dining room attendants may also be expected to dust woodwork, wash mirrors, vacuum carpets, clean and wax floors, and help to clean up spills. They are usually assigned to a station, which consists of several tables, but may help other attendants whose stations get very busy.

In addition to these duties, attendants act as assistants to waitresses and waiters. They get high chairs for children, help serve food, carry heavy trays, and fill water glasses. They clear dishes from tables between courses.

Dining room attendants also act as messengers between the dining room staff and the kitchen staff. Dining room attendants are usually supervised by other restaurant workers. Sometimes the supervisor is the waiter who works at the station with the dining room attendant. More often the supervisor is the headwaiter who manages the dining room. Sometimes the restaurant host instructs the dining room attendants.

Education and Training Requirements

Dining room attendants are not required to have a high school diploma. They typically receive on-the-job training, learning all about the operation of the kitchen and dining room. Their positions are considered starting points for other jobs in a restaurant, hotel, or cafeteria business.

Some fine hotels offer training programs for all their employees, including dining room attendants, so that their customers receive the very best service. Many chain restaurants send their employees to a short training session. Dining room attendants should have a neat, clean appearance, a pleasant manner, and the ability to follow directions. Many states require a health certificate stating that the attendant has no communicable diseases.

Getting the Job

Prospective dining room attendants can apply directly to hotels, restaurants, or cafeterias and answer want ads in the newspaper. The opening of new restaurants provides more opportunities for work. Individuals interested in working during the summer months only should apply to resorts well in advance of the tourist season.

Advancement Possibilities and Employment Outlook

Dining room attendants may be promoted to other positions. They may become waiters or waitresses. If they are interested in preparing food, they may become kitchen helpers. Because of the expansion of the restaurant business, a good worker will have many opportunities for job advancement. Positions for dining room attendants are expected to grow about as fast as the average through 2014. There is one trend to note, however: although the number of restaurants is growing, waiters and waitresses are increasingly assuming the duties of dining room attendants.

Working Conditions

Dining room attendants work at a fast pace and often under pressure. They have to perform a variety of tasks quickly and efficiently. Their surroundings are usually pleasant, well lighted, clean, and comfortable. However, the area where they unload dirty dishes may be hot and noisy. Dining room attendants should have plenty of energy and strength to lift heavy trays and move furniture. In order not to disturb customers, they must work very quietly. Candidates must be good multi-taskers, meaning they are capable of doing many things at once. They have an opportunity to meet many interesting people, both fellow workers and customers. Full-time attendants may work forty to forty-eight hours per week. Some work on a part-time basis. Many dining room attendants belong to labour unions.

Earnings and Benefits

According to the U.S. Bureau of Labour Statistics, dining room attendants earned a median hourly wage of $7.17 in 2004. New dining room attendants often begin at the minimum wage. Those who assist waiters or waitresses usually receive overtime pay. In some restaurants they may also receive a share of the wait staff's tips. Dining room attendants generally receive free meals while they work. Full-time workers may receive paid vacations and holidays, health and accident insurance, and retirement benefits.

ROLE OF DOORKEEPER

Definition and Nature of the Work

Doorkeepers are stationed at the entrances of most large city hotels, restaurants, and luxury apartment buildings, as well as country resorts. These uniformed greeters create a welcoming atmosphere for guests or tenants arriving at their doors. Doorkeepers must be diplomatic, courteous, and helpful to all guests.

Their responsibilities include opening the doors of cars and taxicabs for guests who arrive at their establishment, helping the guests out of cars, shielding them from rain or snow with an umbrella, and opening the door of the building so that the guests can step inside. In exchange for these services, guests frequently tip doorkeepers.

Doorkeepers also hail taxicabs for guests and tenants, carry packages, and watch for unauthorized people who might try to enter the building. They report suspicious people to the building manager or the police. In addition, doorkeepers direct delivery workers to the delivery entrance of the establishment. Those who work in apartment buildings may notify tenants that visitors have arrived by calling the tenants on the telephone.

Education and Training Requirements

A high school diploma is not necessary for this position, but a good command of the English language is necessary to make the best impression on guests and tenants. Doorkeepers are usually trained on the job by experienced doorkeepers. They can start as bellhops in hotels or as kitchen helpers in restaurants. Doorkeepers must have a neat personal appearance and a pleasant and agreeable manner. They should also be polite, helpful, and responsible.

Doorkeepers assist hotel guests and apartment building residents who are in transit. They hail taxi cabs, carry packages, and open building and taxi cab doors for people.

Getting the Job

Interested individuals can apply directly to hotels, restaurants, and apartment buildings for a job as a doorkeeper. The want ads in local newspapers are also a good source for job listings. Candidates who are unable to find work as a doorkeeper can apply for a job as a bellhop or a kitchen helper and advance from that position.

Advancement Possibilities and Employment Outlook

There are very few advancement possibilities for doorkeepers; however, an experienced doorkeeper may be promoted to supervisor of all lobby employees, including bellhops, floor cleaners, and window washers. The employment outlook for doorkeepers is fair. Although openings develop quickly for many hotel and restaurant employees, most hotels and restaurants employ only a few doorkeepers. Turnover is low, so few job openings occur. Additional doorkeeper jobs will likely come from the development of new hotels.

Working Conditions

Doorkeepers typically work a five-day, forty-hour week. They sometimes work evenings or weekends and often work in shifts so that the door to an establishment is covered at all times. Most doorkeepers wear uniforms. Some doorkeepers are provided with uniforms or a uniform allowance. Others must purchase their own.

Since hotel and restaurant doorkeepers are stationed outside, they must endure all kinds of weather. All doorkeepers stand for long periods, which may be very tiring. In spite of physical discomforts, doorkeepers must remain cheerful and courteous at all times.

Earnings and Benefits

Doorkeepers generally start at minimum wage. Those who belong to unions may earn higher wages. Experienced doorkeepers earn an average salary of $17,000 to $19,000 or more per year.

Doorkeepers in New York City earn much more-according to an April 19, 2006 article in the Christian Science Monitor, about twice as much as the average. Those who work night shifts generally receive extra pay. In addition, a large portion of doorkeepers' incomes come from tips given by patrons of the hotel, restaurant, or apartment that employs them. Doorkeepers generally receive benefits such as paid vacations, sick leave, health insurance, and retirement plans.

FAST FOOD FRANCHISE WORKER

Definition and Nature of the Work

Fast food franchise workers are employed by fast food restaurants throughout the country. The most popular restaurants of this type specialize in hamburgers, fried chicken, fried fish, roast beef sandwiches, and other easily prepared food items. Fast food franchise workers prepare and serve food, keep the restaurant clean, and make sure that the customers are satisfied with their service.

In many fast food restaurants the food is prepared in an assembly-line fashion. Workers in some franchises are trained to do all of the jobs in the restaurant; in others each worker learns a specific task.

In a typical fast food chain, a counter worker takes the orders and gives them to the cook, who prepares the food and places the order on a plate or packages it in a box or paper wrapper. The counter worker then completes the order with beverages and processes payment. Some fast food restaurants have one counter worker who works as the cashier and takes all of the orders and another who fills them. A counter worker may also prepare sundaes and other ice cream dishes, cook french fries, and toast buns.

Dining room attendants are in charge of clearing and wiping the tables, filling the salt and pepper shakers, stocking packets of ketchup, mustard, and other garnishes, and making sure the napkin and straw dispensers are filled. They also sweep and mop the floors. Sometimes counter workers assist the dining room attendants by cleaning kitchen equipment, sweeping, mopping up spills, and carrying out trash. All fast food franchise workers are supervised by a manager or an assistant manager. Sometimes the owner of the franchise acts as the manager. Managers hire Fast food franchise counter workers take customers' orders, receive payment, and make change. They deliver the order to the cooks, who prepare the food in an assembly-line fashion and fire workers as necessary, oversee the running of the franchise, and make sure the customers are satisfied. The majority of fast food franchise workers are students who work part time. Managers must set up schedules that cover all work shifts.

Education and Training Requirements

There are no formal educational requirements for fast food franchise workers. Most skills are learned on the job. Counter workers, however, should speak proper English and be able to do simple arithmetic. Most counter workers use a cash register or a computerized system for taking orders, totalling the check, and making change. Fast food franchises provide training in the use of these machines. It is helpful but not necessary for cooks to have some cooking experience. Dining room attendants need no special training.

Most fast food franchises have their own training programs in which they teach workers what to say when customers reach the counter and exactly how each food-related task should be done. This is the company's way of making sure that customers get fast, courteous service. In these training programs, cooks gain experience preparing the foods served by the franchise, counter workers practice greeting customers, using the cash register, and making change, and dining room attendants learn how to work efficiently. Training programs may last from two days to two weeks. Counter workers must be able to get along with people and have a pleasant personality and a neat appearance. All positions require good health and physical stamina. State laws often require health certificates stating that workers are free from communicable diseases.

Getting the Job

Interested individuals should apply directly to fast food franchises in their area. Job listings often appear in newspaper want ads or on the windows or signs of franchises that are hiring. New restaurant openings are another source of job leads. The turnover rate for employees in the fast food business is very high, so potential workers are likely to find job openings.

Advancement Possibilities and Employment Outlook

Workers who show enough ability and enthusiasm can become assistant managers or managers. Some workers advance by taking other jobs in the food service industry.

Jobs for fast food franchise employees are expected to grow as fast as the average through the year 2014 because the lifestyle of many Americans is increasingly fast paced and because healthier items are being added to the menus of many fast food restaurants.

Working Conditions

Fast food franchise employees must work quickly and efficiently. They rarely get a chance to rest, and they are always on their feet. The work can be monotonous. Job hazards include falls, cuts, and burns, although injuries are seldom serious. Fast food franchise workers typically have to work their share of weekends, evenings, and holidays. Students must arrange work schedules that allow them to attend classes. Most counter workers and dining room attendants work fewer than thirty hours per week. Cooks may work as many as forty-eight hours per week, although part-time work is available. Workers generally wear uniforms. Most employers provide uniforms or a uniform allowance, but some workers may have to purchase their own uniforms.

Earnings and Benefits

Earnings vary depending on the location of the franchise and the experience of the worker. According to the 2004 Occupational Employment Statistics survey, fast food franchise workers earn a median salary of $7.06 per hour. A few workers also receive tips. Many receive free meals during work hours. Full-time workers generally receive paid vacation time and other benefits.

KITCHEN AND BAR ORDER TICKETS

This is an order pad which remains with the waiter and is used for the purpose of taking down guest orders and placing them at the supply point i.e. kitchens/bar. Normally there are two copies of the KOT.

The top copy goes to the kitchen while the duplicate remains in there as record. If the copies are in triplicate then the top copy goes to the supply point, 2nd copy to the cashier for billing and the 3rd remains there as control record. This system is nowadays done through the electronic cash registers. But the manual system is still very strongly in force in most systems. To ensure that efficient control is maintained all food and beverage staff should enter the records in the KOT for all orders placed.

Restaurant Sales Summary: These summaries are also known as *Restaurant Analysis Sheets, Bill Summaries or Record of Restaurant Sales.* The summaries provide sales in each category which can be totaled and analyzed. They provide for:

1. Reconciliation of items with different gross profits.
2. Sales mix information.

3. Records of popular/unpopular, fast/slow moving items.
4. Records for stock control.

Electronic point of sales (EPOS) as mentioned before performs the duties of producing Restaurant Sales Summary with fewer errors and at a faster pace. One should understand that controls are essential, yet no control system should cost more than the items being controlled. It makes sense to account each strip of steak, but it would be foolish if controls are designed to account for each green pea. Additionally, controls should not be designed that they cause inconvenience to the guest by slowing down the service.

FOOD AND BEVERAGE SERVICES

Food and beverage services are among the most visible locations at ski areas, and a ski area's environmental commitment is often judged by the environmental practices within these establishments.

Pollution prevention (P2) opportunities for restaurants address a broad range of operations, including solid waste management, grounds and facility maintenance, and restaurant supply purchasing. A restaurant's pre-tax profit is typically only 3 to 9 percent of its total revenue; therefore, money saved through reductions in operating costs (that is, through reduced energy consumption and water use) can significantly increase the profit margin. While some restaurants have already taken advantage of the many P2 opportunities available to them, a survey by the National Restaurant Association shows that for some of the most common P2 techniques and best practices, there is still room for improvement across the industry.

Numerous programs exist for the food and beverage service industry that help restaurants and their customers minimize environmental impacts. These programs have established systematic approaches to help restaurants reduce their environmental impacts. This chapter uses the Green Restaurant

Association's approach as an outline to present the environmental practices a restaurant should consider. Some relevant topics, such as managing office wastes, purchasing environmentally preferable cleaning supplies, using energy-efficient lighting, and environmentally responsible landscape management.

GREEN RESTAURANT ASSOCIATION

Involvement in environmental programs is a good way for a restaurant to learn more about environmental best practice opportunities. An environmental resource for the food service industry is the Green Restaurant Association (GRA), which helps member restaurants reduce environmental impacts with twelve "eco-steps". The GRA's primary operational components are research, environmental consulting, education, public relations and marketing, and community organizing and consumer activism.

To become a member of the GRA, a restaurant must sign a statement of its commitment to making environmental improvements based on the 12 "eco-steps" listed below. After a member restaurant has made positive environmental changes, the GRA will include the restaurant in the "Green Restaurant Guide," which serves as a directory for environmentally conscious restaurants. The GRA also offers fee-based consulting services to member restaurants and initiates public relations and marketing initiatives, such as having restaurants featured on CNN, to increase restaurant exposure and consumer awareness.

GRA's 12 eco-steps are outlined below:

1. *Elimination of Polystyrene Foam (commonly known as styrofoam).* Replace all polystyrene foam products with environmentally friendly alternatives: paper, bamboo or sugarcane paper, recyclable plastic, biodegradable plastic, and so on. *This is the minimum environmental standard for becoming a member of the GRA.*

2. *Comprehensive Recycling.* Initiate or improve recycling programs for glass, plastic, bi-metal, cardboard, and mixed paper.
3. *Waste Reduction and Reuse.* Increase bulk purchasing and reduce excessive packaging for food, condiments, and so on. Replace disposable products with reusable alternatives: eating ware, aprons, tea strainers, cups, and so on.
4. *Biodegradable Plastic.* Transition to corn-based "plastic" products that are biodegradable and petroleum-free: cups, utensils, garbage bags, and straws.
5. *Recycled Products.* Transition to recycled products with the highest postconsumer content available and non-tree-fiber paper products: napkins, paper towels, toilet paper, office paper, take-out containers, coffee jackets, plates, and bowls.
6. *Non-Chlorine-Bleached Paper Products.* Transition to non-bleached or non-chlorine-bleached paper products: cups, wax paper, plates, take-out containers, bags, pastry bags and grabbers, napkins, paper towels, coffee filters, and office paper.
7. *Nontoxic Cleaners, Landscaping and Pest Management.* Replace hazardous chemical products with biodegradable and nontoxic alternatives; dish detergent, germicides, disinfectants, toilet; bowl cleaners, drain cleaner, floor wash, floor; polish, glass cleaners, degreasers, and laundry detergent. For landscaping, switch to nontoxic, nonsynthetic, and organic fertilizers, pesticides, or herbicides. For pest control, use nontoxic products or services.
8. *Energy Efficiency.* Improve the energy efficiency of lighting, refrigeration, air conditioning, gas appliances, and so on. Obtain assistance with using government and private rebate programs. Make connections with energy consultants to learn about more extensive programs.

9. *Water Efficiency.* Improve the water efficiency of toilets, faucets, laundry, sprinkler systems, and so on.
10. *Composting.* Divert food waste from landfills and create nutrient-rich soil for gardening and landscaping.
11. *"Green" Electricity.* Change to an energy provider that uses solar, wind, small-scale hydroelectric, geothermal, or methane-based power that is renewable and less polluting to ecosystems.
12. *Employee Education Program.* Train all employees, managers, and owners. Topics covered should include
    - An environmental profile of the restaurant industry
    - A history of environmental issues relevant to food service: landfills, water pollution, air pollution, clear-cutting, and global warming
    - Data describing the restaurant impacts (positive and negative) on the environment

ELIMINATION OF POLYSTYRENE FOAM

Polystyrene foam (Styrofoam) is widely used in restaurants in insulated cups for hot beverages and take-out containers. Production of polystyrene involves use of known (benzene) and suspected (styrene and 1,3-butadiene) human carcinogenic substances (styrene and 1,3-butadiene). Styrene is also known to be toxic to the reproductive system. Polystyrene can be recycled; however, its recycling rates are low. Styrofoam is light in weight, but bulky in size, so hauling Styrofoam to the nearest available recycling facility is often not economically feasible.

The value of a load of Styrofoam may not even cover the cost of shipping. To reduce environmental impacts, restaurants should consider switching from Styrofoam to non-bleached paper wraps, cardboard containers, or other sustainable food packaging.

According to a report published by the Environmental

Defense Waste Reduction Task Force, McDonalds has completed the switch from polystyrene foam "clamshells" to paper-based wraps for packaging its sandwich items. The wraps provide a 70 to 90 percent reduction in packaging volume, resulting in significantly less space being consumed in landfills. Compared to the polystyrene foam boxes they replaced, the new sandwich wraps also offer a substantial savings in energy used and substantial reductions in pollutant releases measured over the full life-cycle of the packaging. McDonalds is also testing EarthShell packaging products in 300 of its restaurants throughout the U.S.. These sustainable containers are made from potato starch, natural limestone, 100 percent postconsumer recycled fiber, biodegradable polymer and wax coatings, and water.

COMPREHENSIVE RECYCLING

The "Recycling Guidebook for the Hospitality and Restaurant Industry" provides a general overview of developing and implementing a comprehensive recycling program.

The first step mentioned in this resource is to conduct a waste audit in order to evaluate the waste stream, enabling a restaurant to better target the commodities that should be included in a recycling program. Materials that are commonly recycled in restaurants include

- *Paper,* including cardboard, computer paper, register tape, and telephone books
- *Metals,* including aluminum, tin, and steel cans
- *Green, brown, and clear glass*
- *#1 Polyethylene* (PET) and #2 *high-density polyethylene (HDPE)* plastics
- *Printer cartridges*

Convenience is the key to a successful recycling program. An EPA Waste Wise tip sheet notes that a convenient collection system will encourage both customers and employees to carefully sort recyclables by material type and to eliminate contaminants.

Collecting uncontaminated recyclables (commodities that are properly sorted and free of excess food and beverage waste) will save time otherwise spent in sorting out contaminants. Further, uncontaminated recyclables have higher value if they are sold. Presented below are other restaurant recycling tips listed in the "Recycling Guidebook for the Hospitality and Restaurant Industry."

- Recycling and trash bins should look different from each other and be clearly marked. Both types of bins should be conveniently located in the kitchen and bar areas so that employees will use them.

13

The Waiter's Glossary of Terms

Appetizer : A small first course dish that is presented before the entree. Some guests mistake appetizers for entrees.

Assistant Manager : See Manager.Has the same responsibities, but gets paid less.

Back-Of-The-House : Usually consistes of: Manager's Office, storerooms, and/or the kitchen.

Bill : 1} A itemized totaling of purchases before tips. 2} Perhaps someone you work with.

Break Room :A place where servers can take a moment to relax, smoke, gossip, and plot to get the manager to give them some of their free food.

Bring Back : 1} An entree that is returned to the kitchen because the guest did not like it for some reason. Usually means free dessert.

Busser : 1} One who cleans off utensils, plates, and trash from empty tables. 2} One who mistakenly cleans off utensils, plates, and trash from guests who are not done with them. 3} One who puts clean utensils, plates, and linen on tables. 4} One who mistakenly puts dirty utensils, plates, and linen on tables. 5} One who drives a bus.

Campers : A guestwhom sits at your table for an excessive amount of time. Use in a sentence: "Man! Those people have been camping out at my table since 5:30 pm! Anyone got a tent?" (Erin B.)

Check :1} See also bill. 2} Something for cheapskates to ignore.

Check Back : 1} A visit a server will make to the table to make sure all the food and drink(s) tastes good. At this time the guest will say everything is fine, or has the option of saying everything is not fine. A third option is to say everything is fine now, and then later say everything was not fine. If the third option is taken, then free dessert might be offered.

Check Cover : 1} A book used to present the check to the table and/or temporarily store credit cards during transactions.

Chef : 1} A very grumpy man or woman who is in charge of creating foods and food combinations. 2} One who has access to very large knives.

Dessert :1} A confectionery course usually at the end of the meal. 2} The first thing a manager will suggest when their is a problem with a guest.

86 : 1} A term used when you are out of something completely. i.e.: "The prime rib has been 86'd." 2} Can be applied to servers also.

Entree :1} Main course dish. 2} Not the same as an appetizer.

Expeditor : 1} Also known as "Expo". 2} One who is in charge of line cooks and/or plate presentations. 3} One who works in place of, or with, a chef.

Folding Napkins : To take a napkin and fold, twist, or tie into a new shape so it resembles a napkin that has been folded, twisted, or tied into a new shape. i.e. shell, hat, candle, folded napkin.

Front-Of-The-House : Any area a guest might see including: dinning room, lobby, bathrooms, a show kitchen, and/or side station.

Guest : 1} One who dines in restaurants. 2} A term to replace "customer" to make them feel more welcomed. 3} One who might get free dessert if there is a problem with their entree.

Line Cook : 1} One who cooks and/or assembles food onto the plate. 2} One who works with the chef.

Manager : 1} One who is in charge of the daily operations of a restaurant. 2} One who performs such tasks as; scheduling, inventory, budgeting, and supervising. 3} One who eats free food in their restaurant.

Manager's Office : A place for Managers to do paper work, make important phone calls, and hide.

On-The-Fly : 1} A term used for needing right away. 2} A term used when the server forgot to order some part of the entree. 3} A term used to get a new dish in place of a bring back. 4} A good place to put the dish if their is one on the table.

Postal : 1} A term used for a Server who looks way to stressed. 2} A term used for a Post Office Worker who looks way to stressed. i.e. "John looks like he is going postal!"

Rolling Silverware : 1} To take a napkin and wrap it around a fork, spoon, knife, or any combination there of, and tie off with a piece of string or sticky paper. 2} To mug or rob silverware.

Scrumps : The opportunistic feeding of stray entrees, appitizers, or desserts by Waiters. Verb examples: Scrumpping, Scrumpage (Gerald.)

Seating Host/Hostess : 1} One who shows the guest to their tables. 2} Your best friend. 3} Your worst enemy.

Server : Also Waiter, Waitress, Slave. 1} One who takes menu orders. 2} One who brings the meals and drinks to the table. 3} A person who acts as a representive of the guest to the kitchen.

Server's Assistant :1} One who assists a server waiting on tables. 2} A back-up to the server. 3} One who assists in staying out of the weeds. 4} One who performs busser-like duties.

Shift : The amount of hours spent at one's job, measured from moment you walk into the door, till the time you walk into your house. (Has no relation to what the time clock might actually tabulate.)

Show Kitchen : A kitchen that has been placed in the dinning room for full guest viewing.

Side Station : A station set-up in the dinning room for use by servers, Server Assistants, and Bussers. Usually contains extra china, utensils, and linen. Also may or may not consist of a beverage area. Also may or may not be stocked, depending on who's Side Work it may be.

Side Work : Tasks performed by servers other than waiting on tables. These tasks can be performed before, during, or after a shift. i.e. folding napkins, cleaning, rolling silverware, kissing up to the manager for free food.

Skate : 1) For a server to leave without doing closing sidework. ie:rolling silverware 2) To move on shoes with blades or rollers attached. (Elaine)

Slammed : 1} See Weeded. 2} What One Becomes In The Local Bar After Being This All Day Long. (Inspired By A Contribution From Gerald.)

Slave : 1} See server.2} One who is indentured to another. 3} One who has no rights as a human being. 4} One who is owned by another.

Stiffed : 1} No tip was left for the server. 2} No money was given in an exchange for services. 3} A bad, bad, evil, thing.

Tip : 1} Money left in exchange for a service performed. 2}In restuarants usually 15 to 20%, unless British.

Tip Card : 1} A card that explains in serveral different languages, including English, the custom of tipping 15 to 20%. 2} A card placed in english-speaking peoples check covers that explains in several different languages the custom of tipping 15 to 20%.

Waitron : A slang term that is an androgenous form of waiter or waitress.

Weeded : 1} To have to much to do. 2} To not be able to keep up or accomplish all the tasks set before you. 3} A feeling or act of being behind in one's work. 4} A very bad place. i.e. "I have too many tables, I'm very weeded!"

Wig :Term used to describe a server reacting in an adverse manner to being Slammed. Closely associated with postal behaviour. Also known as: Wigging, Wigged-Out, Toupee. (Gerald)

Bibliography

Morendy Octora.: *Introduction to Wine Waiter*, New York, University Press 2002.

Baran, A.: *Why we given Tipping*, New York, Modern Readers, 1975.

Caplin, A.: *How to become a Waiter or Waitress*, London, Oxford University Press, 2006.

Desmond, Glenn: *Waiter/Waitress Prepare for Tables*, Mumbai, Valuation Press, 1995.

Fruhan, W. E.: *Duties and Responsibility of Head Waiter*, Canada, Homewood, 1979.

Goleman D.: *Side Work Duties as a Waiter in a Restaurant*, New York: Bantam, 1995.

Harrigan, K. R.: *Duties of a Waiter for Food and Beverage Operations*, Lexington, MA: Heath, 1980

Knapp, C. L.: *Instructions to Waiters at Summer Breakfast*, Matthew Bender, 1993.

Loomes, G.: *Food Service, Bartending, and Waitress Careers*, Morroco, St. Martin's Press, 1989.

Martin, Gerald D.: *Work of Dumb Waiters*, Santa Ana, CA: James Publishing, 1995.

Plous, S.: *Training Programs For Waiters*, New York, McGraw-Hill, 1993

Roth, A. E.: *Careers Series: Waitress/Waiter/Restaurant Server*, Princeton, Princeton University Press, 1995.

Smith, V. L.: *Bar Service*, Cambridge, Cambridge University Press, 1991.

Index

♦♦♦